FOOD

A LOVE STORY

ALSO BY JIM GAFFIGAN

Dad Is Fat

FOOD

A LOVE STORY

JIM GAFFIGAN

CROWN ARCHETYPE ✑ NEW YORK

Published in the United States by Crown Archetype,
an imprint of the Crown Publishing Group,
a division of Random House LLC,
a Penguin Random House Company, New York.
www.crownpublishing.com

Crown Archetype and colophon is a registered trademark
of Random House LLC.

Library of Congress Cataloging-in-Publication Data
Gaffigan, Jim.
  Food: a love story / Jim Gaffigan. — First edition.
    pages cm
  1. Gaffigan, Jim—Anecdotes. 2. Comedians—United States—Anecdotes.
3. Food—Anecdotes. I. Title.
  PN2287.G28A3 2014
  818'.602—dc23
                            2014022619

ISBN 978-0-8041-4041-6
eBook ISBN 978-0-8041-4042-3

PRINTED IN THE UNITED STATES OF AMERICA

Book design by Elizabeth Rendfleisch
Illustrations and maps by Ellen Byrne
All photographs are courtesy of the author excluding the photograph on
page 168 by Richard Newell and the photographs on pages 257 and 339 by
Corey Melton.
Jacket design by Michael Nagin
Jacket photography by Justin Metz

10 9 8 7 6 5 4 3 2 1

First Edition

DEDICATION & ACKNOWLEDGMENT

If you read *Dad Is Fat,* you know that I do everything with the help of my wife, Jeannie. She is my writing partner, eating buddy, and best friend. I would not be an author, father, successful comedian, or the man I am today without Jeannie. She was by my side while I struggled through writing this book, and she helped turn my incoherent blurbs into something readable and much funnier. This book would not be a book without Jeannie. Jeannie believed in me even before people were yelling "Hot Pocket" at the airport. She was the first person I convinced shellfish were bugs and bacon was candy. Making Jeannie laugh remains one of my greatest accomplishments.

CONTENTS

CONTENTS

WHY FOOD?

As many of you know, I am a comedian who, with the immeasurable assistance of my wife, Jeannie, wrote a book called *Dad Is Fat,* which chronicled my life as the father of five young children in a two-bedroom apartment in New York City. The book enjoyed some success and changed how people raise their children! Well, okay, fine, the book enjoyed some success.

Here's me and my basketball team.

Anyway, I was approached about the possibility of writing another book. I thought long and hard. I knew if I did a second book, I wanted it to be as good or even better than *Dad Is Fat*. (I know, impossible, right?) I didn't want only to be known as the really good-looking guy who wrote one terrific book. So, like a good author, I spent some time reflecting while I rewatched all six seasons of *Lost* on Netflix. I then thought about who I am and what I know. Then I had a breakthrough. In the comedy world, what was I known for? What was my comedy associated with? Obviously I'm known for and associated with . . . you guessed it . . . being good-looking. But what else did my comedy say about me? Boom. I was a good-looking comedian who talked about food. This, of course, led to a brilliant idea. What if I wrote a book that was edible? I pitched it to my publishers, who were so trapped in the old publishing model that they got caught up in how bookstores don't have refrigerators, how to deal with digital delivery, and a bunch of other book-nerd stuff. Whatever! It was at that point that I decided to do the next logical thing. I ate a ham sandwich. Then I decided to write a book about food.

CURRICULUM VITAE

What are my qualifications to write this book? None, really. So why should you read it? Here's why: I'm a little fat. Okay, to some I might not be considered *that* fat, but the point is, I'm not thin. If a thin guy were to write about a love of food and eating, I'd highly recommend that you do not read his book. I'm not talking about someone who is merely in good shape. I'm talking thin. Skinny. I wouldn't trust them skinnies with food advice. First of all, how do you know they really feel passionately about food? Well, obviously they are not passionate enough to overdo it. That's not very passionate. Anyway, I'm overweight.

I'll admit it. I consciously try not to take food advice from thin people. I know this may not be fair, but when Mario Batali talks, I always think, *Well, this is a guy who knows what he's talking about.* He actually has experience eating food. This is why some sportscasters *wonder* what's going on in a player's head during a tense moment in a game, but the sportscaster who was once a player *knows* what's going on in a player's head. When I talk about food, I like to think

I'm like one of those sportscasters who used to play professionally. I'm like the Ray Lewis or Terry Bradshaw of eating. I'm like the Tony Siragusa of eating. Well, that's a little redundant.

When a thin person announces, "Here's a great taco place," I kind of shut down a little. How do they know it's so great? From *smelling* the tacos? If they only ate one taco, the taco could not have been that great. Or maybe it *was* great, but the thin person cared more about the calories than the taste: "I had to stop at one taco. I'm on a diet." A taco that won't force you to break your diet just can't be that great. Fat people know the consequences of eating, but if the food is good enough, they just don't care. Overweight people have chosen food over appearance. When a fat person talks about a great place to get a burger, I lean in. *They know.*

Speaking of thin people, another person it makes no sense to take advice from is the waiter. Why do fancy restaurants always hire thin, good-looking people to be the waiters? "I'll have the hamburger, and I want someone who is at least an 8 to bring it over to me. Can I see some headshots?" Why would we care what the waiter looks like? Even if we did, why would we take the waiter's advice? We don't know him. He is a stranger. "Well, he works there." Does that make him have similar taste in things you like? Does that make him honest? Not to sound paranoid, but the waitstaff does have a financial incentive for you to order something more expensive: "Well, I highly recommend the 16-ounce Kobe Beef with Lobster and the bottle of 1996 Dom Perignon."

What restaurants really need is a fat-guy food expert. Many fine-dining establishments have a sommelier—a wine expert—to assist in wine selection, but if a restaurant really cares about food, they should have a "Fattelier."

FATTELIER: Well, I'd get the chili cheese fries with the cheese on the side. You get more cheese that way.

ME: Thank you, Fattelier.

Although they can't be thin, the food adviser can't be *too* fat. If they are morbidly obese, then you can conclude that they will probably eat everything and anything and do not have discerning taste. This is not to say that they won't have valuable views. I'd still trust an overly fat person over a skinny one any day. The best adviser would have a very specific body type: pudgy or just a little overweight. This makes it clear they have a somewhat unhealthy relationship with food, but not a clinical problem. They are eating beyond feeling full. Sure, I am describing my own body type, but that's why I am qualified to write this book about food. What other credentials do you need, really? Stop being a snob. Read the book already.

AN EATIE, NOT A FOODIE

Now that I've convinced you to read this book, I should clarify something. I have strong opinions about food, but I am not a food expert or a "foodie." I couldn't name more than three celebrity chefs, and I've never posted on Yelp. I have five young children and work nightly as a stand-up comedian, so I rarely go out to dinner. What I have is a general and very personal knowledge of food. I know which food I enjoy. I know which food I hate. I know how food makes me feel. I realize that because of my food obsession, the fact that I am writing a book about food could mistakenly give some people the impression that I think of myself as a "foodie," but I don't. I think of myself as an "eatie." I don't have anything against foodies. I appreciate their love of food and I envy their knowledge and culinary escapades, but I'm generally satisfied with what I've been eating. Foodies seem to be on a never-ending search for new restaurants and interesting dishes. I don't have an insatiable desire to discover what *makes* something taste good or to find exotic combinations. I guess I'm not that bored. This is not to say that I don't appreciate today's chefs trying to expand the horizons of the culinary arts. I just don't need a Japanese taco or cranberry sauce on my steak. There is plenty of *regular* food I still want to enjoy. I wish it were more complicated than that, but it's not.

Me doing my thing.

I am also way too lazy to be a foodie. Foodies will travel for miles in search of the perfect hamburger. "There is this place in Greenpoint that's only an hour by train and a forty-minute walk from the subway that has the best burger in town!" It can't be better than the burger I can get across the street. Mostly, I just want the *closest* best burger in town.

The reason I know about so many great places to eat all over the country is not because I traveled to those cities and towns to seek out those restaurants. It's because I was in those cities and towns to perform stand-up comedy. All I have to do is ask a food-loving follower on Twitter where to eat in that particular city, and *bam!* Shortly thereafter I am cramming my face full of the best food in town. Yes, I'm lazy, but I'm resourceful.

I travel a lot and I like to eat. Besides asking my followers on Twitter or approaching strangers in cities I visit about where I should eat, I do no research. Most cities have at least one food place that locals recommend with pride. "Well, while you are here you have to eat at this place." Unfortunately, this is not the case everywhere. Once I was in Rapid City, South Dakota, and asked a cab driver for a local restaurant that was unique to Rapid City. He replied in a very matter-of-fact manner, "There's nothing. You should go to Outback Steakhouse." Nothing? I didn't believe him. So I pressed on. "Well, where did you go before chain places like Outback Steakhouse were here?" "Nowhere," he replied. Is it possible the fine people of Rapid City did not eat outside their homes prior to the arrival of chain restaurants? Of course not. Well, hopefully not. I don't know. I didn't do the research. I asked another two people in Rapid City, and nobody had suggestions. Therefore, in this book there is no reference to some local Rapid City food specialty. This isn't meant as a slam on Rapid City. This is a commentary on my research method or lack of a research method. If your favorite local food place isn't referenced in this fine book, it's because I didn't go to your town or the local stranger I asked didn't suggest it or someone didn't mention it on Twitter. It is also possible that I'm too dumb and lazy to remember the place. After all, I'm an eatie, not a foodie.

WHY DAD IS FAT

I can't stop eating. I can't. I haven't been hungry in twelve years. Once a writer at *Entertainment Weekly* described me as a human garbage can, which I think he meant as a compliment. Last night I had the following train of thought: *Ugh, I'm so full. I guess I'll have some cheese. Hmm, I don't even like this cheese. I guess I'll finish it.* I know it's not right. On more than one occasion while eating something, I've thought to myself, *Maybe this will make me hungry.* It's either that or feel my feelings. Jeannie likes to point out, "You know you are only eating your feelings." I always respond, "Yeah, but these feelings are delicious. Especially the ones at night. I wish I had more feelings." Have you ever eaten so much that you feel sick? Well, I love that feeling.

I treat my body like a temple. A temple of doom, but a temple nonetheless. I often find myself thinking about what I will eat at my next meal while I'm in the middle of eating a meal. I always eat like I'm on vacation or about to begin a period of fasting. I've eaten things and not noticed that they tasted horrible until I was taking the last bite. Afterward, that horrible taste only leads me to want to eat something else to cleanse my palate. I'm a stand-up comedian, and I've contemplated ways that I can incorporate eating while onstage into my stand-up routine. If other comics bring a beer up with them, why can't I bring up a cheeseburger? Comedians with a drink onstage usually wait for an applause break and then take a sip. I could do that. "I support the troops!" Crowd applauds. I take a bite of my Baconator.

Always conducting research.

When I don't want to eat something, I assume I'm sick and most likely dying. I try to stick to three meals a day and then an additional three at night. The only time I stop eating is when

I'm sleeping. I'm not really comfortable watching television while not eating—it's just too weird. I don't know what to do with my hands. As a result of all this behavior, I'm always full. When the instructions on medication say, "Never take on an empty stomach," I think, *Not a concern of mine.* I'm sure your mother told you to not go swimming until an hour after eating. This is a virtual impossibility for me. Technically, I should never go swimming. Thank God this hour rule is not actually against the law, because if you ever saw me in a pool you would think, *Arrest that man and ask him not to wear a Speedo.* And, in this hypothetical scenario, if I went to prison because I ate too soon before swimming and I wanted to protest the injustice of my sentence, a hunger strike would not be an option. I'd cave after fifteen minutes. Yes, not having food for a short time compromises my principles. If I went to a shaman for help with this problem, he would never tell me what my spirit animal was for fear I would eat it. My wife thinks I'm eating myself to death, and if I am, it's taking longer than I thought.

I like to have my name baked into my food.

NOT SLIM JIM

As a result of my constant eating, I'm not thin. Sure, my beard probably hides none of it, but at least I know why I'm not thin. When most people gain weight, they rarely admit that it is due to the food they constantly shove into their mouths. We blame external forces. "Well, work has been stressful." "That was a brutal winter." "I have young kids, which makes you more hungry, right?"

I'm not in denial. I realize I could lose half an ounce or two of weight. I take full responsibility for the reality I've created, even if at times I feel like I'll never lose this baby weight. That's the price of being a father.

The truth is that it was I alone who caused my weight gain. Luckily for me, most of my girth is intentional. I don't mean to brag or anything, but I'm preparing for a very big role. Sure, it's a cinnamon roll, but I don't want to look like I can't finish it. Or spell it. Some people lie about their age. I lie about my weight. Sometimes I catch myself telling total strangers that my belly is not real. That I actually had to get stomach implants to ward off female suitors. This strategy generally fails, because

I've caught women staring at my gut. I usually point to my eyes and say in a very condescending tone, "Hello, I'm up here." After all, I'm not some piece of flab for anyone to ogle.

Once, after a show, a woman told me, "You're not *that* fat." Like it was a compliment. I held myself back from answering her, "You're not *that* polite." I'm not sure how overweight I am, because you are supposed to find out this information by calculating your BMI. Once I found out that did not stand for "Big Mac Included," I stopped trying.

There was a time when I was thin. Sure, I was six years old, but I'm confident I can get back into those clothes. Actually, around the age of seven it became very obvious that I had the body type of someone who would have to work out twice a day just to look out of shape. I struggled through my twenties and thirties, and then one day I looked in the mirror, saw my belly, and said, "I give up. It's all over." It wasn't defeat as much as it was acceptance. I figured, *I got a hot wife. If she leaves me for getting fat, that means she's shallow.* "Honey, do you think looks are important? No? Good. Now pass the gravy."

A lifelong passion.

Around the time I tricked Jeannie into marrying me, I lost a primary motivator for staying thin. Additionally, my career as a comedian was never affected by my waist size. Even my occasional acting roles were as a character actor. "Character actor" is, of course, entertainment industry code for "not attractive." It became clear that being thin was never going to put me in competition with Brad Pitt. By my thirties I'd auditioned to be Matthew McConaughey's unattractive friend in three movies. I didn't get any of those parts because I wasn't "cute-unattractive" enough. The other reasons to be thin just seemed downright esoteric: "You'll feel better and have more energy." Next. "You'll live longer." Next. Then the reasons just get silly. There's an old Weight Watchers saying: "Nothing tastes as good as thin feels." I for one can think of a thousand things that taste better than thin feels. Many of them are two-word phrases that end with *cheese* (Cheddar cheese, blue cheese, grilled cheese). Even unsalted French fries taste better than thin feels. Ever eat fries without salt on them? I always think, *These could use some salt, but that would mean I'd have to get up and move. I guess I'll just imagine there's salt on them.* Eating fries without salt feels like a sacrifice. "What am I, a pioneer?" When I have to eat unsalted fries, I often feel like I should be a contestant on *Survivor* or something. I look forward to telling *Survivor* executive producer Mark Burnett: "Once I had fries without salt on them, so I could probably live anywhere."

I realize weight is a serious issue in America, but I also believe some people *should* be fat. We all have that friend who has lost tons of weight, and whenever you see them you secretly think, *You looked better fat. Go back to being fat. You're thin, but you look exhausted. Even looking at you makes me want to sit down.* Obviously, losing any amount of weight is an accomplishment. Obesity is a big problem in our society. This is a well-known fact. Another fact is that there seems to be a general insensitivity to our obese fellow citizens. It seems once a week there is a news segment on American obesity. They always show some big person walking. They don't show their face, but that person has to know that's them. They are probably just sitting at home watching TV. "Well, that shirt looks familiar—oh crap! Looks like I can't wear that again." That poor guy probably gets to work and is greeted by a coworker, "Hey Fred, I saw your fat ass on the six o'clock news."

Now it seems like obesity is an industry. At this point the countless number of documentaries on obesity just makes me hungry. I feel like the insensitivity toward obesity reached its peak with the television show *The Biggest Loser*. The show seems to be an elaborate insult masked by stories of inspiration. The following is what I think occurred in the meeting when the show was pitched.

PRODUCER: Hey, I got an idea for a show. We get really, really fat people to lose weight, and everyone watches them struggle and fail.

NETWORK EXECUTIVE: That's good! Ha, ha, ha. I'm laughing already.

PRODUCER: So wait, wait. So we make these really, really fat people run around. Jump up and down. More or less torturing them.

NETWORK EXECUTIVE: Funny. So we get to abuse them. Love it.

PRODUCER: Just thin people get to yell at the fat people.

NETWORK EXECUTIVE: Of course.

PRODUCER: So there will be these thin, attractive judges, and we will have the fat people weigh in on national television.

NETWORK EXECUTIVE: Do they have their shirts off? That would be extra humiliating.

PRODUCER: Fine, no shirt. Now, here is the kicker. Whichever fatty loses the most weight wins the title—wait for it—*The Biggest Loser*. Get it?

NETWORK EXECUTIVE: Because they are all losers, because they are fat, right?

PRODUCER: Of course. But the winner is the *biggest* loser because he or she has humiliated themselves the most on national television and, I suppose, maybe lost some weight.

NETWORK EXECUTIVE: We could probably pay them in Twinkies and Ho Hos, right?

PRODUCER: Sure, some kind of food, of course. While we are torturing them, we make them wear these huge insulting T-shirts that say . . .

NETWORK EXECUTIVE: The Biggest Loser!

PRODUCER: Their big fat bodies will serve as slow-moving billboards for the show.

NETWORK EXECUTIVE: Ha, ha. I love it. I have to go. I have a Pilates class now.

PROUD AMERICAN

If obesity is an epidemic in America, then what caused it? I can only speak from my own experience, but I will just go out on a limb here and guess it was caused by American eating. I'm very American. I don't mean that in a boastful way. I'm just saying my habits and passions surrounding food are those of a typical American. Not to generalize, but generally most Americans have an unhealthy relationship with food. Unless, of course, they are damn Commies! Maybe it's the exposure to a lifetime of McDonald's commercials. Maybe our country couldn't handle the post–World War II financial boom. Maybe we are just better than all the other countries at eating. In any case, consuming food of any kind feels a little more important in the United States. We seem to always be eating. If aliens studied Earth, they would come to the conclusion that the United States is somehow consuming food on behalf of other countries. In America we have gone way beyond sustenance. Eating is an activity. "Why don't we get lunch, and then we'll grab some pizza." Most Americans eat constantly. And when we're not eating, we're chewing gum. We are literally practicing eating. We chew gum with a swagger and purpose that says, "Yeah, I got a big meal coming up. I'm training for Thanksgiving."

There are many elements that make up the American attitude toward food, but some are consistent. There always seems to be an unending dissatisfaction with, and constant need to improve upon, the status quo of food. Americans are never satisfied when it comes to a food item. The hamburger could never remain just the hamburger. "You know what would be good on this hamburger? A ham sandwich. Instead of a bun, let's use two doughnuts. That way we can have it for breakfast. Look out, McGriddle, here comes the Doughnut Ham Hamburger." I came up with this silly concept for my 2006 comedy special *Beyond the Pale*, and then in 2012 Dunkin' Donuts made me a sort of food prophet by introducing the very food item that I had hyperbolically predicted. I wasn't surprised, really. Dunkin' Donuts is only responding to the ongoing public desire for innovation and variety in our food. It's the new American Manifest Destiny. We are the ones who for some reason needed a potato chip that tastes like steak and Jim Beam Jalapeño–flavored sunflower seeds. The variety of flavors is only matched by the speed at which we need them.

This makes perfect sense.

Of course, when the word *fast* is associated with American eating, it is the opposite of the word *fast* as it relates to abstinence from food. When people in other parts of the world hear the term "food fast," they envision a time of spiritual and physical cleansing. I hear "food fast" and I envision a drive-thru. I like things fast. I don't like lines. Whenever I find myself in line for an ATM behind two people, I always think, *What is this, Russia?*

Americans want our food fast. That's why those fast-food value meals are so successful. It's less the value and more the speed. You just have to say a number. "Two!" and your food is on its way. Soon you won't have to speak a word. It will just be a noise—"Eeeyah!"—and your meal will be placed in front of you. Fast and easy is the American way. We start indoctrinating our children into this mindset at a very early age. My children eat this yogurt that comes in an astronaut tube that they just squeeze and the entire serving of yogurt is expelled into their mouths. We don't want them to waste their time lifting up a cumbersome spoon. They are even starting to package baby food in a squeeze bag. I hear soon they are coming out with a variety of kid foods where these squeeze bags come with an elastic strap so they can just put them around their heads and walk around all day wearing a squeeze feed bag. Why should they even have to lift their hands to their mouths? What a waste of energy. Let's keep it fast and easy.

I am a fast eater. I normally am the first one to finish eating my entire plate of food at a restaurant, and then I have to just sit there and stare at everyone who has barely unfolded his or her napkin. I never know what to say. "Do you think they're gonna bring back that basket of bread?"

My wife likes to pause before the meals with our kids and say grace. While I think this is a great opportunity for our children to learn to appreciate the gifts that God has given them, I view grace as kind of the "On your mark, get set . . ." and the "Amen" as the "Go!" I am pretty sure that's the way God intended it.

The faster we eat, the fatter we get. Statistics show that the amount of money spent on weight loss programs in the United States alone is much larger than the amount of money it would take to solve the world's hunger problem. The answer to this dilemma seems perfectly simple: Americans should just start eating people from starving countries.

When you watch late-night television, it becomes abundantly clear that as a culture we are struggling with our weight and have little desire to make any real effort to remedy the situation. The exercise equipment and weight loss techniques sold late at night emphasize painless alternatives to actually eating less. Machines and routines that only take moments out of our busy lives between meals are constantly touted. I have even seen a late-night commercial for a pulsating belt that works your abs while you watch television. All these weight loss techniques point to the fact that we can't stop eating. There are diet programs where all your meals are mailed to your home. How absurd. We can't even be trusted to go out and buy the food we know we should eat. "You'll just screw it up! I'll do it!" We are totally out of control. We're a country that loves to eat so much that instead of learning how to eat less, or honestly exercising, we find ways around it, like wiring our mouths shut and undergoing surgeries in which our stomachs are stapled smaller. "I don't want to do something barbaric like exercising, so I'm just going to have someone vacuum the fat out of my body."

Instead of eating less or spending money on get-thin-quick schemes, I have just accepted the fact that I, like most Americans, also have a totally unhealthy relationship with food and, therefore, as a result, I'm overweight. As I mentioned earlier, the meal isn't over for me until I feel sick. Instead of food giving me energy, I am always tired after I eat, which explains why I am always tired. I go to the gym just so I will stop eating for an hour, which, I believe, is the American form of fasting.

THE BUFFET RULE

If anything defines American eating, it is the quantity of food we consume. This would explain why the "All-You-Can-Eat Buffet" is such an American phenomenon, and it makes perfect sense that it started in Las Vegas. Some of the most amazing restaurants in the world are in Las Vegas, but the real local specialty is the All-You-Can-Eat Buffet. Buffets are as common in Vegas as glitter and regrettable behavior. The Vegas casino buffets are expansive and ridiculous. In other words, completely American. You can get sushi, mac and cheese, and doughnuts all in the same meal. God bless America. One of the main reasons that the all-you-can-eat buffet is a perfect fit for casinos is because the all-you-can-eat buffet is the food equivalent of gambling. And like all other forms of institutional gambling, it's rigged for the house.

The all-you-can-eat buffets always feel like a challenge. "All-YOU-can-eat." The unspoken rule of the all-you-can-eat buffet is that you must eat the food value of more than the cost of the buffet. My wife, Jeannie, finds this approach ridiculous, but then again she married me, so she doesn't have the best judgment anyway. If the buffet is twenty bucks, you must eat at least twenty dollars' worth of food. If you eat twenty-one dollars' worth of food, you make money, right? It's a rule everyone knows. Eating your money's worth at the buffet is a rule that should be known as the "Buffet Rule," but apparently this term was already used for some tax theory proposed in 2011 that has absolutely nothing to do with buffets. I mean, where are our government's priorities, really? I'm not saying my interpretation of the Buffet Rule is a wise one. I've never learned my lesson. I always approach a buffet with the same bluster. "All I can eat for twenty dollars? Ha, ha. This place is going to lose so much money." Unfortunately, after half an hour I am always uncomfortably full and mumbling, "Let's get out of here. This place is trying to hurt people. Why did I do this to myself?" It's the overeating equivalent of losing your shirt at the craps table. It's dangerous.

The all-you-can-eat title is especially hazardous for someone like me who likes to follow directions. When I approach a buffet, aside from seeing it as a challenge, there is a compliant part of me that hears "all you can eat" and says, "Okay, I will try my best. I don't want to let you down, buffet." The assumption is that I can control myself, that I understand self-restraint and portion control, and that I am some kind of nutritional scientist or an adult. There is something very American about the term "all-you-can-eat." "Do you love your country? Prove it. Let's see all YOU can eat." Sometimes I hear other words in the phrase emphasized. It's all you CAN eat, not all you WANT to eat. There's part of me that is relieved that the CAN part is never enforced. I could see trying to leave a buffet, only to encounter some big bouncer: "Hey, hey, where do you think you're going? Get back up there!" "But I don't want any more food." "Look, chubby, no one said this was an 'all-you-want-to-eat' buffet. It's 'all-you-CAN eat.' Read the sign! I've seen your stand-up. You can eat more." Really what most of us need is an all-you-*should*-eat buffet. "Wait a minute there, fella. Here's your brunch. One apple and fifty sit-ups."

CUP OF GRAVY

I suppose I've become desensitized to the level of unhealthy eating in America. An 80-ounce soda, all-you-can-eat buffets, and a Wendy's Triple only seem like logical options to me. I love the rare moments when I'm truly surprised by American eating.

A while ago I was back in Indiana in my hometown walking around the Kmart, or, as we called it, "the mall." You can typically find just about anything you need in one of these "big box" stores like Walmart and Kmart. What I especially love about Kmart is the ambience. I always feel like I've entered a store that was just attacked by a flash mob. Everything always looks and feels a little disheveled. There will be some random empty shelf. There's always a huge corner display tower of sale products that looks like it will collapse on you if you breathe on it. There will be a broken jar in one aisle and an abandoned sock in the next. The selection and layout suggest that this might not be the ideal place to buy a suit or use a public restroom. Anyway, on this fine day I was looking for diapers when I saw a seventy-year-old man walking around the Kmart drinking something I realized later was a cup of KFC gravy.

Now, in full disclosure, I love gravy. Who doesn't, really? It's *gravy*, after all . . . but I've never considered gravy a beverage. Even in my most private moments with gravy I've never contemplated taking a swig. This is coming from someone who drank a product called Yoo-hoo on many occasions as a teenager. The thing I found most impressive was that not only was this stranger drinking gravy, he also wasn't even trying to hide it. When I first spotted the stranger, I saw the KFC Styrofoam cup, saw him take a drink, and assumed . . . well, obviously this guy is *not* drinking gravy. Then I encountered him again standing in front of me in the checkout line. It was at that moment I saw the thick brown liquid in the cup and confirmed that it was, in fact, a cup of KFC gravy he was drinking. And then, almost as if to prove a point, he turned around and took a sip right in front of me. Our eyes met, and he gave me a warm Midwestern smile as if to say, "Hey, how's it going?" I nodded and said hello and was only a bit more than slightly tempted to exclaim, "You realize you're drinking gravy, right?"

I don't know what the events were that led up to this stranger drinking the cup of gravy in that Kmart. I like to think he walked into KFC with the intention of drinking gravy. Maybe his order was simple.

"Yeah I'll have the large mashed potatoes and gravy. And hold the mashed potatoes." Maybe in order to avoid judgment or scorn, he ordered the mashed potatoes, got the gravy on the side, and just threw the mashed potatoes away. Or maybe he really could have cared less what anyone thought, which is more likely, since he seemed like a proud gravy drinker greeting the cashier while she scanned his heart medication.

I'm no health nut, but I can only imagine what this guy's next medical checkup was like. I picture a doctor in a white coat glancing down at a chart as he walks into an examination room with our gravy drinker sitting on the examination table.

The doctor would then tilt his head to the right, perplexed by the results on the chart:

> DOCTOR: Mr. Jones, I've got your cholesterol levels here. (*beat*) Okay, you are aware your blood is not moving?
> GRAVY DRINKER: (*nods*)
> DOCTOR: This is kind of a strange question. Um. You haven't been drinking gravy, have ya? Because based on the test results you're, like, 90 percent meat by-product.
> GRAVY DRINKER: (*nods*)
> DOCTOR: We're going to have to register you with the government.

I guessed the age of our gravy drinker to be around seventy, but I have no idea how old he was or how long he had been drinking gravy. Maybe he was younger. Maybe gravy drinking is one of those rapid-aging behaviors, like smoking. Or maybe he was an even older guy and the gravy-drinking habit had plumped out his wrinkles so he actually looked younger. I suppose his unique consumption of his gravy cup was voluntary, but I honestly don't know. Maybe his wife was just trying to kill him.

> GRAVY DRINKER: Honey, I'm going to Kmart.
> WIFE: Well, why don't you have a cup of gravy?
> GRAVY DRINKER: Well, I guess I could . . .
> WIFE: And why don't you sign this additional life insurance policy?
> GRAVY DRINKER: Boy, you love buying life insurance.

THE GEOGRAPHY OF
AMERICAN FOOD

People look at a map of the United States and see different things. Some people see red states and blue states. Some see North and South. Some see East and West. I see food. I'm not saying the geographical areas of the United States actually look edible to me (not yet, anyway), although I once saw a potato chip shaped like Alaska. Unfortunately, I ate it before I could take a photo. Anyway, my point is, I travel a great deal as a stand-up comedian. I've performed in all fifty states and eaten my way through pretty much every major city. After my fourth or fifth lap of performing and eating across our beautiful and delicious country, I started to think of the geography of our country as it relates to food.

My food geography of the United States, while unscientific, is very personal (and brilliant, in my personal opinion). My hope is that one day, schools, businesses, and prisons will have the Jim Gaffigan American Food Map hanging in their librar-ies and/or bathrooms. We all have our own unique dreams.

THE
JIM GAFFIGAN
FOOD MAP

SOUTHERN COMFORT

SEABUGLAND

SUPER BOWL SUNDAY FOODLAND

STEAKLAND

MEXICAN FOODLAND

EATING BBQLAND

Wineland

Food Anxietyland

Coffeeland

Blubberland

Luauland

I believe the United States is composed of five major food areas:

- Seabugland (Northeast Coast)
- Eating BBQland (Southeast/Parts of Midwest)
- Super Bowl Sunday Foodland (Midwest/Parts of East)
- Steakland (Texas to Upper West)
- Mexican Foodland (Southwest to Texas)

And smaller unique areas:

- Wineland (Northern California)
- Coffeeland (Pacific Northwest)

Some of my geographic areas of food blur into other food geographic areas. The greatest example would be Texas, which is a convergence of Mexican Foodland, Eating BBQland, *and* Steakland. I'm not being generous here. It would be unfair to not put Texas in all three of these major food geographical areas. They just do things bigger in Texas. Louisiana and New Orleans in particular are unique to the food geography of the United States. It's almost as if the Mississippi River flowed all its special food excellence down, and it drained into New Orleans. There are, of course, other exceptions to my regional distinctions, but first let's explore these major areas on the Jim Gaffigan American Food Map.

SEABUGLAND

You will notice on my food geography map that I've identified the northeast coast of the United States as far south as Maryland as "Seabugland." By *seabugs* I mean those so-called food items you call "shellfish." On the surface, naming an entire section of the country after shellfish might appear like an oversimplification. After all, the Northeast boasts many other regional food specialties, and most coastal areas of the United States are littered with shellfish, and I emphasize the word *littered*. However, shellfish are an integral part of the northeastern identity. Whenever someone does a bad Boston accent, it's either to say "wicked" or "lobstah." Lobster is as much a part of the New England personality as is the hating of all things New York City. All along the northeast coast you find this obsession with things that live in shells. Coastal Connecticut, New York City, and Long Island have a long-standing love affair with oysters. Maryland is not Maryland without crab. I know, technically Maryland is "Mid-Atlantic," but it must be included as part of the East Coast bug-loving culture. If you can catch something in a net and crack it open for food, those bug lovers will eat it.

Shellfish are not for me. I'm from the Midwest, and outside of the occasional shrimp cocktail, I had limited exposure to shellfish—or any other kind of seafood, really. I'm still not sure I (or anyone, for that matter) would recognize a scallop in its natural form. Are those the things that stick to the side of the aquarium? Who knows? The French may refer to seafood as the "fruit of the sea," and scientists may call shellfish "crustaceans," but to me they are creepy-crawly giant insects on the bottom of the ocean. I have a rule that if food looks like something that would crawl out from under a refrigerator, I don't put it in my mouth. If you like shellfish, do me a favor: next time you see a really big cockroach, just tell yourself, "If that could swim, I'd eat it." I always imagine fish in the ocean swimming along, looking down at the ocean floor, seeing shellfish and thinking, *We have to get an exterminator up in here.* There is a reason why Red Lobster and exterminators have the same image on their signs. Shellfish are bugs. They have a shell like a bug. They have tons of spindly legs and crawl around like bugs (I have a four-leg maximum on things I'll eat). They even have antennae like, well, like monsters, frankly. Shellfish are probably monsters. You don't have to watch any sci-fi movie from the '60s to understand my point. Consider the following: If you went home and saw a chicken in your house, you'd think, *Why is there a chicken in my house?* If you saw a lobster in your house, you'd think, *We have to move.* This is because there is not a nickel's worth of difference between a lobster and a giant scorpion.

New England: Lobster

"Lobstah!" Finding lobster on the menu is fancy. It is rare and pricey. "Oooh, they have lobster." Lobster is so special, restaurants go so far as to have tanks of live lobsters with rubber bands on the claws. The lobsters always seem to be peering out with a curious expression.

LOBSTER: What are you doing here?
PATRON: I'm going to eat you.
LOBSTER: Ha, ha. Yeah, right. Hey, Harvey, this guy
thinks he's going to eat . . . Harvey? Where's
Harvey?

In some lobster tank restaurants, diners can choose their own lobster. I always found this strange. "Um, I guess I'll take that one that is really struggling with the rubber bands. He seems rather appealing. Why don't we boil him to death?" I'm always perplexed why I'm involved in the decision process. I wanted to have dinner, not play executioner.

All this ritual that I imagine makes PETA members squirm is supposedly justified, given everyone's love of lobster. And people do love lobster. For many, it just doesn't get better than lobster. "I love lobster!" I usually nod in agreement and say, "I like butter too." Really, butter is what makes lobster so good. Each bite of lobster is usually submerged in a small bowl of paradise, also known as butter.

GUY 1: How can I eat three sticks of butter?
GUY 2: Well, I found this giant swimming sea scorpion.
Maybe if we boil it to death . . .

Drawing my inspiration from Julie Andrews in *Mary Poppins*, I think it really comes down to "a spoonful of butter helps the bug meat go down." In, of course, "the most delightful way."

Even the experience of ordering lobster contributes to its mystique and popularity. Lobster is often listed on the menu as "Market Price," which is code for "you can't afford it." The "market" always seems to be the most expensive market in the area. Lobster also is a unique food that requires its own wardrobe, the lobster bib, which indicates not only that consuming lobster is messy, but also that people don't mind looking like a toddler while they do it. A nutcracker is conveniently provided to the lobster connoisseur so that those who dare seek it out may earn the bounty of the lobster meat in the claw. A lobster knife is used to expertly dissect the tail. The ultimate entrée in some steakhouses is often lobster tail served alongside a steak. Yes, somehow the tail of a giant scorpion that can survive in saltwater is the gold standard of accompaniment to a steak. I feel that in life these two animals would have been enemies, but there they are together on the plate in some kind of phony, glorious unity: cow and bug tail. I don't even feel completely comfortable eating a chicken's wing, and some people crave eating the tail of a lobster? "Is that the area near the lobster butt? That's what I want, a little turf and bug butt. Mmm."

The World Is Your Oyster

A century ago a visit to New York City involved a mandatory stop for oysters. It was like getting lobster in Maine or a house for five dollars in Detroit. You had to do it. New York City was where you would see a Broadway show and eat a boatload of oysters. Oysters and clams piled up along every murky dock on the East Coast. Oysters were so abundant that Long Island even has a town called Oyster Bay. I imagine Oyster Bay one hundred years ago as a big hole filled with oysters with just a little bay in it. Now finding clams and oysters in their natural habitat is a rarity. What happened? You guessed it. We ate them all.

Scientists have recently declared oysters to be functionally extinct. Apparently 85 percent of the world's oyster ecosystems have been destroyed. Only 1 percent of the natural oyster population remains intact as a result of our voracious consumption. Oysters are now an expensive delicacy. I just don't get it. I don't even understand how mankind started eating oysters. I'm not saying there were tons of food options back in the 1700s . . . but oysters? Really? How hungry would you have to be to make that leap? Maybe two guys were having an unproductive day of fishing.

MAN 1: Nothing biting over here.

MAN 2: Nothing here either.

MAN 1: I'm hungry.

MAN 2: Me too. Hey, I found a rock with a snot in it. I was thinking of eating it.

MAN 1: Um, okay. Go ahead.

MAN 2: (*slurps up the oyster*)

MAN 1: What does it taste like?

MAN 2: Pneumonia.

Often on the menu, oysters will be listed as "oysters on the half shell." As opposed to what? "In a Kleenex?" Even the way you are supposed to eat an oyster indicates something counterintuitive. "Squeeze some lemon on it, a dab of hot sauce, throw the oyster down the back of your throat, take a shot of vodka, and try to forget you just ate snot from a rock." That is not how you eat something. That is how you overdose on sleeping pills.

It's not just the East Coast that follows this weird and disgusting tradition. These rare and endangered oysters are found in many coastal areas across North America. It seems wherever there is a murky dock with brackish water, oysters and clams can grow or spawn from whatever creates them. There are East Coast and West Coast oysters. There are oysters from Prince Edward Island and the Puget Sound, and supposedly they all taste different. "Oh, this snot from a rock from this filthy dock area around San Francisco tastes more snotty than this snot from a rock from a filthy dock area on the Gulf Coast." I'm not sure how the price of an oyster is determined. "Oh, *this* snot from a rock is from the filthiest dock in Nova Scotia! Let's charge two hundred dollars for it."

I only ate the lemon.

I understand I am in the minority in my view that oysters are only slightly less disgusting than their culinary cousin, the Rocky Mountain oyster. Some of the arguments in favor of oysters seem absurd: "Oysters are an aphrodisiac!" We know this is a scientific fallacy, but why would anyone ever believe such nonsense? I could just see some guy approaching a woman in a bar. "What do you say you and I get some snots from a rock and see what happens? Maybe we'll end up at my place. Maybe we'll end up at the emergency room. Let it happen, baby." Aphrodisiac? It is more believable that after you eat an oyster you're so happy to be alive you'll sleep with anyone.

Once I had a friend defensively point out to me, "Pearls come from oysters." I never really understood his reasoning, but I explained I make a rule to not eat things that also make jewelry. Diamonds come from coal, but we aren't dipping that into cocktail sauce. I would think that, given that pearls do come from oysters, we would NOT eat them. It seems like a prank played on some not-so-bright business partner.

PEARL GUY: I'll tell you what. Why don't I take the rare jewel and you can have the snot from the rock.
NON–PEARL GUY: Um, okay. What am I supposed to do with that?
PEARL GUY: You can tell people it's an aphrodisiac.
NON–PEARL GUY: Deal.

Maryland Is for Crabs

Maryland is for crabs. Not for "crabby people," although that would make the state more appealing to me, but for actual crabs. This slogan was initially a parody of neighboring Virginia's state tourism slogan, "Virginia is for lovers," but it pretty much sums up Maryland's attitude toward crabs. Those Marylanders just love them some crab. Maryland is for crabs. And by *for*, I mean rooting for. The University of Maryland's team may be called the Terrapins, the state's football and base-ball teams might be respectively named the Ravens and the

Orioles, but I think the people of Maryland would have preferred it if all the teams were simply named "the Crabs." You just enter the state of Maryland, and the incessant crab sell commences. "You should get some crab! Are you going to have steamed crab? Why don't you get a crab cake?" I usually politely ask if I can just pay my toll. There is a fascination with the crab that goes way beyond the fact that it is an important industry and export for Maryland. Once Jeannie and I were out to dinner at a crab restaurant on the Eastern Shore of Maryland, and a stranger, not even a waiter, approached our table and addressed me directly: "I couldn't help but notice you aren't eating crab. Is there a reason?" I didn't know how to respond. After a moment of stunned disbelief, I just was honest. "I thought I'd order what I want." I didn't have the courage to tell the guy I wasn't really in the mood for bug meat.

I feel the same way, Patrick.

The crab is embedded deeply in Maryland culture. It is common knowledge that every Maryland vacation home must have an image of a crab in every room. Images of crabs even appear in kitchens on potholders, towels, and bowls, where one would think any logical person would never want to see the image of a bug. "Ooh! There's a bug at the bottom of my soup!" I do not exaggerate. I have seen this crab obsession firsthand. Every summer I attend a weeklong family reunion hosted by my amazingly generous Aunt Katie on the Eastern Shore of Maryland. The climax of the reunion is a gathering at my aunt's house, where picnic tables are covered with newspaper. Wooden mallets and sharp knives are arranged neatly in empty wooden bowls, and a crate of steamed crabs is placed like a treasure chest as the centerpiece of the table. There are even oyster crackers shaped like crabs. The irony! Over the course of hours, relatives sit down to experience the ritual of eating crab. From a distance it may appear as if a pinewood derby car is being constructed as the wooden mallets crash to the table, and the pounding and hammering is deafening. The conversation is light and convivial. It's like a coed knitting circle, except people are eating bug meat.

Giving little kids a hammer is always a good idea.

Aunt Katie hosting her annual "Find the Bug Meat" party.

I don't participate. Being the father of five young children, my time is normally spent stopping any given member of my basketball team from drowning in the nearby pool. Well, that's my excuse. Even if I were kid-free, I wouldn't partake in this barbaric bug-smashing ritual. Is any meal worth that much work? Are we really supposed to be eating these things? Isn't it a red flag that you need a hammer to eat a crab?

> WAITRESS: Oh, you're having the crab? Let me get you some tools so you can crack open the bug shell and get that half a bite of bug meat.

Crab is like the pistachio of shellfish. In my estimation, there is too much effort for too little reward. An experienced crab eater can find "plenty of meat" in other parts of the crab during the culinary autopsy. The most crabmeat is found in the claw or the pincer of the crab. *Pincer?* That does not sound very appetizing. Let's go with *claw.* Who wouldn't want to eat a "claw"? It seems to me that the term *claw* should actually *discourage* people from eating crab. The oversize claw is the crab's natural form of defense, its only weapon against attack. If you've picked up a live crab, it will, with great confidence, try to snip off your finger. "Snip, snip." The crab must think, *Nobody is going to get me because I have these claws.* More irony. It's like carrying around a gun and thinking, *Nobody is going to mess with me while I have this. . . . Why is someone eating my gun?*

There is also that nasty part of the crab that you are not supposed to eat. I think it's called ALL OF IT. Because they are *crabs,* as in the sexually transmitted disease that has the same name because it's the same exact thing. I honestly don't know how people even order crabs with a straight face. I imagine a couple on a romantic date, with the man trying to impress his lady by ordering for her. "Yes, my wife and I will have the crabs. No, actually, I'll get crabs and give her some." Whispering to the waiter, "Don't tell her. I want it be a surprise." Apart from its ill-fated name and frightening body, everything about the crab as a creature is creepy. It only moves sideways. To the right and then jerking to the left. It always looks like it's trying to avoid an awkward situation. "Uh-oh. I owe that guy money," as he sidesteps away.

I'm sure God is up in heaven looking down completely bewildered. "What do I have to do to stop these humans from eating the crabs? I gave it a rock-hard shell! I put it on the bottom of the ocean! I named a *disease* after it! I knew I should have covered it in needles! (*over shoulder*) Jesus, you're going to have to go back down there!"

Lobsters, oysters, and crabs. Oh my!

I'm not just freaked out by shellfish. Seafood in general gives me the willies. With most seafood, I don't understand the appeal. Like anchovies. What is the difference between an anchovy and a sweaty eyebrow? Whenever I see an anchovy I think, *Someone has attacked Tom Selleck. Why would you want to put that on a pizza?* Octopus? Really? *Octo,* meaning "eight"; *pus* meaning . . . really? "Yup, the pus part's my favorite. Them suction cups remind me we need a new bathtub mat." The octopus is really the epitome of the sea monster. Initially delighting people as the frightening subject of seafarers' folklore, now the octopus delights people as high-end cuisine. Eaten, of course, after carefully boiling the octopus properly to rid it of slime, smell, and residual ink. Yum.

Many of these odd and unappealing food items are considered delicacies, which is a food term meaning "unjustifiably expensive." I suppose each culture has its own definition of what a delicacy might be. Things that are presently considered a delicacy in Western culture mystify me. I understand how you can rationalize some seafood as delicacies, such as fish eggs that were from their mother's womb untimely ripped, but snails? "Snails are a delicacy." Compared with what? Barnacles? Slugs? What would you have to be eating on a regular basis to make snails a *delicacy?* "I normally eat just mud and worms, so when I get a snail I'm like, SCORE!" "Snails are hard to come by." Really? Give me a shovel and twenty minutes. I think everyone is aware how disgusting snails are, and that's why they are served in a bowl of wine and butter and called "escargots," which is a French word loosely translated as "denial." Initially, they were probably called "snails" and served in a bucket of sludge. For some reason, no one ordered them.

I think the answer to the perplexing riddle of why we are eating any of these questionable items boils down to a simple fact: humans will eat *anything*, given the chance. Certainly, I can relate to this concept to an extent, but with some of these "edibles," I think we are taking this whole top-of-the-food-chain idea a bit too far. Take the squid. Are we really eating the swimming sea spider? "But I like fried calamari!" Sure, but you could deep-fry a rubber hose and it would taste good. "You know, with a little cocktail sauce, this is good hose!" You ever order calamari? There's always that piece that looks like a deep-fried tarantula. "You can have that one. I'll just stick with the garden hose."

The itsy-bitsy spider went into my big mouth.

EATING BBQLAND

Each city in the southeastern part of the United States has its own unique type of specialty food that can be found only in that city, and it all happens to be called "barbecue." "Oh, we do it different here." Of course, "barbecue" is not exclusively a southern cuisine. As you can see from the map, "eating barbecue" goes as far north as Kansas City, and I've had amazing barbecue in Champaign, Illinois, and in Syracuse, New York, but truly the heart of barbecue is in the South.

Touring around the South doing stand-up often feels more like an "Eating Barbecue Tour." There is a pride in each city's unique recipe for barbecue. It seems in every southern city you encounter the same guy who brags about the same two things: that a president ate at their famous barbecue place and that people have it shipped around the world. "Obama ate there, and you can get it shipped anywhere you want." There is such pride in the fact that their local food is mailed to people. I never have the nerve to point out that Spam is also delivered all around the world. The subtext of all their boasting seems to be "You know we got the best barbecue, and you're a fat guy . . .

so you should get some shipped to yourself." Lest I be considered rude, I always oblige. I've found barbecue to either be some of the best or the worst food I've eaten. There is no in between. Either it's an amazing meal I can't stop talking about, or I'm angry that I wasted the energy to lift the food to my mouth. Of course, I still finish the whole plate. As I mentioned before, I am not rude.

The inconsistency of the quality of barbecue almost seems to match the inconsistency of the meaning of the word *barbecue*. When you read the word *barbecue*, a multitude of different images comes to mind. Some of you may think of the surface on which the food is barbecued—for example, a grill. Some of you may think of a gathering of friends. Some may think of the sauce: *This chicken leg needs more barbecue.* You get the idea. *Barbecue* is a noun, a verb, an adjective, and even a potato chip. Barbecue is one of the only food genres I can think of that has its own acronym, "BBQ." This actually started out as "Bar-B-Q" but continued to get progressively shorter as the person who penned it ate more BBQ.

Kansas City

Now, I'm not saying I've tried every type of barbecue in this great land, but my most memorable experience of eating BBQ was not even in the South. It was at Oklahoma Joe's in Kansas City, Missouri. Yes, that is right, a barbecue place in Kansas City named Oklahoma Joe's. That makes as much sense as a Kansas City being located in Missouri. To make matters more confusing, this glorious meal was purchased and eaten in a gas station. Not a converted gas station. A functioning gas station. Jeannie, the kids, and I were on a bus touring the country, and it was highly recommended to me that I eat at this great BBQ place in a gas station. I figured, Why not? If the food is bad, at least it will be a great experience for the kids to eat surrounded by flammable liquid.

When we arrived at 11:00 a.m., I was surprised to see a line out the door. Not like a line at a cash machine. I mean a long, long line. Initially I was concerned that the kids wouldn't be able to last and Jeannie would once again confront me on my supposedly unhealthy attachment to food. The kind of unhealthy attachment that would have me risk waiting in a forty-five-minute line with five kids and there being no roller coaster at the end. Luckily I was able to find an open table for Jeannie and the kids, and as I returned to the line, I realized something unique. This substantial line was populated exclusively by men. Predominantly pudgy, balding, exhausted men in their thirties or forties. I fit right in. The most impressive thing about the line was the fact that all these middle-aged line-waiters were happy. At first glance, this would be the crowd that you would never want to be caught waiting in line with. The type of guys who would give up and leave if confronted by a line at the store while picking up some milk or diapers for their kids. "We'll make do. The kids can drink water and pee on a towel. I'm not an errand boy!" As we all know, lines are usually filled with angry people. Not that angry people wait in lines, but a lot of normal folk morph into antsy, angry, resentful people about five minutes into the queue. Not this line. You'd think all the men were waiting to turn in a winning lottery ticket, lost in a daydream of impending happiness. Occasionally one would turn to the absolute stranger behind them and giddily exclaim, "I'm getting the brisket! What are you getting?" I imagined that at the end of the line there would be a door that opened into a beam of light. "Welcome to fat-guy heaven. Come on in! There's always an NFL game on. The beer is free. You don't have to wake up tomorrow. You have no responsibilities. And you can eat all the barbecue you want in the middle of a gas station." Eventually I got up to the counter to place my order, and by the time I returned to the table with two heaping trays of Oklahoma Joe's barbecue, two of our kids were asleep, and the other three were under the table playing "fort." There were empty Saltine cracker wrappers, piles of crumbs, and broken crayons all over the table. I'm pretty sure that I saw smoke coming out of Jeannie's ears as she shot daggers at me with her eyes. I guess she didn't want the pulled pork. Who knows? *Women.* Anyway, the barbecue was delicious and we could fuel up the bus before we left. Eat and get gas. What a perfect afternoon.

Southern Comfort

People are just nicer in the South. They are. Even when they are rude they are polite. Maybe it's the singsong of the southern drawl, but even a "Y'all can go to hell" from a Southerner sounds friendly. "Well, thank you kindly. Y'all can go to hell too. An' y'all come back now, y'hear?" People in the South are nicer, but they are slower. I don't mean they are slower intellectually. I mean they just move slower.

FIREMAN: You have to get out! Your house is on fire!
SOUTHERN GUY: All right. All right. I'll leave. But first I have to drink me some sweet tea. Then I'll deal with that pesky house afire.

Biscuits and Gravy

I think I've identified why people in the South behave in such a nonchalant manner. It's the biscuits and gravy. Everyone in the South seems to move like they've just had two helpings of biscuits and gravy. They are moving like you might after

Thanksgiving dinner. You know, when you are uncomfortably full but pleasantly satisfied as you drag yourself over to the couch for a nap. That is how everyone below the Mason-Dixon Line moves in everyday life. I really believe it's the biscuits and gravy. The feeling you have after eating biscuits and gravy is identical to the feeling of chaining a bowling ball to your foot.

Most amazingly, people in the South are eating biscuits and gravy for breakfast. Yes, breakfast. They aren't coming home drunk late at night slurring, "I'll eat anything." They are waking up thinking, *Time for cement!* Then at lunch they are having fried chicken and waffles. And this is all before 2:00 p.m. It could be that the South will never rise again because they don't have the energy. Most of their cooking involves the same ingredients as papier-mâché. They are, in essence, eating piñatas down there. I'm convinced this is even the explanation for why Southerners talk the way they do. After you eat biscuits and gravy, you can't be expected to say both the words *you* and *all*. After a plate of biscuits and gravy, all anyone can muster is "Sho was some good biscuits and gravy, y'all." Then there's lunch. I never understood how someone rationalized eating fried chicken *and* waffles in the same meal.

"What should we serve with the fried chicken?"

"French fries?"

"No, something elegant like . . . a waffle or a gyro."

It's like someone thought, "I know it's lunch, but I'd also like to have breakfast *and* a heart attack." Mind you, I'm not criticizing the biscuits and gravy or the chicken and waffles. I find them delightful. I'm just saying if I lived down there I would be dead. On one bus tour I had biscuits and gravy for breakfast for nine days straight. I still haven't gone to the bathroom. That bus tour was twenty-five years ago!

Grits

You can't really discuss southern food without bringing up grits. When I reference grits during a stand-up show, Southerners will clap like I mentioned the college they attended or that I support the troops. Being southern means liking grits. Grits are not for everyone. It's almost as if someone was like, "If you like the taste of biscuits and gravy but without the taste of biscuits and gravy, then you'll love our man-made wet sand." I want to like grits. I try. I order them, but eventually I end up muttering to myself over my plate, "Are these undercooked? Overcooked? No wonder you guys came up with moonshine." When I've expressed this to Southerners, they always point out, "All y'all need to do to the grits is add a pound of cheese, a cup of sugar, and thirty candy canes." One of the many things I love about the South is that they don't even try to hide the fact that they are eating unhealthily. The following is a reenactment of me ordering in a restaurant in Roanoke, Virginia:

ME: (*looking at menu*) I'll have the bucket of lard and the salt stick.
WAITRESS: You want that deep-fried?
ME: Um, okay.
WAITRESS: Y'all want us to shoot at you while you eat it?
ME: Sure.

The South seems to be the home of comfort food. While I pride myself on making all food comfort food, there is uniqueness to the southern approach. "Southern comfort" to me just means any food in the South. "Southern cooking" almost seems to be code for "we are not counting calories." You will not find a nutritionist at a southern "boarding house–style" meal, and if you do, they will only be there to study what *not* to eat. Looking around at a southern-style dining establishment below the Mason-Dixon Line is very much like seeing the cigarette smoke in casinos. You have the sudden realization, *Oh, yeah, you are still allowed to do that here.* It's an experience of a different era.

Savannah

Allow me to take you along on the journey we had when we visited the famous Mrs. Wilkes' Dining Room in Savannah, Georgia. It's around noon as Jeannie, our five children, and I pile out of the taxi and see a line formed around the block on a beautiful, brick-paved, tree-lined, historic Savannah street. When I see the sheer number of people waiting outside to be seated for lunch, I know Jeannie will, again, be mad at me. Anyone with young children knows long lines don't mix well with toddlers (see "Kansas City," pages 45–47). Leaving the house in general really doesn't mix with toddlers, but long lines just indicate poor parental planning and judgment. That day's adventure was another classic example of "Jim choosing food over family." In a precautionary response I turn to Jeannie: "It will be worth it." The line is filled with nicely dressed retirees. It feels a little like an open casting call for actors needed to play country club members. They are all here for the Mrs. Wilkes southern-style boarding house dining experience. Soon enough we are sitting at one of the large tables for ten that my loud brood will share with strangers, Benihana-style. We don't order. Within a moment the table is covered with every foreseeable comfort food that George Wendt could think of. The meal is amazing. The conversation is minimal. Plates and bowls of fried chicken, cornbread dressing, sweet potato soufflé, black-eyed peas, okra gumbo, macaroni and cheese, corn muffins, and biscuits are shuffled around with the occasional "Oh, you have to try this." Like magic, you could take three scoops of something out of a bowl, and its contents would not diminish at all. All of the separate items would mix together on the plate into new combinations and blend into some other amazing thing that superseded the original taste. The whole was definitely greater than the sum of its parts. Now, I have a powerful appetite, but at this meal the endless bowls and plates of food conquered it. Eventually I had to declare, "The South has won!" Unlike Thanksgiving dinner, where you can, a few hours later, go back into battle to relive some of the more glorious moments with a turkey sandwich, at Mrs. Wilkes, there are no doggie bags. They literally will not allow you to take any unfinished food out of the restaurant. It is like an episode of *The Twilight Zone.* The endless, awe-inspiring food and the ethereally historic atmosphere of the dining room can only exist together. Removing one from the other could somehow diminish the power of the delectable time machine that is Mrs. Wilkes.

The dining room is located on the lower level of the late-nineteenth-century boarding house that the original Mrs. Wilkes ran for more than fifty years. Mrs. Wilkes's goal was to offer her guests comfortable lodgings and southern-style, home-cooked meals in a simple yet elegant setting. I never understood why the boarding house concept was such an important part of the southern culture until I experienced the meal that day. After eating ten pounds of fried chicken and side dishes, what person would ever have the energy to get up and actually go somewhere? Of course you would want to board. It was all I could do to stop myself from crawling up the stairs and passing out in someone's bed. Of course, though, I didn't. That would be ridiculous. I did the right thing and had Jeannie and the kids carry me back to the hotel.

I'm a bad influence on Jeannie.

SUPER BOWL SUNDAY FOODLAND

The first Sunday in February is a special day in the United States. It's the day of the Super Bowl—the championship game between the winners of the American Football Conference and the National Football Conference. People throw parties to watch the game and judge the commercials. I love football and enjoy the commercials, but what I most enjoy is the food served at Super Bowl parties. What is served on Super Bowl Sunday feels like a homecoming of all the great unhealthy American foods. They are dishes that taste great with beer and are all easy to eat while watching television. What could be more American than that? Hot dogs, pizza, and buffalo wings are great examples of Super Bowl Sunday foods. After traveling all around this amazing country, I have discovered that the deepest appreciation of and love for these Super Bowl Sunday foods can be found in the Midwest.

I grew up in the Midwest, or the "flyover" part of the United States. To many on the coasts, the Midwest is mostly boring or, at its best, charmingly boring. While I don't agree, I can empathize with this sentiment. I remember when I was ten years old looking around at my small Indiana town that didn't even have a McDonald's and thinking, *I'm not supposed to be here. There's been some mistake. Was I switched at birth? I am NOT a Midwesterner!* Of course, when I finally got to New York City, the first thing I discovered was that I am a Midwesterner. To the ethnocentric New York City comedy scene of the 1990s, comedians were Jewish, Italian, Puerto Rican, or African American, and I quickly learned that my ethnicity was Midwestern. I was a pale piece of white bread floating in a sea of ethnicity. And I loved it. To make matters more romantic, I was from Indiana, which to many is considered the trailer park of the Midwest or simply an "I-state." I once had someone ask me if I rode a tractor to school. Obviously not, I explained. Only the rich kids had tractors.

In some ways it's understandable why people have an almost dismissive view of the Midwest. It seems like everything in the Midwest was named in an effort to trick people into moving there. After all, the Midwest is not geographically in the West or in even the middle of the country. There must have been an exchange between someone loading up a stagecoach and a government official desperately trying to get people to settle in the Midwest in the early 1800s.

GOVERNMENT OFFICIAL: I see you're moving. Where are you going?

SETTLER: Well, I heard about the gold rush in California. I'm heading out West.

GOVERNMENT OFFICIAL: Have you thought about the . . . Mid . . . west?

SETTLER: Midwest? Where is that?

GOVERNMENT OFFICIAL: It's close to the West! It's in

the middle! Well, it's in the eastern part of the middle
of the western part of . . . well, there's plains. And
those plains are great. That's why it's called the
Great Plains. In the Midwest.

SETTLER: I think I just want to go out West.

GOVERNMENT OFFICIAL: Did I mention the lakes in
the Midwest? Great lakes. In fact, one is so great
they named it Superior. There's Great Plains, Great
Lakes, great everything. Did I mention it's the
breadbasket of the country? Bread is free in the
Midwest.

SETTLER: Uh, okay. I guess I'll go.

So in the true spirit of the American settlers, we set up
camp in the middle of nowhere, were bored and freezing, and
we created delicious food that would be perfect to eat in February while drinking beer and watching football.

Chicago

I grew up in Northwest Indiana, which is a suburb of Chicago.
I love telling people in Chicago I'm from Indiana. There is usually a perplexed look of "Where's that?" I then explain that
Indiana is the bordering state, which is ten minutes away. I had
one Chicago woman describe Indiana to me as "the state with
the road to Michigan in it." All these insults aside, I forgive
you, Chicago. I love Chicago and Chicago food.

Chicago is famous for its deep-dish pizza, but that is not the
only local specialty. If a city is lucky, they will have one food
specialty. Buffalo has wings. Philly has the cheesesteak. Chicago has so many. The best hot dog, the best Italian beef, and,
of course, the best pizza are all in Chicago. Now, before North-

easterners get all defensive about New York–style/New Jersey–style/New Haven–style pizza, let's embrace this fact: there is great pizza in many different cities, but Chicago is the *only* place to get deep dish. It's the only place that deep dish makes sense. Only Midwesterners would be patient enough to wait an hour for deep dish or gluttonous enough to actually eat deep dish.

Just a little snack before I go onstage in Chicago.

Chicago deep dish takes forever to cook and costs as much as four New York–style pizzas. Chicago deep dish is a commitment. You arrive at Uno's, Giordano's, Gino's East, or Lou Malnati's and place your order, and then you wait and wait for what seems like a lifetime. At times it feels like they are purposely tormenting you to make the deep-dish pizza seem all the more appealing. I actually make a point of not showing up hungry when I go out for a Chicago deep-dish pizza. It would be torture. To kill time, you eat a salad with provolone, salami, and pepperoncini in it and drink a pitcher of beer like you are preparing yourself for some kind of long, difficult journey of *waiting*. Finally your pizza arrives in a pan carried by your server with some kind of clamp contraption that I'm pretty sure is the same one they use to shape molten glass. After the first slice you are full, and you should be. You've eaten roughly three pounds of food that is baked on top of a crispy, cake-like crust. There is never a reason to eat more than one slice of deep dish, but you forge on. The wait has built an enthusiasm and excitement in you that can't be quelled by just one slice. Most humans stop after two slices, but I like to think of myself as a superhuman. My brother Joe, who lives in Chicago, makes fun of my love for Chicago-style deep-dish pizza. "It's for tourists." I don't care. Last March I brought my nine- and eight-year-olds for their first deep dish, and they thought it was weird. Weird? I immediately demanded a paternity test to see if they were actually my children.

Wisconsin

Every December Jeannie and I and our five hundred children travel to Milwaukee for the holidays. It's hard enough to eat healthy during the holidays. In Wisconsin, it's impossible. We usually are in Wisconsin for about ten pounds. That means one week for those of you who have never visited Wisconsin. That is how time is measured in Wisconsin. Well, it should be.

"How long have you been in Wisconsin?"

"Forty pounds."

"Oh, you came during Summerfest."

I don't know if it's possible to visit Wisconsin and not gain weight. Eating healthy doesn't seem like an option in Wisconsin. I don't think they even sell salads. And why should they? Wisconsin is the home of the butter burger, the kringle, the bratwurst, and cheese. Lots and lots of cheese. Eating healthy in Wisconsin makes as much sense as going to rehab in Amsterdam. It just doesn't work.

Some of my favorite things on this planet are from Wisconsin: beer, bratwurst, cheese, and, of course, my wife, Jeannie, in that order. Good food is everywhere you look. If you visit someone's house in Wisconsin, a cheese plate is put out. It could be eleven in the morning or ten o'clock at night. There will be a tray with Cheddar cheese and summer sausage. As a result of this plethora of edible happiness, people in Wisconsin eat all the time. Eating is important in Wisconsin. Even their beloved Green Bay football team is called the Packers. The state is about eating. It makes sense that the serial killer from Milwaukee was also eating his victims. He was simply doing what a serial killer from Wisconsin should do.

Cincinnati

Often there seems to be logic behind a local specialty. Omaha and Texas should have great steaks, given the cattle that are raised and packaged there. Italian beef in Chicago and bratwurst in Wisconsin make sense, given the Italian and German immigrants who settled there. From my uneducated viewpoint, chili makes no sense for Cincinnati. Even what they do with the chili in Cincinnati makes no sense. They serve it over pasta. Yet somehow it works. Chili in Cincinnati is not just a local culinary specialty. It is an industry. There are thriving fast-food chili franchises in the Cincinnati area. The story goes that a Greek immigrant in the 1920s wanted to cater to the local taste buds, so he started serving chili over spaghetti at his hot dog stand, which I'm pretty sure makes no sense whatsoever. Either way, Cincinnati chili does appeal to people like me who have trouble deciding between two entrées. I'm always amazed that they have drive-thru chili places. For sure, the most dangerous item to eat in a car would have to be spaghetti, with chili a close second. I'm surprised they don't make you eat it with chopsticks. Texting while driving seems less complicated.

St. Louis

St. Louis is famous for its thin-crust pizza, which almost seems like an overreaction to the Chicago deep-dish pizza, but when I contemplate St. Louis food I think of toasted ravioli. Maybe in St. Louis they call a deep fryer a toaster, because I'm pretty sure St. Louis toasted ravioli is just deep-fried ravioli. Calling deep-fried ravioli "toasted" is a little like calling World War II an extended argument. Toasted ravioli are delicious, but you have to eat them right away or they will turn into rocks. "When did you cook these?" "One minute ago. Now we call 'em St. Louis Diamonds." Many people don't know the St. Louis arch was constructed completely out of toasted ravioli a minute after they came out of a deep fryer.

Buffalo

Okay, Buffalo is not *technically* located in the Midwest, but it is a Great Lakes city with a Midwestern heart. The mere fact that it is the birthplace of buffalo wings makes it an honorary Midwestern destination. I'm not sure how eating chicken wings covered in spicy sauce makes watching sporting events on television so appealing, but it does. I assume most of you savages reading this eat chicken wings, aka buffalo wings. Those are baby chicken wings you are mindlessly dunking in delicious blue cheese dressing. I don't like to eat the baby bird's wings. I'm not a barbarian. This is why I prefer to eat their legs. I'd rather not take away a bird's ability to fly. I realize some of you are thinking, *Jim, while you are brilliant and handsome, you must realize chickens can't fly.* How do we know chickens can't fly? Maybe the chickens have become too dependent on those legs. Legs are just making birds lazy. Have you ever seen footage of a hippo crossing a river? There's always a bird sitting on its back. How lazy is that bird? It's going to take that hippo ten minutes to cross that river. That bird could just glide across. It's pathetic, really. That bird sitting on the back of the hippo, I want to eat its legs. Mostly because I'm pro hippo. I relate to the hippo. The hippo kind of looks like what would happen to the rhino if it ate only Super Bowl Sunday foods. Based on the appearance of the hippo, it is surprising that it is not indigenous to the Midwest.

MEXICAN FOODLAND

I hope it's not considered offensive that my favorite food from the southwestern part of the United States is the food from the neighboring country of Mexico. It shouldn't be insulting, given that Texas and parts of the southwestern United States were once part of Mexico. We may have taken the land after the Mexican-American War, but at least we were polite enough to keep the food, culture, and most of the street names. I'm convinced that anyone who doesn't like Mexican food is a psychopath. Mexican food is so good, you'd think the real immigration problem would be fat guys like me sneaking across the border *into* Mexico. I always imagine a pudgy blond guy being led by handcuffs into a paddy wagon saying, "I just needed some *good* guacamole!" It is a known fact that it is impossible to eat quality Mexican food and not be in a good mood afterward. Even bad Mexican food is better than 90 percent of all other foods.

I used to be a waiter in a Mexican restaurant in Indiana. Yes, Indiana. That's where you want to go for Mexican food—Indiana or Belgium. Actually, Indiana, like much of the Midwest, has a vibrant Mexican American community, so the Mexican food where I'm from was quite good. Then again, it's hard to screw up basic Mexican food. The Midwestern suburban Mexican food I grew up with consisted of the same four ingredients. As a waiter I was asked a lot of questions with the same answer.

> PATRON: What are *nachos*?
> ME: Nachos are tortillas with cheese, meat, and vegetables.
> PATRON: Oh, well then what is a *burrito*?
> ME: Tortilla with cheese, meat, and vegetables.
> PATRON: Well then what is a *tostada*?
> ME: Tortilla with cheese, meat, and vegetables.
> PATRON: Well then what is . . .
> ME: Look, it's all the same stuff. Why don't you say a Spanish word and I'll bring you something delicious made out of tortillas, cheese, meat, and vegetables?

It's all the same stuff in different shapes. It almost seems like a conspiracy. Like they had a meeting two hundred years ago in Mexico and some guy stood up and said, "Hey look, the reason I got everyone here is pretty simple. I figure we can give this same entrée seven different names and sell it to the Americans. Now, who's in on it?" Then one guy in back stood up and said, "Wouldn't that be dishonest?" "Well, if you keep your mouth shut, we'll name one of the entrées after you. What's your name?" "My name is Chimichanga." That's a true story.

The best Mexican/Mexican American/Tex-Mex food is found in places like San Diego, Los Angeles, Albuquerque, and, of course, Texas. Here are some of the great Mexican Foodland specialties.

Guacamole

I eat a lot of guacamole. If I died right now, I'm sure some of my children would just remember me as the balding guy who brought home the overpriced, delicious green dip. I hope at one point some really important person sat the inventor of guacamole down and told him or her, "You are a great human. We thank you for your contribution to our planet." Guacamole is made with the avocado, which is so delicious I think it should be reclassified as a cheese. When guacamole is on the table, I tend to feel sorry for salsa because guacamole gets all the attention. It is always eaten right away because it is that good and also because exposure to oxygen turns it brown in a matter of minutes. Guacamole should be chunky. Non-chunky guacamole just makes me sad.

Churros

Churros are originally from Spain, but since I've given credit to Wisconsin for the German bratwurst in this book, I should probably blame Mexico for the churro. If you don't know what a churro is, just try to picture a ribbed doughnut stick. A churro is not fluffy like a doughnut but rather hard and crunchy. It's like the pipe cleaner of pastry. Churros are sold at fairs or anyplace that might sell cotton candy or other foods we should never eat. Churros are also sold at places we should never eat, like a New York City subway platform. I've only had one churro in my life. The guy who sold it to me almost seemed surprised that I was buying it. I then realized I'd never seen anyone actually eat a churro. Maybe the guy who sold me the churro went home and yelled up to a roommate: "Hey, Churro, get down here. Remember that sugary bread wand you came up with when you were drunk? Well, I finally sold one today!"

Queso

Whenever I'm in Texas, I have to get queso. Well, I don't have to, but I do anyway. Queso is an amazing combination of melted cheese and chile peppers that I seem to crave once I enter the Lone Star State. It's a bowl of cheesy nirvana served with chips as an appetizer in Tex-Mex places. It's like that nasty pump cheese they put on nachos at the movies, but not made of recycled park benches. *Queso* even means "cheese" in Spanish. It's like eating a block of spicy cheese but without being interrupted by the annoying cheese chewing. I like to think of queso as the unhealthy cousin of guacamole and a great way to get full to the point of physical discomfort before they even start cooking your entrée.

Green Chile

New Mexico is really passionate about the green chile, and it's understandable. I'm amazed that the green chile does not have a greater national popularity. They are that good. Unlike the taste explosion of a jalapeño, the flavor of a green chile is balanced, consistent, and, of course, delicious. Comparing the jalapeño to the green chile is the same as comparing a burst of freezing cold air on a hot day to sitting in an air-conditioned room. In New Mexico the green chile is more than a simple ingredient—it is a necessity. They have green chile stews, green chile burgers, green chile pizza, green chile hash browns, and these are not stunt dishes. These are the most popular items on the menu in New Mexico restaurants. At times I think the reason why the green chile is not a nationwide phenomenon is because the people of New Mexico are secretly hoarding the tasty green chiles. They are hiding them from the rest of us. Everyone I've encountered in Albuquerque seems to have them in bulk stored in their freezer as if an impending green chile shortage is coming. I had a cab driver once confide, "I've got ten pounds of green chiles in my freezer." I didn't even ask her about green chiles. She just brought it up out of the blue. And you know what? I was impressed and a little jealous. The green chile addiction is one I understand. New Mexicans treat their green chiles like contraband. Sometimes if you drive around New Mexico, you will see locals selling green chile tamales out of an open trunk on the side of the road, and people are pulling over to buy them. Green chiles are exciting and a little dangerous. You have to wear gloves when peeling a roasted green chile, or your hands will burn. If I lived in New Mexico, I'd be eating so many green chiles I would have to get a hazmat suit. I heard there is talk of reshooting all the episodes of *Breaking Bad*, but instead of meth Walter and Jesse sell green chiles. I can't wait.

Fried Bread

The only thing more astounding than the dramatic beauty of the Southwest is the fact that people there are eating fried bread. There is unhealthy eating throughout the United States, but in New Mexico, Arizona, and Utah, there are stands that only sell fried bread. When I first saw that, all I could think was, *I've found my people.* I realize a doughnut is also fried bread, but at least we don't call it *fried bread.* In some parts of the Southwest fried bread is called "fry" bread. It's like a call to action. "If you aren't fat already . . . fry bread! Let's get fat!" Fried bread is very neutral and can pretty much go with anything. It is used in place of the shell for spicy tacos, covered in honey and sugar as a dessert, or just snacked on in its natural form. Fried bread is like the unhealthy Switzerland of the food world.

At what point do you even feel comfortable eating something called fried bread? I'd love to hear the interview to decide if someone is prepared to become a part of the fried-bread culture.

> INTERVIEWER: Have you ever eaten cake in the shower?
> APPLICANT: A couple of times.
> INTERVIEWER: You may be ready for fried bread. Ever eat in your car so you don't have to share with your children?
> APPLICANT: Every day!
> INTERVIEWER: You are definitely ready for fried bread.

Fried bread by its very name goes against all the basic rules of healthy eating. It is the opposite of a diet.

> DIET DOCTOR: Okay, I am putting you on a strict diet. Here are your rules. No bread. No fried food.
> ME: (*interrupting*) Okay, what about *fried* bread? Is there, like, a fried-bread-only diet?

I don't judge the fried-bread eaters. I admire them. They are much more honest than most of us. We eat fried bread, but we do it in code.

"Would you like fried bread?"

"Never! (*sotto*) I'll just have an *elephant ear*."

"Would you like fried bread?"

"Of course not! I am a debutante! I'll just have a *beignet*."

We have a million names for fried bread, but in the end it's all fried bread. We just want to eat fried bread and have no one find out about it. We are like that guy at the party trying to find weed.

"Hey, is your friend *Herb* here tonight?"

"Who?"

"You know. He hangs around that other guy named *Bud*?"

"I still don't know what you are talking about."

"*You* know, he's going out with the girl from Mexico named *Marijuana*?"

"Sorry, I don't know that dude. Hey, you want to smoke some pot?"

WINELAND

It's always fascinating interacting with crowds after shows. I can get a sense of each city or state's identity and what they are proud of while meeting audience members. Some states are very vocal. "We're from New York, and we're tough!" "We're from Texas, and we like things big!" My home state is more like, "We're from Indiana, and . . . we're going to move." After shows in some cities, audience members will express gratitude for the show, and then they will add in an apologetic thank-you for coming to their town. "I'm sorry you had to come all the way here. Can you take me with you?" Being from a small town in Indiana, I can relate to that feeling: "Sorry, there's nothing cool here." The one place I never encounter even a hint of low geographic self-esteem is Northern California. This is understandable, since NorCal is so beautiful, rich, and re-laxed. It's an abundant, good world in Northern California, and the residents know it. It's not arrogance. It's just grate-ful awareness. Everyone in Northern California seems to be healthy, financially stable, and drinking wine. Did I mention the wine? It's flowing everywhere in Northern California. It is wine country, so it's no surprise that fine wine in NorCal is as common as Budweiser in St. Louis. Wine is a key element of the culture, and it is overemphasized with gracious abandon. Bottles of wine are gifted to me at every show I do in Northern California. The outdoor stages are located in wineries so beautiful I feel like I am performing in a painting. Last year I even performed at a wine-themed music festival called Bottle Rock. Yes, "bottle" refers to a wine bottle, and, yes, I was given bottles of wine there too.

I enjoy wine, but I'm certainly not an expert. My knowledge pretty much ends at the difference between red and white. My ignorance is usually hidden from the world until I'm handed a wine list when I go out to dinner. Does anyone really know what they're looking at when they look at a wine list? Because if you do, I think you're probably an alcoholic. "Yeah, I had three of these for breakfast." I pretend to read over the binder of eight thousand wines with an inquisitive look on my face, but I don't know what I'm looking at. I can never remember the names of the wines I enjoyed in the past, because during those times I was, well, drinking wine.

Occasionally I'll make the mistake of asking which wine the waiter would suggest. They always seem to point at one of the more expensive wines. "Well, this wine would complement your meal." I always think to myself, *Is there a box of wine you'd recommend? 'Cause that would complement my wallet.* Wine intimidates me. At fancy restaurants all the names and types of wine seem infinite. It's like no wine name can appear on more than one wine list. Every time I open one of those huge wine list books I try to identify one wine that I've seen before, but I just end up looking like an idiot. It's exactly like that nightmare you have before finals in high school where you don't recognize anything on the test and it all looks like gibberish. When it comes to the fancy wine list, I am 100 percent white-trash hick.

There is an inherent formality with wine. It is absolutely necessary to drink wine out of a wineglass. Drinking wine out of anything else is kind of pathetic. "Hey, can you refill my Yahtzee shaker? Hit this sippy cup too, will ya? *Danke.*" Wine formality reaches its apex when you are responsible for "tasting" a newly opened bottle of wine when you are out to dinner. A feeling of anxiety always comes over me. All confidence seems to evaporate as I take the sample sip. What does good wine taste like? What does bad wine taste like? I usually just look at the waiter and say, "Yeah, that's wine, all right. Fill 'er up."

COFFEELAND

It's impossible to talk about coffee and not think about the Pacific Northwest. Seattle changed the way we drink coffee. Well, at least what we pay for coffee. Starbucks, Tully's, Dutch Bros., and Seattle's Best all come from the upper-left-hand corner of the map. While all have excellent coffee, in a popularity contest, Starbucks wins. Starbucks coffee is everywhere. It's in malls, hotels, and even in some restrooms of existing Starbucks. It's insane to think that one day not that long ago John Starbuck asked his wife, "What if we serve strong coffee at three hundred degrees and charge five bucks for it?"

I like to think coffee comes from beans; therefore, it's a vegetable. Coffee is the only thing most of us have for breakfast—or in my case, when I wake up in the afternoon. Coffee is a staple of our lives. Coffee plays such an important role in my life, I've contemplated getting coffee a Christmas present. I was thinking a mug. A mug that says WORLD'S GREATEST VEGETABLE. I need coffee to get out of bed and get through the day. However, after fifteen cups of coffee I do feel there is a diminishing return. It almost seems as if it starts to have the opposite effect, as processing all that caffeine exhausts my system. At times coffee just feels to me like a sleeping potion with a delayed time release that can only be remedied by additional coffee. Even the person who decided on the spelling of the word *coffee* seems to have had too much caffeine.

Initially, I was reluctant to pay more than a dollar for a cup of coffee. Coffee shops like Starbucks and their boutique coffee shop competitors seemed annoying to me. Why was everyone so pompous and aloof? I'm here for coffee, not to write the next great American novel. I didn't understand why the espresso machine was the size of a station wagon or why I should have to wait longer to pay *more* for a cup of coffee. I thought of coffee as just a caffeine delivery device, but eventually I came to care deeply about the taste. The desire for good-tasting coffee is a secondary step in the coffee addiction. First you get addicted to the crutch of caffeine in coffee and then you find your taste preference. I was seduced by the flavor of good coffee. I like my coffee strong, black, and frequent. "Okay, expensive strong coffee, you win. I'm lost without you. Where do I send all of my money?" At this point, weak coffee angers me, and I believe brewing it like that should be considered a crime.

The wait I encounter in coffee shops still annoys me a little. I hold myself back from barking at the people in line before me, "Just order! You are getting a beverage, not picking a college to attend!" I'm impatient, but I still wait. I am a serious coffee drinker and I have to stand in line with others like me as well as the amateurs. I go to coffee shops for good coffee, and amateurs go for coffee-flavored milkshakes. I find it humorous that adults have found a way to use coffee shops as a means to not look ridiculous by walking around in broad daylight with a huge cup of ice cream with a straw in it. "It's a Frappuccino! I'm an adult!"

I used to not appreciate the employees in coffee shops. They seemed too snobby and nonchalant. And slow. There is not-being-in-a-hurry slow, and then there is "I work-in-a-boutique-coffee-shop" slow. The coffee shop employees always seem like they could use some caffeine themselves. I remember thinking to myself, *Who the hell does that guy think he is?* Now I understand that the people who work in coffee shops are entitled to act self-important. After all, they are the first responders of everyone's day. They are delivering the first fix of caffeine to all us addicts, and they have to take their time or it could become Armageddon. They are heroes, really. Or drug dealers. Either way, they are allowed to be jerks. Thank you, arrogant coffee shop employee.

FOOD ANXIETYLAND

Traveling around doing stand-up, you learn about the uniqueness of certain cities. A stand-up comedian knows they will be competing for an audience with amazing music scenes in Nashville and Austin. In New York, Las Vegas, and Chicago you will contend with an enormous entertainment scene. You'd never schedule a show in any Canadian city if the local hockey team (NHL or minor league) has a game. In New Orleans, it is a different situation. In New Orleans you compete against food. Sure, New Orleans has jazz and binge drinking, but the real competition for live stand-up comedy shows is restaurants and food in general. There is great dining in most large cities, but not like the dining in New Orleans. You don't just dine in New Orleans. You overeat. Not overeating in New Orleans is like going to Paris and not looking at the Eiffel Tower.

Whenever I'm about to go to New Orleans for a show, I always suffer food anxiety. I'm not being cute here. There is actually an angst that comes over me. There are just too many decisions. Where should I eat? What should I eat? How often can I eat? Did anyone watch all the episodes of *Treme*? New Orleans is a food mecca. It's not just the variety; it's the fact that I have never had bad food in New Orleans. I think it may be against the law. Even getting a hot dog from a street cart in New Orleans is a culinary adventure. Typically, a city or a region of the country is known for a particular dish or a type of food that an overeater can track down in a day by asking a local. That is not the case in New Orleans. The bread, meats, and spices of New Orleans are as fun, unique, and diverse as its inhabitants. The dishes are at once pedestrian and simultaneously exotic. Should I eat Cajun, Creole, fried chicken, beignets? I could go on for a page or two. It's too much. I never have enough time.

I think the po'boy sandwich was named after a guy who was trying to decide where to eat for his one meal in New Orleans. Settling on a place to eat there is my equivalent of *Sophie's Choice*. How do I choose one over the other? It's painful. To make matters worse, this issue affects me not only for every meal but also for every moment of the day. Sure, for breakfast you need to get a beignet at that tourist-trap place, but what about Cajun-style biscuits and gravy? For lunch you have to get jambalaya, but what about chicken and sausage gumbo? Breakfast, lunch, snack, dinner, late-night dinner, pre-breakfast ... it's all too overwhelming. I understand people plan actual food vacations to New Orleans under the guise of enjoying jazz, but I'm typically in the Big Easy for one night. One night! That translates into only six meals for me. How will I decide? If I had to make a film about my experience in New Orleans, I would definitely get Meryl Streep to play me.

Some gumbo while I figure out what to order.

AT LEAST I DON'T EAT BLUBBER

Every morning I get up at 6:00 a.m. I meditate, do my yoga, drink a protein shake, run six miles, and then commence lying to everyone about what I do every morning. The truth is, I didn't get a chance to do yoga or jog this morning or any other morning of my life. But those things are more likely to happen than the likelihood of me ever drinking a protein shake. I don't eat healthy. It's difficult to eat healthy. At times I make an effort, but I usually fail. I hate when I try to order a salad and my mouth says, "I'll have a Double Quarter Pounder with Cheese." It's like I have autocorrect in my mouth. My heart may be willing, but my brain abdicated to my taste buds long ago. I'm not a healthy eater. I'm like the Dr. Oz of unhealthy eating. I don't mean this as a criticism of Dr. Oz, who I'm sure is a nice man, but I'm starting to doubt he is really from Australia. Where is your accent, Dr. Oz?

Stages of Eating Healthy

I go through different stages of healthy eating. First it's the "I'm only eating salads" phase. Then I'll get to the "I've eaten salads for half a day straight—I should treat myself to a hamburger" phase. Finally, I get to the last phase, which I'm in right now, the "I don't give a phase."

If you are like me, when you enter this last phase, you begin to justify things. "I'm in a hurry, so it's just an absolute necessity that I go to McDonald's. I don't want to go, it's just that I have to or it's possible I could starve to death." Then all your food choices quickly become an endless stream of irrational rationalizations. "Well, I'll allow myself to eat *that* because I had a salad a month ago. Well, I've earned *that* because I took out the garbage. Well, I'm starting my starvation diet tomorrow, so I really should have five hamburgers."

My favorite rationalization is when the food is free. I have never been able to turn down free food. Maybe it's because I grew up with five siblings, and food was always a valuable commodity. Maybe the inability to resist free food has its roots in my college years, when I couldn't afford food and at one point resorted to eating a can of pie filling. Whatever the reason, I just can't resist it if it's free. Free food is the temptress that can make me give up my morals and cheat on any diet. My diets always end in divorce.

I'm married to a beautiful woman. I'm not just saying that because Jeannie is helping me write this book and she is sitting right next to me. Well, not *right* next to me, but chances are she will probably see this page at some point. But anyway, she is beautiful. When we are in public together and strangers find out Jeannie is my wife, there is usually an audible *Wow!* I used to find this flattering until I realized it was an insult. I'm not a caveman. Anyway, there are so many impressive things about Jeannie besides her beauty and brains. Most noticeable would be that Jeannie has given birth to five healthy babies, and I look like I ate five healthy babies. She is a genetic anomaly. It seems she can eat whatever she wants to and still remain thin and energetic. Jeannie aspires to make everyone in our family healthy eaters, but it's kind of hard with me around.

Jeannie has gone from wanting us to eat healthy, to wanting us to eat organic, to not buying food. She buys this bread that is made from 100 percent organic tree bark. "Why do you need regular bread when you can lick a tree?" Jeannie likes to buy organic whole foods. Organic is probably the biggest scam of the century. For those of you unfamiliar with it, *organic* is a grocery term for "more expensive."

There are people who eat only organic food, and then there are people who don't have tons of money to waste. You can pretty much find anything made organically these days, including healthy versions of unhealthy food. French fries have been replaced by sweet potato fries, which are the Gardenburger of fries and taste exactly like something terrible. We all know hot dogs are bad for us, so that's why there is the tofu dog. I'm pretty sure the guy who invented the tofu dog never actually ate a real hot dog. If he had, he never would have invented the tofu dog. Or maybe he tasted a real hot dog *after* he invented the tofu dog and was then filled with remorse. The tofu dog became his Frankenstein's monster. "Why? Why did I create the tofu dog? We must stop the tofu dog!"

There are even organic candies, cookies, and chips that fall into another category known as "Whole Junk Food." These foods fit into my rationalization pattern very nicely: "These potato chips are cooked with avocado oil, so I can eat ten bags. It's good for me." Usually the only discernible difference between a regular potato chip and a "healthy chip" is the difficulty in opening the bag. Supposedly there are good fats and bad fats. I like to think of myself as a good fat. It helps my self-esteem when I look in the mirror.

Jeannie loves buying vegetables at the farmers' market. Can we just settle down with the farmers' market enthusiasm?

Instead of going to a grocery store and getting everything I need, I can stand outside and buy some dirty vegetables on the street from absolute strangers who supposedly live on a farm but are probably serial killers. How do we know that some of the people selling stuff at the farmers' market didn't just buy that stuff at the grocery store? Some con artist probably came up with the idea.

> CON ARTIST: Psst! C'mere, kid. This is what we're gonna do, see? We're gonna go in that grocery store and buy a bunch of unwashed vegetables. Then we're gonna sell them on the street for ten times the price.
>
> KID: That will never work!
>
> CON ARTIST: Just tell them they're from the *farm*, so they taste better, see?
>
> KID: You're a genius, Mac. A genius! We're gonna get RICH!

It's hard to eat healthy. It's too expensive: *Should I have this salad for twelve bucks or these five hamburgers for a dime?* I resent when I go out to dinner and they try to sell me the healthy food for the same price as the good food. What a rip-off. Even more infuriating is the way the waiter tries to present the healthy choice on the menu as if it tastes as good as real food. "Tonight were having a *delicious* entrée of steamed spinach and tofu over a bed of vitamins." Great. And for dessert why don't we get our teeth cleaned?

I eat kind of healthy compared to some of the Eskimos up in Alaska. They're eating blubber up there. Compared to them, I'm practically dieting by eating a Cinnabon. Whale blubber? Isn't that like eating a fat guy? Actually, it would be healthier to eat a fat guy. I don't want to appear to insult Eskimos and their culture, even though I'm starting to think they don't even make those Eskimo Pies. I realize the weather is not great in Alaska, but consuming something called *blubber* is a little insane. They are actually eating something that is the direct result of eating unhealthy. Isn't blubber like the fattest part of fat? If fat made a noise, it would be *blub-ber*. You'd think at some point one of the Eskimos would stand up at a meal and say, "Hey, I love blubber. Who doesn't like blubber? But I was thinking we could mix in some salads or, maybe, less blubber?" Who knows, maybe the blubber eaters think we eat weird stuff: *Those poor bastards down there don't even eat blubber.* If you are eating blubber, what do you consider bad for you? I'm pretty sure drinking liquefied lard might be a healthier choice. On the other hand, maybe we got lucky because of the blubber. It's possibly the reason why Alaska became part of the United States. Maybe the Canadian explorers made it up to Alaska and saw the Eskimos eating blubber and thought, *Oh, the Americans already got here.*

I look forward to the day we can walk into health food stores and see organic whale blubber for sale. "Oh look, it's *whole* whale blubber. That's really good for you, right?"

NOBODY REALLY LIKES FRUIT

Recently I saw an apple and for a moment I didn't recognize it. Just for a second I was like, *What is that, a paperweight? Oh that's an apple! It's so weird to not see it in a pie.* I'm not proud of this, but let's be honest. Nobody really wants fruit. We only act like we do. A false desire for fruit is woven into the fabric of our culture. We are told that Adam and Eve were kicked

out of paradise for eating an apple. An apple? Would an apple ever really tempt you? I would've looked at the serpent, "An apple? Uh, cover it in caramel and come back to me. You got any cake back there?"

Take this apple.
Nobody wants it.

Sure, people will eat it if there's nothing else around, but, given the other options, fruit just isn't that great. Even when people seem excited to see fruit, they are really just relieved it's not vegetables. Fruit involves too much work. You have to wash it. You have to remove that sticker al-Qaeda put on there. There's work with fruit. Think about the orange. Has peeling an orange ever really been worth it? I always think, *There's not even chocolate in this thing.* Yet people still imagine they like fruit. Some weirdos even convinced everyone that the gathering of a fruit is a fun activity. Once a friend excitedly asked me, "Why don't we go apple picking?" Because I'd rather die. You have to pay to pick apples? "Okay, how much do I owe you to work for you for free? Don't rip me off. I'm no dummy." Once in my pre-Jeannie life I dated a woman who made me go blueberry picking. One August she said to me, "I think I'd like to go blueberry picking. Maybe we should go blueberry picking?" I remember thinking, *No. No way. They can't even get migrant workers to do that.* Yet like ten seconds later there I was in upstate New York, picking blueberries. I remember thinking, *What happened? What am I doing here?* The whole experience was much worse than it sounds. Picking blueberries is not like picking pumpkins. It's not like, "Hey, I got one. Let's get the hell out of here." With blueberries you are never done. Even after three hours you tell yourself things like *Uh, I got four. We could make a muffin. There's got to be a machine to do this!* It's no surprise that I broke up with that woman after that fun date. Irreconcilable differences.

This insane fruit-acquiring behavior is because we think we like fruit. Like it's some prize rewarding us for our labor. Upon further analysis, this is most certainly not the case. We don't actually like fruit. Why did the fruit cocktail disappear? Simple. It was horrible. When you think about it, has a strawberry ever lived up to expectations? I'm convinced strawberries never tasted good but just had fantastic public relations. "Dip it in chocolate and no one will even notice that it's fruit!" If honeydew melons disappeared from the planet, would anyone even notice? We would just continue to eat prosciutto like God intended us to.

Nobody really *wants* fruit. This is why there are so many paintings in museums of just bowls of fruit. You could start painting a bowl of fruit, leave for a couple of hours or even days, and when you came back, no one would have touched the bowl of fruit. On the other hand, if you're painting a doughnut, you better finish it on the first sitting. You can't even take a bathroom break. Upon returning, you might ask, "Hey, what happened to my doughnut?!" Your friend with a full mouth will exclaim, "I don't know. Some fat guy ran in here. Well, I'm going to go get some milk and take a nap." This also explains why there is no doughnut art. When was the last time you saw a painting of a doughnut? The subject always gets eaten. Sad, really. I think anyone would love a painting of a doughnut. Dunkin' Donuts just has two *D*'s in their logo and no picture of a doughnut. Why? It's pretty clear to me that someone ate it before they had a chance to capture the image. Do I have to explain everything?

Edible Arrangements

At some point during the turn of the last century it became acceptable for people to send cut fruit arranged like flowers. I'd like this to stop. I understand you might find nothing wrong with someone sending you a beautiful arrangement of fruit on a stick that you eventually throw out. I realize that instead of sending flowers to say congratulations or sorry for your loss, people want to send these expensive fruit arrangements, but frankly I find it unsanitary. Cut-fruit always seems like it's on the verge of going bad: *Our deepest sympathy . . . for your impending diarrhea.* I always imagine the person arranging the cut-fruit display in a robe watching *The View* and occasionally sneezing. And honestly, why do "edible arrangements" have to be fruit? Can't you just send me a bouquet of meatballs?

EVEN FEWER PEOPLE LIKE
VEGETABLES

If nobody wants fruit, even fewer people want vegetables. This is because, overall, vegetables taste horrible. Don't believe me? Why, then, are we surprised when vegetables taste good? "Oh my God, this beet is delicious." We are surprised because the expectation is that vegetables will taste like, well, vegetables. People eat vegetables, but nobody WANTS to eat vegetables. Think back to the last time you ate a vegetable. Did you WANT to eat the vegetable? Be honest. Maybe it was part of a healthy choice you made: "I'll eat some carrots." Congrats on that healthy choice, but don't confuse a healthy choice with a desire to eat a vegetable. I mean, I don't want to be fat, but I want vegetables less. Of course, I'm forced to eat vegetables when there are children present.

Admiring the pretty colors before going to buy ice cream.

Parents dishonestly announce how good vegetables are in front of young children, hoping that because of the youngsters' absence of life experience and sheer stupidity, they will be tricked into liking them. The lie that "vegetables are good" usually expires around the same time as the belief in Santa and the notion that adults actually know what they are doing.

Let's say I'm wrong. Maybe you do want to eat a vegetable. Let's now subtract deep frying, vinegar, dairy, oil, or an unhealthy amount of salt from the vegetable. Do you still WANT the vegetable? If you say no, you are like me. If you said, "Yes, Jim, I love eating raw radishes by the handful," you are a weirdo and probably need therapy. Okay, I'm jealous.

Mostly I've found that vegetables MUST be deep-fried, drowned in vinegar, or covered with some form of dairy or salt to have any appeal. Even at that point, the improvement is very minimal. It's staggering, the exertion that is put into making vegetables appealing. I'd like to applaud the effort behind grilled vegetables, but I'm pretty sure everyone finds them soggy and a waste of precious grill space.

At their best, vegetables are the sidekicks. The opening band you didn't come to see at the concert. The asparagus next to the steak. The expectation is that the entrée is so good you won't notice that you are eating mutant blades of grass. There is no better sidekick than the potato, mostly in deep-fried form. Even so, potatoes, like corn, are fake vegetables and a great excuse to your wife if you eat a lot of fries and tortillas: "I had *so* many veggies today, honey!"

The Vegetable Tray

Occasionally, raw, naked, unenhanced vegetables are shamelessly presented as if they are actually desirable. This is the case with the elaborate vegetable party tray. When you are at a party and there is a vegetable tray, aren't you a little surprised? I always think, *Wow, that's a waste of money.* A tray of vegetables at a party almost makes me sad. Here is a meticulously arranged tray of neatly cut vegetables for someone to throw out at the end of the night. I think *crudités* is a French term meaning "toss in le garbage at end of le party." The only thing that raw vegetables have ever been good for is the careers of hummus and ranch dressing.

The vegetable tray reflects very poorly on the shortsighted host of the party you are attending. "Who is throwing this party? A nutritionist? Peter Rabbit? Is this a party or a Weight Watchers meeting?" You know they are just there for decoration. Who doesn't want to look at pretty colors while scarfing down pigs in a blanket? But actually *eat* the raw vegetable decoration? Hell, I'd rather eat a candle. What, I'm the only one here who eats the occasional candle at parties? Why do you think they're scented?

I almost feel sorry for the vegetables on the tray. They don't stand a chance against the other party appetizers. I know what it feels like to be the cauliflower next to the chips and guacamole. I've been to the beach and been the pale guy next to the tan bodybuilder. It's not a good feeling.

> CAULIFLOWER: What the hell am I doing on this table? I can't compete with a bowl of peanut-butter-filled pretzels! As if that ranch dressing is going to help sell me.

Some of us have to settle down with the ranch dressing. The usage is getting out of control. "I can't help it. I love ranch dressing. I like to dip my pizza in ranch dressing." That's fine. You are just not allowed to vote anymore. Ranch dressing is rather pathetic, really—after all, it's made from buttermilk and sadness. Prior to ranch dressing, nobody had ever eaten a raw vegetable. Throughout history, mankind has always known that vegetables were primarily put on this Earth for decoration.

> FARMHAND: Done with the harvest. Nobody is eating the Indian corn.
> FARMER: Feed it to the cows.
> FARMHAND: They didn't want it either.
> FARMER: Throw it on the front porch next to the gourd and jack-o'-lantern and remind me not to grow it next year.

Types of Vegetables

A list of different types of vegetables reads like the roster of attendees at an international conference for the barely edibles.

Brussels Sprouts: Clearly some kind of cruel joke by God.

Bell Pepper: Probably what makes cooked bell peppers so special is that they can ruin the taste of any dish they are in. Green, red, yellow, or orange peppers—you can change the color, but when I see one, I prepare for disappointment. Green is by far the worst of the culprits. Green peppers can make the best steak bitter and a grown man cry.

Radish: Interesting fact: No one has ever really wanted to eat more than one radish in a lifetime. Radishes are a fascinating example of how something can be both tasteless and burn your tongue at the same time.

Celery: Celery better get buffalo wings a great holiday present every year.

Squash: The name says it all. Pretty much the only thing that can squash my appetite.

Cauliflower: The unpainted broccoli imposter.

Asparagus: Most interesting thing about asparagus is how fast it makes your pee smell like asparagus.

Zucchini: The cucumber's ugly and disappointing cousin. (Similar to what the raisin cookie is to the chocolate chip cookie.)

Cucumber: The cucumber is just a pickle before it started drinking.

Pickles and Hot Peppers

It seems whenever I identify a green vegetable I enjoy, it is a pickled vegetable or a hot pepper. Pickles are so good you'd think being "in a pickle" would be a good thing. Actually, a great thing. Pickles are delicious. Imagine a Cuban sandwich without the pickle. Wait, don't do it. It's a sad thought, actually. A Cuban sandwich without the pickle is just a ham-and-cheese sandwich with a slab of pork. Who would ever order *that*? Well, I guess I would, but I am a unique case.

If a pickle can define a meal, a hot pepper is there to overpower one. The hot pepper is the marching-band cymbal of vegetables. It's like, "This is a pretty tasty sandwich—WOW, HOT PEPPER!" The super-hot-food thing is weird. It's like, "Eat this thing that will burn off your nose hairs and kill all your taste buds to make the food better." It's surprising that we don't put thumbtacks on our beds to enjoy our sleep more. But for me hot peppers are highly addictive.

I seem to have an abusive relationship with hot peppers. I probably need a support group. I know what they are going to do to me, yet I cannot resist them. At night I'm all "Yay, jalapeños!" The next morning I'm all "Boo, jalapeños!" Still, like a true codependent, I am the person who willingly keeps going back to the abusive relationship. I don't want to give too much information, but they were probably eating jalapeños the night before writing the Johnny Cash song "Ring of Fire." Still, I would much prefer to suffer the aftereffects of an exciting hot pepper than eat a boring vegetable. What am I, a monk?

As a society, I am sure we can all agree that vegetables should be removed from their classification as actual food. I am pretty confident that the food experts agree, because they are giving us subliminal anti-vegetable messages. For instance, remember that "healthy" food pyramid they used to show, where the stuff you are not supposed to eat is in that tiny tip and the things that are good for you are at the bottom? I don't want to sound like a conspiracy theorist here, but I believe that the true purpose of that pyramid is to be a rating system for taste. It's no surprise that the vegetables are the lowest on the scale. I think that the secret engineers of the food pyramid design are the Masons. They hate vegetables too, right? Let's just admit the truth. After all, what is most people's worst fear besides death? You got it: ending up a vegetable.

SALAD DAYS

As a young child I'd see people eating a salad and think, *They must be dying or, even worse, training for a marathon or something.* To me, salad eaters never seemed happy. I just didn't understand the appeal. I still don't. It's a well-known fact that it's impossible to have a good time when a salad is placed in front of you. Why would someone voluntarily eat lettuce? A salad is never anyone's preferred choice. When a waiter asks, "Would you like a salad or fries with your cheeseburger?" does anyone actually say salad? Well, maybe some people say it, but no one actually *means* it. "Hmm, would I like to pretend to eat healthy, or would I like to enjoy my meal?"

Salads are good for you. We all know that. Yet, for having such a terrific health perception, eating a salad still feels like a surrender. Even when someone orders a salad at lunch, it's presented as the decision of a martyr giving up their happiness to the waiter: "I'll just have the salad." Like they are part of a group escaping from prison, but they have fallen down and injured themselves. "No, go on without me. I'll just slow you down." Sure, a salad is a great way to eat greens, get roughage, or re-create a lunch scene from *Sex and the City*. Possibly the most impressive thing about a salad is that you can eat tons and tons of it and never be satisfied. Salads are all about health. No one on death row is ordering a house salad as a last meal. If we found out salads were bad for us, would anyone ever eat another salad? I doubt we'd ever hear someone say, "I was so bad. I just had a salad."

After I've eaten a salad I always feel I've earned something, like a meal, or at least maybe I've raised money to fight cancer. "I will finish this salad if you sponsor me for five dollars a leaf." A salad for me takes so much effort. That's why on the rare occasion I've had a salad as an entrée, I feel less like I've made a healthy choice and more that I'm being punished. Like I'm being sent to bed without a meal. I remember finishing my salad entrée only to realize: *That's it? What a disappointment. I have nothing to look forward to.* This is not to say I don't eat salads. I do. In fact, I had a salad as recently as 1995. Okay, fine. I have eaten salads. Whenever I get a steak, I always order a salad, thinking that will somehow balance it out: *Twenty pounds of meat, two leaves of lettuce. That should cover it.* I guess I do enjoy a salad every now and then. Well, I should say I enjoy salad dressing with just a touch of lettuce. I don't even like lettuce on a cheeseburger. I need salad dressing. Without a heavy dose of salad dressing I feel like I'm eating a bag of yard work. Salad dressing is lettuce gravy. It's there to mask the inadequacies. My salad dressing of choice has changed over my lifetime. As a child it seemed there were only the fake "ethnic" dressings: French, Italian, Russian, and, of course, Thousand Island (I still haven't figured out where Thousand Island is on a map, but I think it may be in the South Pacific). Now there are innumerable dressings. I mostly enjoy blue cheese dressing because it invalidates any possible positive elements of a salad.

Unfortunately, salad dressing doesn't seal the deal for making salads desirable. We've made every effort to make the salad easier to prepare and consume. There is the salad shooter, and for one second McDonald's tried selling cups—yes, cups—of salad: "It's salad you can eat while driving!" The salad people are desperately trying to make it easier for us to eat a salad. There are those prewashed, tossed bags of lettuce in grocery stores that you literally only need to add dressing to, and people still won't eat them. I shudder to think how many landfills are piled with plastic bags of brown slimy lettuce leaves that have withered away, neglected in someone's lower refrigerator drawer. But we still try and try to like salad. It is amazing the effort put into making lettuce or a salad appealing. We add nuts, dried fruit, and I've even seen marshmallows. All in a valiant effort to make salads, well, *not* salads. "Yeah, can I have some more cheese? Some bacon, and can you throw in a Snickers bar? Hey, instead of the lettuce, can I get French fries?" Whenever you go out to dinner, they always try to improve the salad through presentation. They bring it in like it has some kind of importance, when we all know it's just the magazine that you read on the train before you reach your destination. But a magazine has more flavor. "Would you like some fresh pepper on your salad?" Can anyone really tell the difference between fresh and stale pepper? "Hey, wait a minute. This isn't fresh pepper. I grew up on a pepper farm, and this is some stale-ass pepper." I can't even taste the pepper. They might as well ask if I'd like a wooden wand waved over my salad.

ME: Uh, okay.
WAITER: (*waving pepper grinder over salad*) La, la, la.
    Enjoy your magic salad.
ME: I didn't know I was getting a magic salad.

Occasionally, in fancy restaurants they will prepare the salad at your table. This ends up only being awkward because there really is nothing interesting about watching a salad being prepared. It's like a bad magic show. But you have to be polite. "Oooooh, lettuce! Ooooh, oil and vinegar!" I never know what to say to the waiter while he's making the salad. It feels rude to ignore them. "How long have you been in the salad biz?" "Nice wooden spoons." "Oh, yeah, toss my salad!" I feel like some kind of dictator. I always assume people at other tables are judging me. "That guy is so controlling he's having them make his salad in front of him."

Sometimes restaurants will go the whole other way with salads. Instead of preparing it at your table, they'll have you make your own. This really indicates how little people want salad. They have to trick us into eating it.

WAITER: You want a salad?
MAN: No. No, thanks.
WAITER: You can go to the salad *bar*.
MAN: *Bar?* Wait. Are there going to be women there?

A salad bar just doesn't make sense to me. I mean, besides the guaranteed diarrhea. After all, there is virtually no difference between the germ levels of a salad bar and a kiddie pool. But why would someone want to make his or her own salad? I go out to dinner so I don't have to make my own food.

"Over there is our salad bar and just next to it is our dishwashing bar."

"Awesome!"

Salad bars always give the impression that the kitchen is having a garage sale. "We don't need this potato salad anymore. Let's see what we can get for it." To make matters more confusing, the salad bar usually only has small plates. "All-you-can-eat salad . . . off this drink coaster." The plate size is probably intended to dissuade someone from overdoing it on salad. As if that would ever happen. I take it back. There is always one guy leaving the salad bar who doesn't believe he's allowed to make multiple trips. His plate is stacked. He looks like he's emptying the garbage.

"Hey, buddy, you know you can go back up."

"They might take it all away! I'm not getting ripped off!"

There are some items at the salad bar I don't understand. The offerings at the beginning of the salad bar make some sense. It's usually an assortment of things I'd never want to eat: lettuce, celery, and cauliflower. Then there are some premade salads, such as macaroni salad. Has anyone eaten any of that macaroni at the salad bar? There's rarely even a spoonful taken out of there. It's just a festering bowl of germs. That's why they have that sneeze guard up there. To protect us from the macaroni salad. After the premade salads, there are toppings like nuts and raisins and then, for no obvious reason at all, suddenly a tub of chocolate pudding. Hey, I love pudding, but who is putting chocolate pudding on their salad? What is this, *Fear Factor*?

Taco Salad

My favorite type of salad has to be the taco salad. I enjoy the taste, but I find the whole concept of the taco salad deliciously ridiculous. On first glance the most impressive thing about the taco salad is that it is actually called a "salad." When I hear the word *salad*, I think *lettuce*, and I'm pretty sure there is more lettuce on a Big Mac than in most taco salads. Really the only thing "salad-y" about a taco salad is the word *salad* in its name. The taco salad makes no effort to live up to the healthy perception of a salad. Interestingly enough, a taco is healthier for you than a taco salad. From what I can tell, the recipe for a taco salad is pretty simple: dump eight tacos into an edible bowl. The edible bowl may be a key characteristic of a taco salad, but to me it serves no purpose. I understand salads are not everyone's favorite, but dealing with a reusable bowl is not a deciding factor. Nobody is thinking, *I'd get the salad, but I don't want to clean the damn bowl afterward!*

Of course, the taco salad bowl is not only edible, it is deep-fried. Yes, an edible, deep-fried bowl to hold a "salad" that is mostly cheese and meat. I'm pretty confident that eating a wooden salad bowl is better for you. Taco salad? At least the ice cream cone is not called the ice cream *salad*. Maybe the deep-fried taco salad bowl indicates we have reached the end of things to deep-fry. I could just see the following discussion at the Deep Frying Convention.

CHAIRMAN: Well, guys, we had a good run with the deep-frying. It all started with Stan's mozzarella sticks. We had fun deep-frying the candy bar. Hell, we even deep-fried a zucchini, not that anyone wanted that. But unless we think of something new to deep-fry, we're gonna have to shut down the deep-fryer test facility. Yes, Charlie?

CHARLIE: What if we deep-fry bowls, dishes, tables, and chairs.

CHAIRMAN: Ha, ha, ha. Charlie . . . wait a minute . . . a deep-fried chair?

I imagine it was a Charlie who came up with the taco salad. Tacos are one of the many beautiful gifts from Mexico, but the taco salad is filled with so much broken logic it must be an American creation. I imagine Mexicans must look at the taco salad and think, *¿Como se dice "ridiculous"?*

How do you even order a taco salad with a straight face?

"Yeah, I guess I'll just have the Taco Salad. I'm watching what I eat. Do you have a fork made out of bacon? Maybe a bologna napkin?"

Fake Salads

I'm not sure what exactly makes something a salad, but I know I usually don't like it. I don't think chefs even like salads, given that the chef's salad is basically just deli meat. There are salads named after people (Caesar, Cobb) and places (Waldorf, Niçoise). Cultures have their own salads. There is the Greek salad, which I'm pretty sure is an Italian salad with unpitted olives and feta cheese. I'm still not sure how you are supposed to eat an unpitted olive without looking like a giant nibbling on a plum. The Greeks just do things differently. After all, they are lighting cheese on fire. I guess it's mostly lettuce that designates something as a salad. I prefer the fake salads, like potato salad. I'm pretty sure the recipe for potato salad is four potatoes and a gallon of mayo. For some reason, mayonnaise can turn anything into a salad. Take eggs, add mayonnaise, you get egg salad. Take tuna, add mayonnaise, you get tuna salad. Take salmon, add mayonnaise, you get salmonella. You'd think we wouldn't be allowed to combine fish and mayonnaise. They are two things that go bad ten seconds after you take them out of the refrigerator. If someone told you they just mixed mayonnaise and fish together, your first question should be "How long has that been out of the refrigerator?"

Any way you look at them, salads generally are just not that good. But you don't have to take my word for it. Bill Shakespeare himself, another actor who did some writing, used the term "salad days" to mean "green in judgment," which pretty much describes perfectly the people who actually like salads. The Bard has spoken.

WHOLE FOODS NATION

Health trends change and recalibrate every six months or so. When I was a little kid, cottage cheese—yes, cottage cheese—was considered healthy. My mom and my sisters would announce with a straight face, "We are being healthy by eating this tub of cheese curds." I guess the logic was that to be thin, you should eat something that looks like cellulite. "If we eat it, we won't get it on our thighs." Dairy always seems to have a representative in the health trend cycle. Today the belief is that yogurt holds some special nutritional value for women. Apparently *only* women, because in most yogurt commercials you will find only women. There's usually someone like Jamie Lee Curtis winking at the females watching. "Ladies, we need yogurt, right?" Jamie might be talking about calcium or helping ladies poop, but I've seen more men in tampon commercials.

Milk

Milk, of course, is dairy and seems to have its own ongoing role as a health trend subset. Cow's milk is presently viewed, for all intents and purposes, as a poison. "Don't drink cow's milk. You should never drink the milk of another animal. Humans are the only animal that drinks the breast milk of another animal." Then again, humans are the only animal with Internet access. We have all been told for various reasons that we are not supposed to drink cow's milk. First, the suggested replacement was soy milk. After that it was discovered that soy milk is all estrogen and we are not supposed to drink it if we would prefer that our newborn sons have testicles. Then we were told to drink rice milk, which, understandably, was revealed to be identical to drinking a huge glass of liquid carbs. Then we were told to drink almond milk because, apparently, almonds make milk. However, if you have a nut allergy, you should drink hemp milk, which is supposedly like a nut-free almond milk made from rope. Eventually it will be unanimously decided that we should drink the healthiest milk of all, which is a natural form of milk that is big in Europe, called "cow's milk."

Bread

Health trends often originate from other cultures. A basic rule is that if the people of another culture are thin and consuming something regularly, then the thing they are consuming will become a health trend. A great example of this is the Mediterranean diet. It's a well-known fact that if you eat a Mediterranean diet, you are guaranteed to become thin, tan, and a great soccer player. It was this theory that led us to believe that the pita, the bread wallet, was healthy. "Pita is not bread. It's from the Middle East, so it's healthy. Cheese is bad, but when you put it in pita it's okay, because pita is from the Middle East, where people are thin." This is why when I smoke crack I always put it in a pita. Those evil perpetrators of health trends are always trying to find a way to make bread healthy. There is a type of "sprouted" bread that I believe is actually made of soil. The healthy bread trend may have reached its peak with the "gluten-free" trend. By now we all realize two things: (1) we are *all* allergic to gluten, and (2) gluten is apparently the thing that makes bread so delicious.

Granola Bar

Inevitably, health food trends will lead to the corruption of a healthy item. Granola is considered healthy, and we know this mostly because it tastes like gravel. Granola is the classic example of something tasting so bad it must be good for you. Scientists never even had to do research. A scientist just tasted granola: "Oh this must be good for you, since it tastes like it should be on the bottom of a fish tank."

Because of the fact that granola has the same consistency as ground-up animal teeth, the granola "bar" was developed. It could be that some granola-health-inspired entrepreneur named Bob had the following experience.

BOB: Hey, kids are eating candy bars, right? All we have to do is shape granola like a candy bar and then kids will eat the granola. They'll be eating something healthy and not even know it. Idiots. Ha, ha, ha.

Then a week later his director of operations came in.

DIRECTOR OF OPERATIONS: Uh, Bob, kids are not eating those granola bars.
BOB: Well, all we have to do is put chocolate chips in the granola bars. The kids will be eating healthy and not even know it. Idiots. Ha, ha, ha.

Then a week later his director of operations came in again.

DIRECTOR OF OPERATIONS: Uh, Bob, kids are now picking the chocolate chips out of those granola bars and tossing the granola.

BOB: All we have to do is cover the granola bar in chocolate and caramel. Fill it with nougat and get rid of the freaking granola! Do I have to tell you how to do everything?

That man's name was Bob Kudos. Whenever I eat a Kudos bar, my next thought is, "Well, I might as well finish off the whole box. If I'm going to eat healthy, I'm going to eat *really* healthy."

Kale

We want to eat healthy to feel better, but what we truly desire is to increase our life spans. We all want to live longer, but how much longer? You ever talk to an old person? I mean a really, really old person. They always have this exhausted look on their face that says, *I can't believe I'm still here! I would've eaten so much more ice cream. Why did I ever consume kale?*

Ten years ago nobody ate kale. Then someone (probably a kale farmer or Satan) discovered that kale had some health benefits, and off kale went. Now we are in the middle of a full-fledged kale trend or, as I call it, a kale epidemic. There are kale chips, kale shakes, and even kale salads. I don't know much about grammar, but I think kale salad is what they call a "double negative." Kale is a superfood, and its special power is tasting bad. If tasting horrible is an indication of something being healthy, kale is the healthiest thing out there. Kale tastes like bug spray. Once I looked at a can of bug spray, and printed right there on the can was "Made with real kale." The mantra of the kale lobby is "Kale is so good for you. Kale is so good for you." So is jogging, but I'm not going to do that either. I'm not against things that are healthy. Well, not in principle. My issue with kale is a simple one. Kale is not edible. It is amazing the lengths we will go to in order to be able to stomach kale: "All you have to do is freeze-dry it, cover it in cayenne pepper, put it in a shake, and bury it in the ground." It doesn't matter what you do to kale: it still tastes like bitter spinach with hair. I suppose some people don't care what it tastes like. "Kale is so good for you." As for me, taste is too important. They could find out kale cures cancer and I'd say, "No thanks, I think I'll just do the chemo. I've tried the kale." I guess the thing I can't stand the most about the kale trend is the *bragging* that is associated with eating it. People seem to bring up eating kale as if it's something that's going to impress me.

GUY: I just ate kale.
ME: I don't care.

Announcing you ate kale is like the bringing-up-the-SAT-score of vegetables. Nobody asks, but annoying people find a way to work it into a conversation. Haven't we evolved as a species so we would no longer have to eat things like kale? I'm sure that cavemen thousands of years ago were grunting in a field, "One day, son, we no longer forage for weeds. There be long metal fire sticks for me to kill big beast, and then me eat porterhouse steaks and me no longer sound like Cookie Monster. *NUM NUM NUM.*" Recently at a school event for parents, one of the moms was nice enough to make a bean soup. Being a fan of free food, I grabbed a bowl, tasted it, and did the obligatory "This is great!" The soup mom then said with a big condescending smile on her face, "I snuck some kale in there." I nodded politely, but I felt like throwing my bowl at her. This soup mom was trying to impress me with a plant trend that will likely have the life span of a fruit fly. Well, one can only hope.

Whole Foods

If there is one main source of health food propaganda that exists today, it is Whole Foods. Our local Whole Foods store even sells T-shirts that have KALE printed on them. I suppose this does help us identify people nobody wants to talk to. It seems that they are just bored at Whole Foods. "All right, what else can we sell these half-wits? Just hand me a plant. Not that one. That's poison ivy. Wait . . . can we make milk out of that? Just grab the other green plant thing, say it's healthy, and charge fifty bucks for it." If you are someone who shops for healthy food in a large metropolitan area, you probably spend all your money at Whole Foods, or "Whole Paycheck," as it has become known. They should just have a garbage can at the entrance of Whole Foods with a picture of a wallet positioned over it. "How many items do I get? Two? I'll get the grapes for five hundred, and, Alex, I'll have the loaf of bread made of wood for ten. I'll put the rest on my Amazon wish list." I think the business idea was "It's like Costco, but instead of bulk, you get nothing." If you've ever looked at your receipt upon leaving Whole Foods, you've thought to yourself, *Wow, I'm really not good at managing money.* Unfortunately, you only remember how expensive Whole Foods is when you get there. "These prices are ridiculous . . . oh, I'm too lazy to go to another store." You win again, Whole Foods. You win again.

MORE WATERY WATER

Two-thirds of this planet that we call Earth is made up of water. Well, that's what I've always been told and seen in photos. I think that's what all that blue is on the globe. I've never personally checked if it's all actually water. The Indian Ocean could be filled with blue Jell-O and I really wouldn't know. Anyway, my point is, we got a whole lotta water on dis here planet. Not all of the water is potable, whatever that means. We all know that access to drinkable water is a very serious issue in many parts of the world. Luckily, in most parts of the United States we have clean, drinkable water available from just about every faucet. Yet we all buy bottled water because tap water, we have been told by the bottled-water folks, is scary. These anti-tap-water people act as if bottled water didn't at one point come from a tap. It's not like there was some French guy next to a stream individually filling bottles. "Le one, le two . . . Jean-Paul, hand me another bottle . . . le three." In my scenario, the French guys don't speak French very well. Anyway, how did we get to the point where we're paying for bottled water? I imagine it was some weird marketing meeting over in France.

PIERRE: How dumb do I think the Americans are? I
   bet you we could sell those idiots water.

JEAN: Pierre, the Americans are pretty dumb, but
   they're not going to buy water.

PIERRE: Oh, yes they are. Let's just tell them the water
   is from France. They took that enormous lady
   statue from us, didn't they?

And we bought it. Evian is even *naive* spelled backward. I
don't know if you were like me, but when they first introduced
bottled water I thought it was so funny. *Bottled water? They're
selling bottled water?! Well, I guess I'll try it . . . This is good!
This is more watery than water. Yeah, this has got a water kick
to it.* For some reason they have nutritional facts printed on the
side of the bottle of water. I'm no chemist, but I've got a rough
idea of what's in water. I kind of expect to turn the bottle and
see a recipe printed on there. "Oh, that's how you make ice
cubes. Apparently you just freeze this stuff. (*reading*) Oh, but
you need a tray. That's how they get you. They probably want
you to buy their tray. That's how they get you."

For some reason bottled water from another country is
more appealing.

"Oooh, Norwegian water! They got better water than us.
They've been drinking water a lot longer than we have. They
are better at it." The Norwegians have a special relationship
with water. They ski on it.

We need water. Seventy percent of our body is made up of
water. Well, I think. I don't have time to do research about
water. The fact is that water is important. We know we should
drink tons of water every day. Like six glasses or something.
As a result, we are searching for ways to make water more pal-
atable. Flavored waters are everywhere. The most popular is
VitaminWater, which is basically adult Kool-Aid. "I know it's

three bucks a bottle, but this Kool-Aid water has vitamins in it. I'm saving so much money on vitamins!" Supposedly coconut water is like nature's Gatorade. I'm not sure what the difference is between coconut water and spoiled water. Coconut water, which I think is water from a coconut, has surged in popularity. One time while in Jamaica I witnessed a coconut being sliced open and then I drank the one ounce of coconut water. So there have to be at least twelve coconuts used to make one twelve-ounce bottle of coconut water. That's a lot of coconuts to use to get something that tastes that bad.

Recently I tried Smartwater, which has electrolytes in it, and it's supposed to replenish your body better than regular bottled water, therefore making you, I guess, smarter. I tried it, and it totally worked. I am now much smarter. Now I only drink tap water.

SOMETHING'S FISHY

It is probably no surprise to you that I'm not a huge fish-eater, mostly because fish is disgusting. I really wish I could be that guy at the restaurant who looks over the menu and decides, "Well, I rarely get to go out to dinner, but instead of getting a delicious steak I'm going to order the fish, because I like nasty-tasting things." How bored are you with eating if you are ordering the fish? "You know what, just bring me something gross. I like to waste money." I'm not even sure how we are supposed to tell when fish goes bad. It smells like fish either way. "Well, this smells like a dumpster . . . let's eat it." I don't think fish even like fish. That is why fish are always frowning. "What's that smell? Oh, that's me. I'm a fish. Ugh."

Jeannie is a devout Catholic, so during Lent we eat fish on Fridays, which is meant to symbolize the suffering of Jesus on the cross. What? This means at some point some people had the following conversation:

GUY 1: How should we honor the suffering of Jesus on the cross?

GUY 2: Well, we could fast. We could starve ourselves.

GUY 1: No, that's too easy. What if we ate fish?

GUY 2: I'd rather be crucified.

I recognize that many people enjoy fish and that fish is good for you. However, at times it feels like there is an elaborate fish publicity machine at work. "Fish is so good for you. Fish cures cancer. Fish captured two members of al-Qaeda." Well, it still smells like a dumpster. This fish lobby seems so passionate, I'm usually hesitant to express my dislike of fish. I often feel like when I do, I'm treated as someone who doesn't know how to read. "You don't like fish? I could teach you. You could take night classes!"

I sometimes think no one really likes fish. They just won't admit it. Occasionally you'll hear someone say, "I like fish just as long as it doesn't taste like fish." I have news for those people: you don't like fish because I'm almost positive fish is supposed to taste like fish because, well, it's fish. That's the catch with fish (pun intended): the word *fishy* is only associated with something negative. When people compliment a fish dish, they actually say it's "not fishy." You'd never hear "Try this hamburger: it's not burgery." *Fishy* is an indication something is wrong. "Is something fishy going on here?" "No, no. Everything is burgery." Sometimes fish will be complimented by saying it tastes like something else. "Try this halibut: it tastes like chicken." This selling tactic never works for any other food. "Try this steak—it tastes like tofu." I always think, well, instead of eating the halibut that tastes like chicken, why don't I just order the chicken? It doesn't help that most of the things that are supposedly so good on fish seem to be the things that kill the taste of fish. "This deep-fried fish doused with vinegar, then dunked in a gallon of mayo and relish, is delicious!"

I'm surprised that anyone would enjoy fish at all, but I am shocked and amazed we are still serving fish with the head on it. What are we . . . barbarians? I always feel like the eye is looking up at me. "Hey, you don't mind if I watch while you eat my body? Don't be distracted if a tear comes out. You can just tell yourself it's butter." I suppose some people prefer fish served with the head on. "Yeah, I'll have the fish . . . keep the head on there. Oh, and do me a favor—find out if it had a nickname."

In some cultures they eat fish for breakfast. "Good morning. Here's some fish. It matches your breath." There are not a lot of things I like to do in the morning, and eating fish is probably at the bottom of the list. While I was in Iceland doing shows, I went down to breakfast and was shocked to find a large jar of fish oil at the beginning of the buffet next to twelve shot glasses. Yes, they are *drinking* fish for breakfast! I can't think of any time when anyone would want to *drink* fish, but most definitely not after they just woke up. "Should I have orange juice, grapefruit juice, or fish juice?" I bet fish oil at breakfast was the best thing that ever happened to grapefruit juice. "Finally, I'm not the worst thing here."

The Icelandic cure for morning breath.

Sushi

I don't like fish, but somehow I enjoy sushi. I never said I was someone who followed logic. And, no, I'm not a person who thinks that seaweed makes things taste better. (Does anyone?) Well, to be honest, I *tolerate* sushi. I don't really consider it a meal. Once, Jeannie asked me if I had eaten dinner, and I responded, "No, I just had sushi." Sushi in general doesn't make sense. Sushi seems like something someone came up with to get people to *stop* eating fish. I could see some evil dictator demanding:

DICTATOR: From now on, people can only eat raw fish.

CROWD: (*moans*)

DICTATOR: Wrapped in seaweed.

CROWD: (*moans loudly*)

DICTATOR: And you can only pick it up using these long sticks!

CROWD: (*begs for mercy*)

Sushi is a Japanese thing. Don't trust a non-Japanese person as your sushi chef. Nobody believes in racial profiling until they get a red-haired sushi chef with a southern accent. The Japanese have done so many impressive things with art, technology, and science that we all assume sushi was some brilliant achievement. In reality it was probably that some Japanese chef didn't pay his electric bill.

In all seriousness, sushi *is* an art form. It's beautiful. There is the expert cutting of the fish. Putting it on rice. Laying it on the wood plank thing. Rolling it up in that seaweed snakeskin. Planting that little carrot garden on top. Placing it in front of someone and nodding with an uncomfortable smile. I'm not even competent at preparing a box of mac and cheese.

I'm certainly in no way a sushi expert. I would definitely consider myself a wimpy sushi eater. I always order California rolls because they have nothing raw in them and I'm pretty sure that fake crabmeat they contain is made of chicken. I feel California rolls are the training wheels of the sushi community. "I can't ride a bike yet, but I'll pretend I can." There's some sushi I would never eat, like the salmon roe, the fluorescent fish eggs in the seaweed bucket thing. Roe is just a capsule of fish concentrate. Those Icelanders would love it. I don't know how you can eat salmon roe after you've seen the opening scene to the film *Finding Nemo*. The eggs are even orange like Nemo's mom and siblings.

When I do eat sushi, I always make a point of not telling anyone I've eaten sushi. This is in reaction to my observation that everyone seems to have to tell you that they've eaten sushi like it was some impressive activity or adventure. "We just went for sushi!" "What did we do this weekend? We went for sushi!" It seems people never *ate* sushi. They *went for* sushi. I always want to ask, "Did you catch anything?" Some of the posturing may be to justify the cost of sushi, which for some reason is very expensive. This is strange, considering that it's not even cooked.

Marre enjoying some overpriced raw fish.

Cooked or uncooked, fish is scary. My manager and good friend, Alex Murray, was an anti-meat fish-eater (yes, one of those). Feeling generally ill, he went to the doctor for a thorough examination. Turns out his blood contained abnormally high levels of mercury and other toxins to the point of almost poisoning him. Why? That's right! From eating the evil fish. Upon hearing this news, I took Alex out for a gigantic steak, my own prescription for a fish-poisoning antidote, and, of course, made him pay for it because I was right. Fish *is* bad. A part of me felt like the alcoholic who just found out red wine was an antioxidant. I always knew that whole "fish is good for you" story was a little fishy.

ANIMAL EATER

I love to eat animals. I realize this sounds harsh, but it's true. Of course, I'm not going into pet stores and asking, "Which is the most delicious animal you sell here?" Well, not anymore. I have contemplated buying a zoo, eating the animals, and putting my children in the empty cages, but I like to think that has more to do with my parenting style than my diet. I'm kidding. About part of that. Anyway, I do consume food that was once an animal. Some vegetarians refuse to eat meat because they feel it's cruel to animals, which, interestingly enough, is the same reason I don't eat vegetables. In a way I'm a vegetable rights activist. I bet those vegetarian savages don't even feel guilty when they eat baby carrots!

I don't like to think of myself as the type of person who would be mean to an animal. I love animals. I've never looked at a cow and thought, *I want to eat that.* But once that cow has been slaughtered, drained of all its blood, chopped up, and put on a grill, I do get hungry for some cow. I guess I love animals, but I enjoy eating them more. My motto is "Fun to pet, better to chew." It definitely helps when the food doesn't look like an animal or part of an animal. "This ham sandwich doesn't look like a pig to me." Of course, ribs are a different situation because, well, they are *ribs*. There is no denying you are eating actual ribs. Ribs are what protect the pigs' or cows' lungs and are really great with barbecue sauce. I'm still not sure how to eat ribs without looking like a caveman. "Excuse me while I tear the flesh from this bone with my teeth. I need my energy for when I club you later." It's amazing how casually we order ribs. "Yeah, I'll have the baby back ribs, and can you wheel them out in a stroller?" You can order the veal as an appetizer and have an all-baby animal meal. I do feel bad that the animals have to be killed to provide the meat I eat. I'd feel better if it was an animal suicide or if maybe the animal deserved it. "This is a good turkey sandwich, and to think that damn bird tried to steal my car."

Me eating an assortment of vegetarians.

I'm really not interested in seeing the face of the animal I'm eating. At pig roasts they always have the pig head sitting out there on display. This is always sad, because you can tell someone killed the pig while it was eating an apple. The poor pig didn't even get to finish the first bite.

I am a meat lover, but I believe that the people who are really obsessed with meat are the vegetarians. For people who don't like to eat meat, they sure seem to eat a lot of fake meat. There is mashed-up tofu, wheat, or vegetable versions of every type of meat.

> VEGETARIAN AT A RESTAURANT: I find eating meat repulsive! (*to waiter*) Okay, I'll have a veggie burger with soy cheese and tofu bacon, and could you serve it to me dressed like a cow?

If anyone is driving by meat's house seeing if any lights are on, it's the vegetarian.

> VEGETARIAN: Hey, have you seen meat lately? I mean, I don't care, but has meat asked about me? (*singing*) *I ain't missin' you at all (missin' you).*

Some of the meatless meat products seem like something out of *Spy Kids*. "Over here, Agent Cortez, we have what looks like a hot dog, but it's made completely of beans. Whoever eats it will never leave the bathroom."

Recently a waitress asked me if I was a vegetarian. I was flattered. I felt like a seventy-year-old lady who was just carded in a bar. I guess vegetarians and meat eaters are not that different. It's pretty straightforward: some people eat meat and some people are wrong. Of course, I'm only teasing the vegetarians. It is very easy to understand the animal-loving vegetarian's issue with us carnivores, but I'm confused by why some meat eaters take issue with the vegetarians. Why would I care if someone doesn't eat meat? I always think, "You don't eat meat? Hey, more meat for me." The reality is, the vegetarians are winning. The perception has changed since I was a child. It's become more socially acceptable. Recently my nine-year-old daughter informed me that she was a vegetarian. I would love to have seen my own father's reaction if I had said the same thing to him. Without missing a beat, my dad would have said, "(*cough*) No son of mine is gay. Be a man. Eat your meat."

The health benefits of a vegetarian lifestyle are undeniable. In the not-so-distant future half the population will be vegetarian and the other half will be happily in a meat coma. This is not to say I don't find vegetarians amusing when they try to impress me. "I haven't eaten meat in five years." I always say, "I haven't had a banana in a month, but you don't see me bragging about it, because I'm not a food bragger," and I go back to eating my McNuggets. The shocked vegetarian usually replies, "Do you know what they do to those chickens?" "No, but it's delicious. If you could get me the recipe, that'd be delightful."

I do have *some* scruples. I make it my policy to only eat meat from animals that during their lives were strict vegetarians. I find it very unethical to eat the meat of a lion, a python, or a tyrannosaurus rex. Those animals were too cruel toward other animals for me to feel okay about eating them. What can I say? I am just a great guy. One animal that no one in this country wants to eat is a dog. I think dogs don't realize that they are never going to be eaten. Maybe that is why they're so friendly. They are just kissing up to us so we won't eat them.

Jeannie eating a barbecued lung protector.

We eat so many different types of meat and it's also remarkable how many different ways to raise and process meat there are: organic, free range, grass fed, cured, smoked, and, of course, canned. Organic meat is better than other types of meat because those cows did yoga. There is a type of meat for everyone. For example, prosciutto is for people who like to floss while they eat meat. Some people like to eat poultry, but since that's just a nice way to say *bird,* I don't consider poultry a real meat. Sure, I occasionally eat chicken and turkey, but I think there is a reason why birds are categorized as fowl. Turkey has also become normal meat's unofficial stand-in. "Now playing the role of a meatball, here's turkey!" I am not sure how the cow feels about her understudy being a bird. It's kind of weird that we even eat birds. Some restaurants seem a little too eager to serve duck. Duck is all over the menu. "I guess I'll order the duck, unless you have a flamingo or a dove holding an olive branch in its beak." To me, ducks are a little too adorable to eat. The reason I can even stomach chicken is because I don't have the image of a cute duck in my mind.

Adorable and *edible*.

STEAK: THE MANLY MEAT

As a child I was confused by my father's love of steak. I remember being eight and my dad ceremoniously announcing to the family, "We're having steak tonight!" as if Abe Lincoln were coming over for dinner. My siblings and I would politely act excited as we watched TV. "That's great, Dad!" I remember thinking, *Big deal. Why can't we just have McDonald's?* To me, my father just had this weird thing with steak. I thought, *Dads obsess about steak the way kids obsess about candy.* Well, my dad did. I'd watch him trudge out behind our house in all types of weather to the propane grill after me or one of my brothers barely averted death by lighting it for him. He would happily take his post out there, chain-smoking his Merit Ultra Light cigarettes and drinking his Johnnie Walker Black Label Scotch alone in the darkness of Northwest Indiana. He'd stare into the flame like it was an ancient oracle relaying a prophecy that solved the mysteries of life.

Given the sheer joy that standing at the grill gave my father, I was always amazed by how bad he was at cooking a steak. Maybe it was the grilling in virtual darkness, or maybe it was the Scotch, but his steaks were usually really burnt and often had the flavor of cigarette ashes. At the table he would try to justify the charred meat in front of the family: "You like it well done, right?" Again, my siblings and I would politely lie. "It's great, Dad. Thanks." I think I actually grew to enjoy the taste of A.1. Steak Sauce mixed with cigarette ash. A.1. was always on the table when my dad would grill steaks. It seems everyone I knew had that same thin bottle of A.1. It always felt like it was empty right before it flooded your steak. Ironically, the empty-feeling bottle never seemed to run out. I think most people still have the same bottle of A.1. that they had in 1989. Once I looked at the back of a bottle of A.1. and was not surprised to find that one of the ingredients was "magic."

By the time I became a teenager, I generally understood that steak was something unique. It had some kind of a deeper meaning. I still preferred McDonald's, but I realized steak was certainly not something my father would've been able to eat growing up as the son of a denture maker in Springfield, Illinois, in the 1940s. I remember thinking that maybe eating steak was actually my father's measure of success. He wasn't poor anymore. He and his children could afford to eat burnt steak. Even in my twenties, when I would go home to visit my father after my mother passed away, he and I would always eat a cigarette-ash-infused steak that he had overcooked on the grill. Many years later I realized that following my mother's death, my father pretty much ate steak every night. Probably because my mother was not around anymore to say, "Well, obviously you shouldn't eat steak every night!" When I think back to my father eating steak day after day, year after year, I can only come to one conclusion: my father was a genius.

I don't know what happened, but steak makes perfect sense to me now. I was really overanalyzing it as a teenager. My father was not cooking steak on the grill to get away from his family or eating it daily to prove to himself that he wasn't poor; my father was eating steak because consuming a steak is one of the great pleasures we get to experience during our short time on this planet. This was probably one of my most profound coming-of-age realizations. Steak is really that amazing. Steak is so delicious, I'm sure the first person to go on a stakeout was eventually disappointed: "Been sitting in this car all night and still no steak! Not even a basket of bread."

I'm actually relieved I inherited my father's love of steak. Where I was raised in the Midwest, all the men around me seemed to love three things: fixing stuff, cars, and steak. I learned that a *real* man loves fixing stuff, cars, and steak. Well, at least I've got one of those three. If eating steak is manly, it is the only manly attribute I possess. I'm not handy. I can't fix things. Whenever something breaks in our apartment, I just look at my wife sheepishly and say, "We should call someone." I don't even call. My wife calls. I can barely figure out the phone. When the handyman comes over, I just kind of silently watch him work. I don't know what to say. "You want some brownies? My wife could bake us some brownies. I'd bake them, but I don't know how to turn the oven on." I try to act like I'm working on something more important. "Yeah, I'm more of a tech guy. I'm really good at computer stuff . . . like checking e-mail."

I'm just not manly. I don't know what happened. The men in my family are manly. My dad and my brothers loved cars. I mean LOVED cars in a manly way. They'd talk about cars, go to car shows, and even stop and look at other people's cars in a parking lot. I barely have an opinion on cars. I do know that trucks are manlier than cars. The most manly form of transportation is, of course, the pickup truck. My brother Mike has a pickup because he's a MAN. Pickup commercials just give me anxiety. There's always a voice-over bellowing, "You can pull one ton! Two tons! You can pull an aircraft carrier!" I always think, *Why? Why do you need that? I only see people taking their pickup trucks to Cracker Barrel.* My brother Mike, like many other pickup owners, never seems to be picking anything up in his pickup. I find this confusing. It's like walking around with a big empty piece of luggage. "Are you about to travel somewhere?" "No, but I'm the type of guy who would." To be fair, I really can't judge. I don't own a pickup—or even a car, for that matter. Whenever I go back home to Indiana to visit my brother Mitch, who is car obsessed, I rent a car and drive to his house from Chicago. We usually have the same conversation.

MITCH: What kind of car did you rent?
ME: I think it's blue.
MITCH: Is that four or six cylinders?
ME: (*pause*) It has four wheels. I think. Wait, cylinders aren't wheels, right?

But *steak* . . . steak I *get*. If eating steak is manly, then I'm all man. I'm like a man and a half. I love steak so much, it's actually the way I show affection for other men. "You're such a good guy, I'm going to buy you a steak." Men bond over steak. "We'll sit and eat meat together and not talk about our families." I recently toured for two weeks with my friend Tom. When I returned home, Jeannie asked, "How's Tom's family?" I don't know. I only spent like twelve hours a day with the guy. I know he likes a medium-rare rib eye. What else is there to know?

I order steaks from Omaha Steaks. Yes, I order my meat over the Internet, which I'm pretty sure is a sign of a problem. I guess I don't want my steak shopping to cut into my steak-eating time. Ordering Omaha Steaks is very simple. It's like Amazon.com for beef. A couple of days after I place my order, a Styrofoam cooler shows up. It's the same type of cooler that I imagine they will deliver my replacement heart in. Omaha Steaks is nice enough to provide dry ice in case I'd like to make a bomb or something. Occasionally, when I grab my Omaha Steaks cooler out of the hallway I'll make eye contact with a neighbor, who I'm sure will later tell his spouse, "Jim got another box of meat today. That apartment will be available in a couple weeks." The only problem with Omaha Steaks as a company is that you can't get rid of them. Once you order from them, they are like Jehovah's Witnesses calling all the time.

OMAHA STEAKS REP: Hey, you want some more steaks?

ME: I just got a delivery yesterday.

OMAHA STEAKS REP: How about some rib eyes?

ME: I don't need any more steak, thank you.

OMAHA STEAKS REP: How about some filets? You want some filets?

ME: Really. I'm fine with steaks.

OMAHA STEAKS REP: Okay, I'll call tomorrow.

ME: Um . . .

OMAHA STEAKS REP: Hey, you want some turkey? Ham?

ME: I thought you were Omaha Steaks?

OMAHA STEAKS REP: You want some drywall?

ME: Aren't you Omaha Steaks?

OMAHA STEAKS REP: I'm right outside your window. I'm so lonely.

I could never be a vegetarian for many reasons, but the main one is steak. Sure, bacon, bratwurst, and pastrami are pretty amazing, but steak is the soul of all carnivores. Steak is the embodiment of premium meat eating. I'm a meat lover, and steak is the tuxedo of meat. The priciest dish on most menus is the "surf and turf," the steak and lobster. Who are they kidding? The steak is clearly driving the steak-and-lobster entrée. The steak is the headliner. There are way more people going for the steak and the lobster than people going for the lobster and the steak. The people who want the lobster are just ordering the lobster. Lobster's appeal is all perception, and steak is truly extraordinary. Steak has its own knives. There aren't steak restaurants. There are steak*houses*. Steak gets a house. There's no tunahouse. Tuna gets a can. I love a steakhouse. It's really the perfect environment for eating a steak. They always seem like throwbacks to another era. A time when kale was just a weed in your backyard. All steakhouses seem to be dimly lit and covered in dark wood. They are usually decorated with a combination of red leather and red leather. You know there is a huge locker full of hanging carcasses, like five feet away. The waiters are no-nonsense pros. They approach in a gruff manner:

WAITER: (*deep, scratchy voice*) Welcome. Let's not beat
    around the bush. You getting a steak? We serve
    meat here. Want some meat?
ME: Yes, ma'am.

At Peter Luger's in Brooklyn, the waiter usually won't even let you order. "You're all getting porterhouse." Um, okay.

Some steakhouses show you the meat raw. At places like Smith & Wollensky, a tray will be wheeled out with different cuts on it. One by one the waiter will pick up a glob of raw meat and thrust it at the table. "You can get this. You can get this." Men are such visual animals that they'll point at the fat-swirled hunk of flesh and grunt, "That one." It's all very simple and primal. At other restaurants, fancy non-steak items are prepared in a code of complexity: "Al dente." "Braised." "Flambéed." But the way steak is cooked is understandable even to a monosyllabic caveman: "Rare." "Medium." "Well." You barely even have to know how to talk.

Me in the Smith & Wollensky meat locker.

Of course, vegetables are also served at steakhouses, but they are called "side dishes." Like their presence there is only justified by the existence of steak. They're the entourage of the steak. And you can take them or leave them. The sides are not included with the purchase of steak. They are à la carte in steakhouses, like napkins on Spirit Airlines.

Sides are never called "vegetables," because what is done to vegetables in steakhouses makes them no longer qualify as vegetables.

GRUFF WAITER: We have spinach cooked in ice cream.

We also have a bowl of marshmallows with a dollop

of yam. And our house specialty is a baked potato that we somehow stuffed with five sticks of butter. We also have a "diet potato" that is stuffed with only four sticks of butter.

Everything about a steakhouse is manly, so it's no surprise that sports heroes own steakhouses. I've been to Ditka's, Elway's, and Shula's, which all had great steaks, but I'm pretty sure those NFL greats didn't cook my steak. "Hey, you were good at football. Why don't you open a meat restaurant? They have nothing to do with each other." Nothing except the same demographic: manly men. Like me.

My love of steakhouses is sincere. When I die, I would like to be buried in a steakhouse. Well, not buried. Just my casket on display in the dining room. That way people can come in, eat, and stare at me lying in state. Maybe someone will say, "Jim died too soon, but this steak was aged perfectly!" I don't think people in steakhouses would mind that much about my casket. People are in steakhouses for steak.

PATRON: Why is there a casket in the middle of the room?

WAITER: Oh, that is a comedian, Jim Gaffigan. His only wish was to . . .

PATRON: I'll have the rib eye, baked potato, and can I get blue cheese on the side?

WAITER: I'll bring that right away, Mrs. Gaffigan.

I love steakhouses, but I realize there is something barbaric about the whole experience. Going to a place to eat cow hind parts. Eventually, eating steak won't be socially acceptable. In two hundred years I'm sure the following conversation will take place:

PERSON 1: Did you know that in 2014 people would sit in dark rooms and eat sliced-up cow by candlelight?

PERSON 2: Not my ancestors! My ancestors have been vegan since they came over on the *Mayflower*. I read that on Ancestry.com.

KOBE BEEF: THE DECADENT MEAT

The Japanese are better at being human beings. They just are. Have you used a Japanese toilet? (I realize I'm bringing up a toilet in a food book, but I have a point.) The Japanese clearly saw toilet paper as archaic, barbaric, and probably the most disgusting part of human existence, and they fixed it. After using a Japanese toilet, you actually leave the bathroom cleaner than you were before you entered it. That is impressive. Granted, the Japanese are also selling used women's underwear in vending machines at train stations, so I'm not saying they should take over or anything, but they analyzed something that we were all used to and found a way to make it better. They did the same thing with the steak. That's pretty impressive, considering that the steak didn't even need to be improved. After all, it was a steak to begin with. It's sort of like someone adding another day to the weekend. What I'm talking about is, of course, Kobe beef.

Kobe beef comes from cows that are fed beer and massaged with sake. When I first heard this, all I could think was *I want to be Kobe beef. How do I sign up for that gig?* Those must be some happy cows. Beers AND a massage? I've heard of factory farms, but now there are spa farms? I can just see the cows with slices of cucumber over their eyes, guiding the masseuse. "A little lower. Little lower, honey. Oh yeah! Right there! That's a major stress knot." Those cows have no idea they are on cow death row. They are just lost in euphoria. "You know what, honey? THIS cow could go for another beer. Ha, ha! (*pointing up*) You Japanese love design. You really made that sake bottle look like a giant hatchet. . . . Ow! I said NO deep tissue on the neck!" I guess it is a pretty humane way to go. The cows are probably too drunk to see the end coming.

We are basically eating an intoxicated cow, and yet it seems appealing. "Yeah, that sounds good." I suppose we can look forward to chicken raised on grain whiskey and pigs that are given champagne with their slop. Kobe beef is an indication of how decadent we have become. Not only do we live lives of luxury, now we need to eat things that have lived a life of luxury. I envision a demanding diner asking a waiter who's just delivered his steak, "Did this cow go to private school? I only eat cows that went to private school. (*chewing and nodding*) It did. Do you have anything on your menu that owned a boat?"

I'd like to know who came up with this idea for Kobe beef.

FRIEND AT GRILL: Do you like that steak?

STEAK EATER: (*chewing*) This is the best steak I've ever had. Amazing.

FRIEND AT GRILL: You know, I fed that cow some beers.

STEAK EATER: (*chewing*) Ha, ha. You got the cow drunk. That's awesome.

FRIEND AT GRILL: And then I massaged it.

STEAK EATER: (*stops chewing*) What? Why? Why would you massage an animal you gave tons of alcohol to?

FRIEND AT GRILL: The cow liked it.

STEAK EATER: I'm not hungry anymore. I'm going to call Special Victims Unit.

No matter who came up with it or why, in the end it just matters how something tastes. When I first tasted Kobe beef, my thought was *We need to start massaging vegetables.* I finally understood why Kobe beef is sold by the ounce like gold and silver. And, like all fine things sold by the ounce, its enjoyment comes at a cost. If you order a very large Kobe steak, be prepared for a credit check. Maybe even take out a policy. What if the Kobe beef accidently falls on the floor, or, even worse, some kid knocks their water over onto your plate? Then you'll regret not getting flood insurance. Of course, you could always get imitation Kobe beef, "Wagyu" beef, which is the same thing but not from Japan. Like champagne that's not from the Champagne region of France, Kobe beef not from Japan is, well, not Kobe beef. Wagyu beef is the sparkling wine of beef. Why is this important information? Take it from a steak expert like me with a distinguished palate: Who cares? They're both amazing. Anyway, thank you, Japan, for the steak, the toilet, and now can you please fix my bald spot?

NOT THE CITY IN ITALY

On the continuum scale of meat, on one end is steak and on the other end is bologna. All other types of meat fall somewhere between these two extremes. Steak and bologna are the alpha and omega of meats. Steak is premium, and bologna is, well, bologna. If steak is the tuxedo of meat, then bologna is the stained Members Only jacket. Maybe that analogy did not make sense, but neither does bologna. I honestly don't even know where bologna comes from. I know it's a type of deli meat, but *what* is it? We know that ham and bacon come from pigs, and that hamburger comes from cows, and turkey and chicken come from, well, turkeys and chickens. Bologna is just bologna. No one is really sure what animal or animals produce bologna. Occasionally bologna will be labeled as "beef bologna," but if you look really close you can see a tiny question mark next to the word "beef." I like to imagine bologna is just a slice of a giant hot dog (a meat that also has questionable origins).

Bologna isn't even spelled close to the way is is pronounced.

I'm not sure how we decided on the commonly used pronunciation.

> GUY 1: All right, how do you want to pronounce this word?
>
> GUY 2: "Baloney!"
>
> GUY 1: Uh, I don't know if you noticed, but there's a *g* in the word.
>
> GUY 2: I don't see no *g*. Let's go with "baloney."
>
> GUY 1: Okay. Well, the word does end with an *a*.
>
> GUY 2: Baloney. We're going with baloney. Trust me, I decided on the pronunciation of the word *colonel*.

Regardless of where the pronunciation (or the meat, for that matter) comes from, there are definitely negative connotations associated with bologna. "That's a bunch of baloney." "You're full of baloney." That kind of implies bologna makes you a liar. I enjoy bologna. I really do. Or maybe I don't. Maybe that's just the bologna talking. Its *spelling* is even baloney.

Most of my childhood I ate bologna for lunch. A bologna sandwich with ketchup. This is valid proof of my white-trash heritage and that my parents were not very discerning about what I stuck into my mouth. "Jimmy, for lunch do you want bologna or rat poison?" Part of me is always a little surprised when I still see bologna on sale in the grocery store. I thought you only ate bologna when you were five years old in the '70s or in prison. Otherwise, I imagine bologna getting banned along with trans fats and gigantic soft drinks.

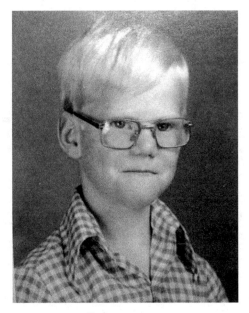

Bologna eater.

As gross as the concept of bologna is in and of itself, the most revolting bologna is bologna that has olives in it. I never knew who that was for. Maybe there was a time when bologna was served in restaurants.

WAITER: And how would you like that bologna prepared?

MAN: I like my bologna like a martini, with an olive.

WAITER: So, dirty?

MAN: Very.

The only thing positive I can say about bologna is that it is a half step above Spam, which actually does not appear anywhere on the meat continuum.

BACON: THE CANDY OF MEAT

If I bought this book, I'd probably go right to this section. Bacon is, after all, bacon. Bacon makes people happy. If you walked up to a stranger and said, "Bacon," they would probably respond with a smile or a "Yes, please!" Everyone loves bacon, but bacon holds a special place in my heart and, I guess, my stomach. My affection for bacon goes beyond any appropriate relationship a man should have with a food item. Even when I look at photos of a stack of crispy bacon, sent to me by the lunatics on Twitter, an involuntary "Aww" creeps out of my mouth like I'm looking at a newborn. Bacon is the candy of meats. Bacon even defies its categorization as a food and becomes a metaphor for wealth. You take care of your family by "bringing home the bacon." When I bring home the bacon, I just buy more bacon. What else do we *really* want to spend our money on but bacon? I love everything about bacon. I even love the name Bacon. You can't tell me some of the success of Kevin Bacon isn't somehow tied to his name. After all, nobody wants to see a Kevin Tofu movie.

MAN 1: Want to go see this movie with me?
MAN 2: Who's in it?
MAN 1: Kevin Bacon.
MAN 2: Sounds good.

The Good

The power of bacon seems to know no bounds. It's not just the taste, which is like eating pure joy. The frying of bacon even sounds like applause. As it is cooked, the crackle of the grease cheers, "Yea, bacon!" The smell of bacon can make a vegetarian renounce their lifestyle. Bacon is so good it is used to improve other foods. If it weren't for bacon, we probably wouldn't know what a water chestnut is or why anyone would eat a fig. Bacon bits are like the fairy dust of the food community, sprinkling magical taste on undesirable dishes.

MAN: I don't want this baked potato.
FAIRY BACONMOTHER: (*waves bacon wand over the potato*)
(*SOUND EFFECT of magic dust: Brrrring!*)
MAN: Now it's my favorite part of the meal! Thank you, Fairy Baconmother!
WOMAN: I don't want this salad.
FAIRY BACONMOTHER: (*waves bacon wand over the salad*)
(*SOUND EFFECT of magic dust: Brrrring!*)
FAIRY BACONMOTHER: Bibbity, Bobbity, Bacon!
WOMAN: Oh my! You just turned it into a delicious entrée. Thank you, Fairy Baconmother!

Of course, once you put bacon in a salad, it's no longer a salad. It just becomes a game of find the bacon in the lettuce. I always feel like I'm panning for gold. "Found one! Eureka!"

Bacon has special powers. I bet if you sprinkled bacon bits on a strip of bacon you could travel back in time through a tasty vortex. This would be redundant for me, because I would just travel back to a time when I was eating bacon. It would be a bacon-to-bacon time-space continuum.

Bacon can even keep you warm.

Preparing and Serving Bacon

The journey of bacon starts from humble beginnings. A package of uncooked bacon is, well, to be generous, not attractive. Taking the raw bacon out of the clear, flesh-filled FedEx envelope doesn't help its appeal. You know bacon is bad for you when you see it raw. Zebra-striped raw meat and fat strips are not easy on the eye. Everyone has this same reaction. "Oh my God, fry that up before I realize what I'm putting into my body." There are not many ways to prepare bacon. You either can fry it or die of trichinosis. Sadly, as bacon is cooked, an amazing amount of shrinkage occurs. You start with a pound and end up with a bookmark. The shrinkage while cooking foreshadows the main problem with bacon. There never seems to be enough.

I never feel like I get enough bacon. At a traditional American breakfast it seems we are rationing bacon. "Here are your two strips of bacon." Eating two strips of bacon seems cruel. "I want more bacon!" At a breakfast buffet there is usually a whole metal tray filled with upward of four thousand slices of bacon (I've counted). Everyone seems to linger over the bacon tray at the buffet like they've discovered the location where bacon originates. You almost expect a rainbow to be shooting out. "I've found it! I've found the source of all bacon!" Everyone pauses at the bacon tray, trying to evaluate what a socially acceptable amount of bacon to put on your plate might be. The bacon tray is always at the end of the buffet. This is a crafty attempt by the chef to preserve the limited and endangered resource that is bacon. You always regret the items you already have on your plate. "What am I doing with all this worthless fruit? If I had known you were here, bacon, I would have waited! I'd eat only you, bacon!"

Busted! I guess he is my son.

Types of Bacon

When I talk about bacon, I'm talking about the American version of bacon, which is pork belly bacon, the kind Jesus ate. Besides normal bacon and Canadian bacon, I didn't even know other types of bacon existed until I traveled internationally.

Canadian Bacon

I was always confused by the term "Canadian bacon." Sure, you have to love a country that has its own type of bacon, but I remember thinking, *When is someone going to tell Canada that its bacon is really just round ham?* Canadian bacon is a different type of bacon that comes from the side cuts of the pig. Canadians don't even refer to Canadian bacon as Canadian bacon. They call it "back bacon," and they call real bacon (strip-style bacon) "American bacon." The bacon the British eat seems like a combination of Canadian bacon and American bacon. They call it "bacon," but it's really not bacon. Then again, they call a cookie a "biscuit," so they have a different word for all the important stuff.

Fatback

Supposedly fatback is like bacon on steroids. I've never tried fatback. Probably 'cause it's called "fatback." I don't know which word creeps me out more: *fat* or *back*. Why didn't they just throw in *hairy* while they were at it? "This is some delicious hairy fatback. That reminds me, your uncle called."

Turkey Bacon

Our health concerns over bacon have led to horrible bacon alternatives. The most popular fake bacon is turkey bacon (I refer to it as TB), which tastes like an airline food version of bacon. I think we can all agree turkey bacon was a valiant but failed experiment. Some believe 70 percent of all disappointment we feel in life is from turkey bacon. I'll stick with good ol' American pig bacon, thank you.

The Bad

Sadly, you shouldn't eat bacon all day, and, according to my overly protective wife, you can't. Eating a doughnut is a healthier choice. I've heard each piece of bacon you eat takes nine minutes off your life, which means I probably should have died in early 1984. To me, the only bad part of bacon is that it makes you thirsty . . . for more bacon. Apparently bacon affects the brain in the same way as cocaine, overloading pleasure centers and requiring increasing amounts of bacon to feel satisfied. That doesn't necessarily sound horrible to me, but we all know the negatives of bacon. A strip of bacon gives you high cholesterol and has a fat percentage that a normal person should only consume over a decade. Bacon is the opposite of medicine, but if I died choking on a piece of bacon, I'd liken it to being murdered by a lover. We've known bacon has been bad for us for thousands of years. Eating bacon is literally a dietary restriction in certain religions.

> MAN 1: Our rules to join this religion are: no killing, no cheating on your wife, no bacon—
> MAN 2: Whoa, whoa, whoa. What was that last one?
> MAN 1: Um, no bacon.
> MAN 2: I'm in the wrong cult. Is there a bacon cult around here?

The bad news for bacon goes on and on. Bacon prices are always rising, and recently researchers discovered that eating bacon lowers sperm count. This study also determined that researchers waste time and money on useless studies rather than finding a cure for cancer. I don't understand why we even need to understand the correlation between bacon and sperm count. I would have loved to have been there when that research grant was pitched to the board.

> RESEARCHER: I'd like to study the effects of bacon on fertility. You know, the possibility of bacon as a contraceptive?
> GRANT BOARD MEMBER: (*beat*) Are you even a scientist?

Contraceptive or not, I've always consumed enormous amounts of bacon, and I have five children. I guess if I didn't eat bacon I'd have thirty children and probably be dead from exhaustion. Really, what I'm saying is, bacon saves lives. How do we know swine flu isn't caused by not eating bacon?

The negatives associated with bacon have forced us to restrict our bacon consumption to the morning. I guess the idea is that before noon we are too tired to care that we are eating something entirely made up of nitrates. After the morning, bacon goes into hiding. The word *bacon* is not even spoken after 11:00 a.m. Bacon becomes He-who-must-not-be-named. You would never be crass enough to order a bacon sandwich in the afternoon. You must speak in code. You have to play dumb and order a BLT. "Oh, I didn't even know bacon was in the BLT. I just love lettuce and tomatoes." You're like the underage kid trying to buy liquor while attempting to distract the cashier by also purchasing a pack of gum. "I just need something to drink while I chew my gum." The word *club* in "club sandwich" is meant to signify the exclusive group that does not like to admit they like bacon with their turkey.

Bacon, of course, comes from the pig. The pig is an amazing animal. If you feed a pig an apple, that apple will be metabolized by the pig and eventually turn into bacon. The pig is converting a tasteless piece of fruit, essentially garbage, into one of the most delicious foods known to man. The pig has to be one of the most successful recycling programs ever. When you think about it, that is more impressive than anything Steve Jobs did. The pig is remarkable on so many fronts. Bacon, ham, and pork chops come from pigs. The pig should really have a better reputation. You'd think calling someone a pig would be a compliment.

"You are such a pig."

"Well, thank you. I try."

It is actually the pig who should be known as "man's best friend." I love dogs, but pigs would make great companions, and when they die you could have a barbecue. "I'm sorry to hear about your pig passing. When is the luau?"

A scary bedtime story.

PASTRAMI PLAYDATE

After reading this book so far and seeing how I spend most of my time and energy, you may wonder if I ever think about or see my five young children. At the writing of this book, I have a nine-year-old, an eight-year-old, a four-year-old, a two-year-old, and a one-year-old. I should really learn their names. Being the father of five is a heavy responsibility. I try to make an effort to spend as much quality one-on-one time with each of my children. To my wife's chagrin, this usually involves me taking them to get something to eat.

My favorite place to go on my daddy-time dates is Katz's Deli to split a pastrami sandwich. A true New York Jewish deli, Katz's has an authentic Old New York environment. Even the process of getting a sandwich is a throwback to an era of Industrial-Age-bureaucracy. It's an insane system, really. Upon entering Katz's you are given a ticket. If there is more than one adult in your party, you get a ticket for each adult. You have to hang on to this ticket the entire time you are at Katz's so they can write down everything you have ordered. You must present the ticket when you leave. If you lose the ticket, they kill you. I think. I'm not sure. I just know I don't want to find out. Either way, you don't go to Katz's for the service or hospitality. This is not to say people are rude. It's just more of a do-it-yourself place. There is a self-service water dispenser, stacked high with vintage water glasses, that looks like it was in the movie *On the Waterfront.* Anyway, you go to Katz's for the deli. Specifically, I go for the pastrami. After you receive your ticket from the pastrami TSA, you approach a counter where you order your sandwich. As you wait, you are given a sample hand slice of your selected sandwich meat, which is placed in front of you on a small plate right next to a makeshift paper tip jar. I am always suspicious of a free sample next to a tip jar. It never seems as "free." Your sandwich plate is then placed on a school cafeteria tray, your ticket is marked up, and you can go to other stations to get fries, a hot dog, cream soda, or a knish (for those of you who don't know what a knish is, it's sort of a fried dumpling of dough filled with potatoes, or, as I call it, *the carboholic's ecstasy*). Then you show yourself to an open table and enjoy your monstrous sandwich. It's not just a deli. It is an experience.

I always enjoy sharing a pastrami sandwich at Katz's with one of my kids and not simply because they eat so little. "Okay, Daddy will finish your half of the sandwich." I have taken a photo of each of my children with an enormous pastrami sandwich and a plate of pickles at Katz's deli. One time when I went to Katz's with my son Jack, they took a picture of us and framed it to put on their wall. Now whenever we go back there we get to see a photograph on display for the entire community proving that I am the type of father who feeds a five-year-old smoked meat. It's kind of like a mug shot or a posted bad check. My kids love Katz's. When she was six, my daughter Marre asked, "If there's a Katz's deli, is there a dog's deli, too?" My helping out with the kids does not only involve me taking them to Katz's Deli. After we return, I always volunteer to take a nap with them. Sure, I couldn't really do anything else after a Katz's pastrami sandwich, but I'm only napping to help Jeannie with the kids. When she rolls her eyes at me, I like to think of it as her way of saying "Thank You."

CORNED BEEF: THERE'S SOMETHING
ABOUT REUBEN

I have a confession. I never had a Reuben sandwich before
March 2014. I admit this with a bit of shame now that I know
how delicious they are. I was in Erie, Pennsylvania, and was
unabashedly told that the Reuben from McGarrey's Oakwood
Cafe was "out of this world," whatever that means. I never understood why food is always described that way. Out of this
world? You mean like the blue milk Luke Skywalker had on
Tatooine? Anyway, I was hesitant to have a Reuben because
as an Irish American I don't have a great history with corned
beef, but, being a tireless researcher, I obliged. I just always assumed corned beef was so horrible-tasting they had to rename
the corned beef sandwich the Reuben so people would actually order it. Every Saint Patrick's Day my mother would make
corned beef and cabbage, we would eat together as a family, and
then I would spend the rest of the day questioning the palate of
my Irish ancestors. How drunk were those people to be eating a
big tasteless, greasy ball of cabbage and the even less appealing
corned beef? The stuff didn't taste like corn *or* beef. It was just a

big fatty, chewy hunk of unnaturally coral-red meat that tasted like cabbage. It was only in 2014 that I realized that my mother, while perfect in many ways, simply made horrible corned beef. Sorry, Mom. It was you, not the corned beef.

The Reuben is rumored to have been created in Omaha, Nebraska, which should have made sense to me, seeing how great they are at beef (you may recall my penchant for Omaha Steaks). However, I was personally shocked that corned beef came from Omaha, since it was the first time in my life that it dawned upon me that corned beef was actually made of beef. I never said I was smart.

Reuben, whoever he was, got really lucky with the sandwich. For me, all indications would be that the sandwich wouldn't work. Let me break it down:

Corned beef: Hate
Sauerkraut: Hate
Swiss cheese: Hate
Russian dressing: Not a fan
Rye bread: Like my eighth choice
Reuben sandwich = Delightful

Apparently, Reuben took a bunch of crap no one wanted and turned it into bliss. Maybe Reuben was just a guy cleaning out the refrigerator. I can see it clearly. It was late March 1920 in Omaha, Nebraska. During those long, cold days after Saint Patty's Day, Reuben and his brother were playing jacks at the kitchen table.

REUBEN'S MOM: (*offstage*) Reuben! Clean out the icebox. It's starting to smell in there. Get rid of that Swiss cheese, sauerkraut, and corned beef. No one wants that junk.

REUBEN: Gross!

REUBEN'S MOM: (*offstage*) Do it!

REUBEN'S BROTHER: I dare you to eat all that nasty stuff at once.

REUBEN: How much will you pay me?

REUBEN'S BROTHER: Two bits!

REUBEN: Deal! Hand me that Russian dressing and the George Foreman Grill.

(*scene*)

Don't you think it's a little weird that Russian dressing is called *Russian dressing*? It's not from Russia. It's a lot like Thousand Island, but it has no relish in it. It's just mayo and ketchup mixed together to make *red* mayo. The use of the color red to define Russian dressing is clearly an outdated slam against Russians, because Russia used to be a Communist country. Since I am a very evolved human being and feel above perpetuating that kind of senseless bigotry, I refuse to call it that. That's why I've started referring to Russian dressing as "North Korean dressing," and now I feel way better about eating my Reuben sandwich.

HOT DOGS AND SAUSAGES:
THE MISSING LINKS

Mikey eating a kabanos sausage at East Village Meat Market.

A hot dog, of course, is a sausage, and it is the most popular sausage. The hot dog has become so famous it is considered as

American as baseball and that car company that went bankrupt. I am a true hot dog fan. Even my favorite hors d'oeuvre is pigs in a blanket, which I affectionately refer to as the midwestern California roll. When I was a kid, I loved hot dogs so much my sister Pam gave me a package of Oscar Mayer hot dogs for my tenth birthday. And, yes, it was my favorite present. That all being said, hot dogs are not even my favorite type of sausage. To me, the bratwurst is the king of sausages.

Bratwurst

On the sausage scale of greatness that exists in my mind, bratwurst is off the charts. It has no rivals. Although I also love Italian sausages, chorizo, andouille, and those thin Polish kabanos sausages, my heart with all its clogged arteries belongs to bratwurst. When I was dating Jeannie, I found myself comparing her to a bratwurst. It was then that I realized I was serious about her. Unlike Jeannie, a bratwurst is not pretty to look at and frankly does not sound appealing. I remember as a six-year-old being at a friend's house on some breezy summer afternoon. My friend's mother received a call from my mom and announced, "You have to go home now. Your dad is making bratwurst." I remember thinking, *Ugh, anything with* worst *in the name has to be horrible.* Of course, I went home and realized that the frightening-named things my father was making were what my family referred to as "brats." I loved the tasty, juicy sausage with the crisp grilled skin. I'd had no idea the unfortunate formal name of my favorite summer food was brat*wurst*. No wonder it goes by *brat*. I mean, if my parents had named me Jimwurst, I'd probably say, I'm going to just go with "Jim."

Now once the weather starts getting nice, around May, I think only about bratwurst. I eat bratwurst exclusively during the summer. I guess it's the seasonal popularity that makes it even more appealing. Luckily I get to spend some time every summer in Wisconsin, America's bratwurst basket. Sure, it's always nice to visit Jeannie's family, but the easy access to a perfect bratwurst is a huge draw. I've heard if you eat bratwurst for more than a week straight anywhere in the United States, you have to pay taxes in Wisconsin. Bratwurst are so associated with Wisconsin, I'm surprised there isn't a delicious brat in the middle of the state flag. But by the end of the summer you realize why hot dogs are the most popular sausage. You can eat a hot dog year-round. You can eat brats only in three-month increments. Sure, it's fun to pull a muscle eating a bratwurst because it contains roughly the same amount of fat and calories as two Thanksgiving dinners, but the body cannot survive on brats. So around September I'm back to my loyal friend the hot dog.

*I should have probably made some brats for
Jeannie and the kids too.*

Hot Dogs

There is good reason why hot dogs are the original fast food. They just make everyone happy. Hot dogs are like the antidepressant of food. Hot dogs are always associated with fun things like carnivals, block parties, and eating hot dogs. Hey, hot dogs are that fun! You're never at a baseball game thinking, *Let me get a beer and a turkey sandwich.* You get a beer and hot dog. Compared with the hot dog, a turkey sandwich at a baseball game sounds like a form of punishment. Hot dogs make every experience better, with the exception of maybe a circumcision.

Jack at Crif Dogs in the East Village.

While many of us associate hot dogs only with happy times, there are the party poopers who get all caught up in facts. The contents of hot dogs are not something anyone wants to think about. Lately, hot dogs have experienced a perception problem. When you are eating a hot dog, there is always that annoying friend there to rain on your parade: "Do you know what those are made of?" I always think, *I don't want to know. I just want to enjoy my hot dog.* Hot dogs are like strippers, really. Nobody wants to know the backstory. We don't want to think about how they came to be in their present form of employment. "Well, when I was twelve, my stepfather . . ." "Not interested! Now put some mustard on that."

At this point I don't care. Meat scraps in a tube sounds more appealing than caviar (tiny fish eggs) to me. I think we hot dog fans should fight back and tell it like it is: "I love animal scraps stuffed in intestines. I only eat Hebrew National, which means I'm eating kosher cow lips!" I just love hot dogs.

I prefer the Icelandic hot dogs to the fish oil.

I've come to the conclusion that hot dogs could be made up of just about anything and I'd still eat them. Well, anything but kale. I have some boundaries.

Hot dogs are a worldwide phenomenon. Every culture seems to have their own special hot dog. One of the best hot dogs I've eaten was in Iceland. Served with fried onions and sweet mustard, it was delicious, but it also brought back memories of when I was ten and my parents brought my siblings and me to Europe. One of my favorite memories was a stop at Tivoli Gardens in Copenhagen, where I had my first hot dog with fried onions. Initially I thought it was strange, but then I was mesmerized by the combination. As I normally did during that European summer trip, I followed my blond parents in their cardigans while I enjoyed the most brilliant hot dog I had ever had. When I finished the hot dog, I pleaded with my mother to get another one, but when my mom turned around, she wasn't my mom. She was just a blond lady in a cardigan, and my father was another blond stranger in a cardigan. I looked around, and every adult in Tivoli Gardens was blond and in a cardigan. For a moment I felt like I was trapped in a Hans Christian Andersen story until I found my parents back at the hot dog stand sharing another hot dog.

Hot Dog Alley

There seems to be a part of the Midwest that really appreciates hot dogs. I call it Hot Dog Alley. In these cities it is almost a requirement to get a hot dog when you are in town. This hot dog–obsessed geographical area even looks a bit like a hot dog. Starting in Chicago, one must get a Chicago-style hot dog, which for some reason comes with a salad on top. It's probably the only time I'm excited to eat vegetables and fluorescent-

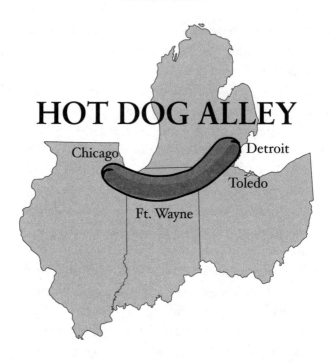

green relish. The combination of onions, tomato wedges, pickle spears, sport peppers, celery salt, yellow mustard, and the unique bright-green sweet pickle relish on a sesame seed hot dog bun is amazing. I've been in parts of Chicagoland that have had three hot dog places on the same block. And, yes, they are all busy.

In Fort Wayne, Indiana, a must-stop is Fort Wayne Coney Island Wiener Stand, where you get the hot dog with way too many fresh-cut onions and a dollop of chili on top. Hot dogs that are prepared this way in the Midwest are known as "Coney Island hot dogs" but have really nothing to do with Coney Island, New York. The only thing that I can figure out about the origin of the name is that a hundred years ago when someone from Fort Wayne, Indiana, decided to open a hot dog place, they named it after Coney Island, because that seemed like a faraway place where people ate hot dogs and they would probably sell more "Coney Island hot dogs" than "chili dogs" (as everyone else called them) because Coney Island sounded more romantic. Yes, to people in Fort Wayne in 1914, Coney Island seemed romantic. Fort Wayne Coney Island Wiener Stand has been serving their hot dogs that way since, well, since people wanted a pound of fresh onions and chili on their hot dog.

In Toledo you must get a hot dog at Tony Packo's, the place Klinger used to talk about on the TV show *M*A*S*H*. The Tony Packo "hot dog" is really a Hungarian sausage called *kolbász* and is roughly the width of a baseball bat. Tony Packo's is also famous for all the signed hot dog buns, because someone's signature on a perishable item made sense to someone, and who doesn't want a little ink on their bun?

Hot Dog Alley ends in Detroit, where the onion and chili-laden Coney Island hot dog returns and seems to take center stage. Detroit is passionate about their Coneys, but unlike the Fort Wayne version, the Detroit Coneys have a meatless chili that is mostly beans. Aside from onions, chili is the most important element to the Coney Island–style hot dog, and all these locations have their own spin on the chili. Different parts of Michigan have their own varieties of chili sauces, from chili made with Hungarian spices to a dry topping made of finely ground beef heart. The vendor proudly announced this special ingredient while handing me my hot dog. Frankly (pun intended), I would have been more comfortable not knowing that information until several days after eating the hot dog, but I ate it nonetheless.

Recently I did a stand-up tour through Hot Dog Alley with my friend (and opening act) Tom Shillue, who commented in Toledo, "I don't think people are supposed to eat hot dogs four days in row, right?" Oh, we are, Tom. And I did. After all, we were in Hot Dog Alley.

Grocery Store Hot Dogs

Like many people, whenever I'm at a ball game or a movie I enjoy eating four or five hot dogs. Sure, the hot dogs at these places might be like six bucks a pop, but, hey, we're talking about hot dogs here. Anyway, early one recent morning, right before heading to bed, I was in the grocery store buying a block of cheese and a six-pack of beer for breakfast. I saw this sign that announced a package of ten hot dogs on sale for four dollars. I thought, *Huh, this must be a typo or something. Surely the store must mean twenty dollars.* I picked up the package of hot dogs, and, sure enough, right there on the package the price tag clearly stated four dollars, but I still didn't believe it. I picked up another package and, sure enough, four dollars. So I held up the package and asked some old woman near me, "Have you seen this, or am I dreaming?" Well, she scrunched her face and looked at me like I was drunk or something. Granted, I was, but not stumbling or anything, so she didn't have to look at me like that. I mean, what a Gloomy Gus. Leaving that black cloud in my dust, I skipped up to the cashier, paid four dollars for a ten-pack of hot dogs, brought them home, and then I, Jim Gaffigan, actually cooked them. Believe it or not, in my very own kitchen. I swear I'm not lying. Sure, it wasn't that easy, but I figured it out.

Jim's Homemade Hot Dog Recipe

Being a person who likes to share his good fortune, I would like to now give you my recipe for homemade hot dogs that are as good as the half dozen we all buy at the ball park. I might be backtracking, but first you're going to have to do a little shopping. Since we're making hot dogs, definitely buy hot dogs. I find it best to buy hot dogs in the hot dog section of your grocery store. Okay, so if you've got hot dogs, let's get started. Don't be afraid to write down some of these instructions, because cooking hot dogs can get complicated.

Step One: opening the hot dog package. Take your hot dog package and open it up. I like to tear it open with my teeth unless my wife is in the room. Then I'll use a knife, a key, or a ballpoint pen. Either way, be careful. That package isn't only filled with fresh hot dogs; there is also hot dog juice in there. You don't want to spill that juice on your shirt. The shirt will smell like hot dogs for a month—unless, of course, someone washes the shirt for you.

Step Two: prepping your hot dog. Take a hot dog out of the package with your fingers. Put the hot dog in the microwave. If your wife or mom is around, put the hot dog on a plate or something paper before you place it in the microwave. That way they can't complain about having to clean up your greasy mess later on.

Step Three: the microwave. The microwave can be the most confusing part of making a hot dog. If you're like me, I find it hard enough trying to figure out how to open the damn microwave door, let alone how to set the cooking time. Don't worry, you'll get it eventually—just keep hitting random buttons. Set the microwave for any number of seconds under a minute and push START. This will most likely be the button with START printed on it. If you can't find the START button, yell for your wife or mom.

Step Four: cooking your hot dog. Once you hit START, you should hear some noise, and sometimes the inside of the microwave starts spinning. I always sit back and watch the action. The window on the microwave is there for that reason. Like a lot of people, I like to hum along to the microwave: *MMMm-mmmmm*. I'm a very musical person.

Step Five: the *bing*. When you hear a *bing*, stop staring at the microwave. Once you've figured out how to open the door, grab the hot dog with your fingers. Warning: this sucker is going to be hot. If someone is around, use a fork or something to stab it with.

Step Six: bunning your hot dog. If you still live at home or are married, you might have hot dog buns, so check around the kitchen. If you do have a hot dog bun, put the cooked hot dog in the pre-sliced part of the bun. I recommend the top-sliced buns. Your hot dog is less likely to roll out. I learned that the hard way. Now, if you only have hamburger buns, cut or tear the hot dog in half and eat it like a hamburger. Do not attempt to cut the hamburger bun in half to try to shape it like a hot dog bun. It's extremely dangerous. Cut the dog. However, get ready for way too much bread.

Step Seven: dressing your hot dog. Now you're ready to put whatever you like on your home-cooked hot dog. Your choices are endless. You've got your mustard, your relish, your on-ions . . . hell, you could put peanut butter on it for all I care. Hey, it's your hot dog, buddy. Unless you're a ketchup–hot dog or mayo–hot dog person. In that case I really have nothing to say to you, weirdo. Warning! Don't try to force your bunned hot dog into a mustard jar. Not only could the hot dog break in half, but you're also going to end up with way too much mus-tard on that puppy. Another warning: don't put the condiments directly on the bun, unless you're a soggy-bun person—in that case, I have nothing to say to you either, weirdo.

Well, there you have it. A homemade hot dog you made yourself, at home. I hope you've learned something. Lord knows there are no hot dog–making schools out there, and those microscopic directions on the package are just too darn confusing. Feel free to pass along this Jim Gaffigan homemade hot dog recipe to any of your friends you meet at the unemployment office.

GYRO: THE "LAST CALL" MEAT

The gyro is from Greece, but it's actually the national food of drunk people. One of the only things I remember about attending college was eating gyros with melted American cheese prepared by Korean immigrants at a pizza place in DC. Ain't America great? I'm not sure how or why gyro meat is cooked on that oversize metal paper-towel holder and then sliced with a hunting knife, but from what I can tell it's just Greek bologna and it's delicious. Unlike that American-cheese bastardization I had the pleasure of experiencing in college, the proper way to eat a gyro is to pack the slices of Greek bologna into a pita pocket with onions and tomatoes and drench it with garlicky yogurt tzatziki sauce. There is an ongoing debate about the pronunciation of the word *gyro*. Some say "gi-ro," some say "yir-o," but on the inside we are all saying, "We are drunk and want more happiness." The last gyro I ate sober was in the Newark Airport on February 3, 2009, a day that will live in infamy. I remember turning to Jeannie and saying, "Well, that was a mistake," which I've often said after I eat something, but this time I meant it. I felt so bad, I could barely finish Jeannie's burger before we got on the plane. It was a long, uncomfortable flight. I quickly learned that the only advantage to eating a gyro at the airport is that you don't care if the plane goes down. I realized then that my gyro at the Newark Airport was missing a key ingredient. Alcohol.

THE CHEESEBURGER:
AMERICA'S SWEETHEART

Someone once told me there was a study that found the average
adult is supposed to eat red meat only once a month. Of course,
this study was actually conducted by cows. Not being a fan of
studies, I eat a lot of cheeseburgers. If you called me and asked
me to list the last three meals I've eaten, at least two of them
would be cheeseburgers. The third meal was because I couldn't
find a cheeseburger. If steak is the tuxedo of meat, and bacon
is the candy of meat, then a good cheeseburger is the mother's
hug of meat. There should be way more poetry written about
cheeseburgers. I've always felt that a cheeseburger could be a
rating system for the pivotal moments in my life. First time
doing stand-up equals two cheeseburgers. Marrying Jeannie equals three cheeseburgers. Receiving a free cheeseburger
equals four cheeseburgers. You get the idea.

If I were advising a suicide hotline, I'd recommend start-
ing every call with "Hey, how about a great cheeseburger?"
I'm talking about a *cheese*burger here, not a plain hamburger.
I don't know who is eating a hamburger without cheese, but

he's probably an alien impersonating a human. In my world a burger must have cheese, and preferably Cheddar. Cheese was such an important topping to the hamburger, the name had to be changed to cheeseburger. A world without cheeseburgers is not a reality I want to partake in. Non-ethnic restaurants that don't offer cheeseburgers are like a *USA Today* without a sports section. What's the point? I don't expect a great Indian restaurant to offer a cheeseburger, but then again, I'm going to an Indian restaurant because I couldn't find a place that serves cheeseburgers.

A cheeseburger a day keeps the feelings away. Cheeseburgers seem to put me in a trance. I usually remember I was going to start eating healthy around the last bite of a cheeseburger. I eat my cheeseburgers in a ritualistic manner. The first bite is always done with a bit of hesitation. "Am I going to like this cheeseburger? Am I going to love it? How is the meat? Do I need more condiments?" The second bite is the "getting to know you" bite. I might think I like the cheeseburger, but I haven't given over fully. The third bite is when I give in. I am enveloped in pure happiness. I say things like, "This is amazing!" or "No, you can't have a bite" or "Go tell your mother you're hungry." The fourth bite always has a twinge of sadness to it. It means I'm more than halfway through with my cheeseburger. The fifth bite is always a small nibble because I've suddenly decided I should ration the cheeseburger so I can make the experience last. Then, before I know it, the cheeseburger is gone. It's a memory. A beautiful memory.

Here are some great cheeseburger memories:

Schoop's

Calvin Trillin once wrote, "Anybody who doesn't think that the best hamburger place in the world is in his hometown is a sissy." This is a brilliant observation that refers to the inherent provincial affection we all have for our hometown burger. It's an attachment that extends beyond taste or logic. So I guess I'm no sissy when I say one of the best burgers on this planet is a Schoop's burger from where I grew up in Northwest Indiana. I understand and appreciate the wisdom of Mr. Trillin's point, but I naively believe that even if I were from Kansas City or New York City, I would find the Schoop's burger to be the most excellent. Schoop's does two things to their burgers I normally dislike. Their burgers are well done and flattened—hamburger sins in my mind. Magically, at Schoop's these sins are forgiven. Their burger is flawless. The meat is crispy but not burnt, the cheese proportion is perfect, and the pickles are a sharp accent without being overpowering. I've yet to eat a Schoop's burger during a return visit to Northwest Indiana and be anything but completely satisfied. Calvin Trillin has spoken.

One of the greatest accomplishments of my life.

Shake Shack

I've lived in New York City for over twenty years, and during that time I have enjoyed some of the finest burgers of my life. Jackson Hole, PJ Clarke's, and Corner Bistro hold special places in my heart, but Shake Shack is something even more special. Where else other than Shake Shack would you find people in New York City lining up in zero-degree weather? Well, maybe a Broadway show or a place that sells mittens. The Shake Shack cheeseburger is one of the juiciest, most flavorful burgers—and with its not-too-hard, not-too-soft bun, it is well worth the wait. I asked the owner of Shake Shack to build one of his restaurants in my apartment. I figure the kids don't need a bedroom.

Bonding with Marre at Shake Shack.

Burger à Cheval

A cheeseburger with an egg on it is called a Cheeseburger à Cheval at Balthazar in New York City. In French, the translation of this is "on horseback," but the reference to horses does not stop anyone from eating this burger, because most people don't speak French and those who do probably are poetic enough to understand that this phrase refers to the over-easy egg on top of the meat. I like to add bacon, so I cover the three major animal-meat categories of cow, pig, and chicken. It's my way of supporting farmers. I love a fancy restaurant that is serious about its cheeseburger. Balthazar delivers every time for me. The perfectly cooked yolk is soft enough to be liquid but not liquid enough to be disgusting. It's nature's ideal sauce.

Butter Burger: Kopp's/Culver's

Growing up, I never realized exactly how seriously Wisconsin took its title of "Dairy State." It all became clear when I was exposed to the Wisconsin butter burger. I can only assume the butter burger was inspired by someone's desire to use as much butter as possible. A pat of butter is put on the bun, another is put on the burger, and the onions on top are grilled in butter. Not surprisingly, the burger tastes a lot like butter. Any state that puts cheese and butter together should get *two* stars on Old Glory.

Undead Gaffigan: Zombie Burger

Zombie Burger is a gourmet burger restaurant in Iowa that combines everyone's two favorite things: burgers and the postapocalyptic world of zombies. You can get burgers like "The Walking Ched" or "George Romero's Pittsburgher." When Zombie Burger asked me over Twitter what I wanted on an "Undead Gaffigan," I instantly knew—bacon, Cheddar, white bread, five patties (one for each of my kids), and jalapeños, because I'm a hot Latina! Here is the beauty that was created for me.

Given that I had a show that night in Des Moines, I went with the one-patty version.

Juicy/Jucy Lucy

I love Minneapolis and not just because I enjoy being in cities where I'm not the only pale blond guy with an oversize head. My head is so large that in middle school I had to use a football helmet from the high school. I don't know why my head is so large. You could store a normal-size head inside my head. I like to think my head is like a head case. Okay, I will stop now. Anyway, whenever I bring my large head to Minneapolis, I always head over (sorry) to Matt's Bar and get a Jucy Lucy. Then I usually go to the hospital for burns to my mouth. A Jucy Lucy (yes, that is how it's spelled) is a cheeseburger where the cheese is, for some reason, cooked inside the burger. I suppose Matt from Matt's Bar had the insight "Hey, instead of putting cheese on top of the burger, let's burn people." After all, who doesn't like their cheese at a thousand degrees, or roughly around the same temperature at which they melt swords? There is another place in Minneapolis called the 5-8 Club that also claims to have invented the Juicy Lucy (yes, they spell it that way). This Juicy Lucy is pretty much the same, except for the *i* in *juicy*. I guess they did this to distinguish themselves from each other because they are otherwise identical. Kind of like Protestants and Catholics. Apparently the rivalry between the Jucy Lucy and the Juicy Lucy is rather serious, so I try to eat at both places just to keep the peace. Blessed are the peacemakers, for they shall inherit the burgers.

In case I die, I'm gathering a list of advice for my kids. All I have so far is:

1. Mustard on a cheeseburger is amazing.
2. Ignore lists.

FRENCH FRIES: MY FAIR POTATO

Sometime in the late 1940s, the Geneva Convention declared it a crime against humanity to sell burgers with anything but French fries. Well, they should have. Whenever you get served a cheeseburger with bland-ass potato chips, don't you feel a little ripped off? "Where are the French fries? Did your deep fryer break? I better get a discount!" A burger and fries together is one of the great culinary marriages of all time. French fries are amazing and, as logic would have it, horrible for you. If you are eating fries, you definitely are treating yourself. I think we should just rename taking vacations "eating French fries." French fries are like Crocs. You know you shouldn't, but your life is pretty much over anyway. French fries are deep-fried. Unquestionably the most important deep-fried item ever created. I doubt the inventor of the deep fryer realized the impact his contraption of a heated-up bucket of grease would have on the otherwise bland root vegetable. Like a Hollywood rags-to-riches fairy tale, the deep fryer turned the lowly potato into a food star desired by millions. With all its success, I can't help but feel the French fry still remains one of the more underappreciated food items. I'm not sure if it's a mental block on our part or the fact that they are mostly classified as a side dish, but we don't give enough credit to French fries. French fries are like one of those beautiful images hidden within another image. Often we just don't see the French fries. We always want fries with our meal, but we don't realize how important they are to the enjoyment of the meal. Not only are French fries a key element of fast food, they are possibly the one food item keeping most restaurants open. As I calculate, French fries are served with 90 percent of all non-ethnic entrées. Aside from the obvious pairing with a burger, we serve French fries with everything: steak, fish, a grilled chicken sandwich, a hot dog, even a gyro. French fries are so good, they change political thinking. When Congress was furious with the French for refusing to send troops to Iraq, they didn't dare ban the actual French fries—they just changed the name to "Freedom fries." Our government would not let a measly war interrupt their lunch.

French Fries as an Entrée: Poutine

I love our North American neighbors, Canada and Mexico. Americans really scored when you think about it. We could have easily been sandwiched between countries like North Korea and Albania. Phew! There is nothing to dislike about Mexico or Canada. If anything, they are the ones who have to put up with us Americans. We are like the obnoxious rich neighbor leaning over the fence, "Hey dudes, wanna come over and check out my new space program?"

Mexican food is one of the greatest accomplishments of mankind, but let's not forget Canada. I've always had a strange affinity for Canadians. They always seem so nice, calm, and health insured. Because of their voluntarily living in perpetual winter and their almost absurd love for hockey, I never understood the Canadian character until I ate poutine for the first time. Like that last scene in *The Usual Suspects*, all the pieces seemed to come together. While poutine is a dish unique to Eastern Canada (Montreal and Ottawa), the concoction of French fries covered in cheese curds and (for no apparent reason) gravy, clearly deciphers Canadian culture. First, heart-blocking poutine is the easiest explanation for Canada's adoption of universal health care coverage. I'm pretty sure I'm still digesting the poutine I had in May 2006. Poutine also serves as a sedative, making you so drowsy and serene you find yourself saying "a-boot" instead of "about." The extra pounds you immediately gain help shield you against the bitter climate. The irrational love of hockey still remains a mystery to me, but I'm convinced it has something to do with poutine.

It's normal for me to make unhealthy food choices, but poutine almost appears sadomasochistic. Poutine seems like the result of someone's goal of making French fries even less healthy. "Well, the most unhealthy thing we could do is to cover the fries with every other food item that causes heart disease. Let's get to work." And that is what some brilliant Canadian did, and the results were incredibly successful. It tastes as amazing as it is bad for you.

I attended one of Ottawa's Poutine Fests (they had two this year), where twenty-six vendors find creative ways to serve poutine. There is Philly cheesesteak poutine, popcorn chicken poutine, and for some infuriating reason, vegetarian poutine. While I was eating my second portion of poutine, I actually heard my heart say, "Oh no. What are you doing? Are you mad at me?" I could feel my arteries tightening. But my brain said, "It's all right. It's all right. There's going to be some sweating. Well, a lot of sweating, but you'll get through it. Bowels, you can take the weekend off."

In Ottawa you get the squeaky cheese that sounds like you are cleaning a window when you chew it. I always get smoked meat added to my poutine. It's not just the flavor of the smoked meat that I enjoy, it's also the fact that no effort is made to explain what type of smoked meat it is. The following is a conversation I had with a waitress in Montreal in 2008.

ME: This meat is amazing. What kind of meat is it?
WAITRESS: Smoked meat.
ME: Yeah, I know, but what kind of smoked meat?
WAITRESS: The delicious kind of smoked meat.
ME: Sorry. I don't know what you're talking a-boot, but suddenly I want to watch hockey.

This is triple-bacon poutine, for people who are seeking a heart attack after the third bite.

French Fries as a Condiment

Pittsburgh and Cleveland, while very different, share a common phenomenon. Besides the fact that they are both rust belt cities with a passion for football, they both have the strange and unique habit of putting French fries inside sandwiches. Sandwiches are normally one of the few items that do not come with French fries. Pittsburgh and Cleveland snuck them in. I don't know or care who did it first, because it doesn't matter. It's like sneaking an extra person in the trunk into a drive-in movie. Putting fries in a sandwich is just a beautiful thing. The efficiency and convenience of this idea is nothing short of brilliant. I'm not suggesting these are the only cities where this excellent behavior has occurred; it's just that it has been perfected in Pittsburgh and Cleveland.

In Pittsburgh I go to Primanti Brothers and get a ham sandwich with coleslaw and crispy French fries piled high between two pieces of soft Italian bread. I'm not sure which Primanti brother came up with the fries-in-the-sandwich idea. Maybe the brothers had a meeting:

BROTHER 1: Okay, you jagoffs, we need to boost sandwich sales. Any ideas?
BROTHER 2: How about yinz guys put coleslaw on every sandwich?
BROTHER 1: Interesting. Maybe.
BROTHER 3: And French fries.
BROTHER 2: On a sandwich?
BROTHER 3: Yes, fries on a sandwich.
BROTHER 1: Are you drunk again?
BROTHER 3: No, but that's when I thought of it.

In Cleveland I love to eat at a place called Panini's that is legendary for putting fries and slaw in their sandwiches. This is different from the Pittsburgh version because in Cleveland the sandwich is ironed. By the way, they love to drink in Cleveland too. I imagine this is what you would call a "happy accident" created when someone in Cleveland was eating the Pittsburgh-style sandwich while ironing and drinking at the same time. This idea is not too far-fetched, considering that in Cleveland their river always catches on fire.

TOP MICROWAVE CHEF

Whenever a politician gives a speech about getting America working again, I always cringe a little. Not just because it's an empty political promise, but also because I'm not a fan of work in general. I usually think, *Ugh, I hope this* work *isn't going to involve movement. It better not be yard work!* I'm a fan of relaxing, and when I get tired of relaxing I like to do nothing. I view cooking as work. I don't enjoy cooking, so I don't follow the logic sometimes presented to me: "Hey, you love food, so you must enjoy cooking." I also enjoy sleeping, but that doesn't mean I like making a bed.

Thankfully, other people enjoy cooking. Even more thankfully, some other people *really* enjoy cooking. I guess I feel the same way about *not* cooking that those people feel about cooking. It's really a win-win for everyone involved, especially if the food is free. I occasionally enjoy watching people make food. It's relaxing, I guess. I have noticed that the Food Network is far more interesting when I'm hungry. When I'm full I usually think, *Well, this cooking show is silly. Why would anyone watch this?* But when I'm hungry, really hungry, the Food Network is amazing, a visual spectacle. I watch it like some of you degenerates watch porn. "Oh yeah. Whip it up, baby!"

As you know by now, I'm an eater, not a cooker. Besides the microwave, I don't even know what half the stuff in my kitchen is for. Most kitchen appliances just feel like an unnecessary waste of space. Has anyone not on a cooking show ever even used their blender for anything other than mixed drinks? Before I got married, I stored blankets in my oven. Yes, it was that nice of a place.

Most of the times when I cook I'm using a microwave, which, of course, is not cooking. It's just me pressing buttons and waiting for the *bing.* As I mentioned in my homemade hot dog recipe, I barely even know how to use a microwave. I've never tried to light one, but mostly all I know is you aren't supposed to put metal or wet cats in there. This is not a good thing, given I'm occasionally in charge of feeding a gaggle of small children. "Okay, for lunch here are your options: you can have hot dogs, popcorn, or cold hot dogs." The manufacturers understand there are people like me, which is why microwaves have buttons like REHEAT and POPCORN. I once stayed in a hotel that had a microwave that had a DINNER button. I pressed the DINNER button, but when I opened the microwave door, there was no dinner there. I guess the microwave was broken.

When I cook something in a microwave, I rarely read the directions on the packaging. That's right. I just wing it. I'm dangerous like that. I'm like the Evel Knievel of microwave cooking. I don't even understand why some microwavable foods *have* instructions. If you're cooking a frozen burrito in a microwave, are you that interested in quality? It might as well say, "Toss this into the microwave for a little bit and then shove it into your mouth after it cools, you tub of gluttony." On Amy's Bowls you are instructed to "Stop, rotate this dish, and stir the contents." Like that would happen. I might as well be making something from scratch out of *The Joy of Cooking.* If microwavable food has any directions beyond "Stick in microwave and press a button," I assume they were trying to add wording to the packaging to fill space.

> BOSS: It's kind of empty on the back of the package. Maybe add some writing.
> EMPLOYEE: About what? It's a burrito.
> BOSS: I don't know. Tell people how to open the microwave door. The packaging is going to look weird without writing on it.

Microwaves are like winter coats. They warm quickly, people never clean them, and they look ugly after a year. Nothing that you put in a microwave is that exciting. That's why there is always forgotten food in there. At times a microwave just seems like a box to hide half-full cups of cold coffee in. The microwave is an odd way to cook anything, when you think about it. From my uninformed viewpoint it seems as though someone thought, *Hey, you know the technology of the atomic bomb? What if we used that to make popcorn?*

MUSEUM OF FOOD

If you are eating at home, this means you or someone you live with went to the grocery store. I've always had a strange attachment to grocery stores, and I don't say this just because many of my stand-up set lists are indistinguishable from my grocery store lists. One summer in high school I had the pleasure of working in a grocery store. My job title was "stock boy," which involved stocking shelves with cans and boxes of food while I fielded never-ending questioning from my well-intentioned but relentless born-again Christian coworkers. "Have you been saved?" "If you died right now, would you go to heaven?" "Why are you putting headphones on?" To make matters more inspiring, the soundtrack that played over the grocery store sound system that summer was a single cassette of Country Music's Greatest Hits. On repeat. All day. Day after day. Near the end of August I was a devout atheist who knew all the words to "Elvira" and never wanted to enter another grocery store. El-vi-RA!

Now, by God's grace and probably thanks to the prayers of those born-again Christians, I love going to the grocery store.

For me it's like going to an art museum of food I've eaten. Ah, the work of Frito-Lay. What a lovely exhibit. Peanut butter and jelly in the same jar? A masterpiece. What is this Double Stuf Oreos? How abstract. In grocery stores food is on display at its finest. All the produce is shiny and color coordinated. All the boxes and cans are colorful and organized. I love the food packaging. It's like the clothing of food. "Oh, what are you wearing there, cookie? A lovely Mint Milano bag?" "Candy, let me help remove your wrapper." It seems the fancier the food, the nicer the packaging. While Pepperidge Farm bread is packaged in the equivalent of a three-piece suit, generic cereal comes in plastic bags and lives on the bottom shelf like it's homeless. I always think, *We should find you a box to live in.*

I couldn't fit down the aisle of this NYC grocery store.

The variety at most grocery stores is staggering. There are innumerable kinds of peanut butter: smooth, chunky, natural, sugar free, crunchy, and even extreme chunky. I'm pretty sure if I bought the extreme chunky, I'd open it up only to discover it was just peanuts. It would be *extreme* trying to spread those peanuts on bread. "This is radical!" The "extreme" products of any kind make you feel like a coward eating the regular stuff. "Hey, look at that wimp eating regular Doritos. You can't handle the *extreme* Doritos, can you?" "Uh, I'm working my way up to it." Grocery stores show how complicated we humans have made food. Dogs would definitely conclude that we are really putting too much thought into this food thing. This is probably why dogs are not allowed in grocery stores.

I'm happily married, but supposedly the grocery store is a great place for singles to meet. I'm not sure how this works. "I see you got the Charmin there in your cart. It really is more absorbent. Wanna grab a cup of coffee?" It's impossible to buy toilet paper without some level of embarrassment. We all need it, but I am always self-conscious wheeling around the toilet paper in my cart. It normally comes in these giant twelve-packs, and I feel like everyone is staring at me. "Does that guy ever leave the bathroom?" I never want to see *anyone* in a grocery store, let alone *singles*. I was only hit on once at the grocery store. I remember it was early one Saturday morning and I was buying my daily bacon, when I got tapped on the shoulder. I turned around and I saw a rather short and very feeble eighty-year-old lady looking up at me. She said in a weak, scratchy voice, "Excuse me, young man, could you reach up and grab some ketchup for me?" Well, I'm no dummy. I know when I'm getting hit on. I smiled politely and reached up for the ketchup, knowing full well that she just wanted to get a gander at my derriere. As I handed her the ketchup, she said, "Thank you," like I was some piece of meat, a boy toy, or something. Finally I just blurted out, "Look, I'm married, lady!" She acted all surprised and confused. "Excuse me? I don't understand!" I shook my head with a smirk, raised my left hand, and showed her my wedding ring. "Married!" I loudly told her. "I'm taken!" A stock boy at the end of the aisle looked at us and inquired, "Is everything okay?" "I'm fine," I assured him. "I know how to deal with predators." Well, suddenly this sex-crazed lady got all angry at *me*. Like *I* was out of line. She huffed off. "Well, I never!" "And you ain't gonna with me either," I yelled after her. I have to admit, it was nice to get the attention.

One of my favorite parts of a visit to a grocery store is the free samples. "Ooh, free sausage." Unfortunately, there is always that awkward moment after you consume a free sample. Before you get the sample, you usually act like you are considering buying the product. "Well, this would be good for a party (*eat sample*). Nah. Well, gotta go!"

Checking out at a grocery store can also be an awkward experience. The checkout person gets such a window into your personal life. I imagine they are judging me for everything I am buying. "Should you really be eating that? No wonder you're buying this Ex-Lax." The total amount of the receipt seems to get higher and higher every time I check out at the grocery store even though I feel like I'm buying less food. It's also become necessary for us all to be members of these grocery store clubs.

CASHIER: Are you a member of our club?

ME: Um, I'm just getting hot dogs.

CASHIER: That'll be four thousand dollars . . . or you can join our club.

ME: Um, I can't come to a lot of meetings, but I guess I'll join.

CASHIER: It's really convenient. Fill out this personal information for the next ten minutes.

I used to feel uncomfortable when the cashier would bag my groceries. Talk about feeling lazy. "Hey, thanks for putting my groceries in my bag. I could help, but I'll just watch. Yeah, I'm pretty exhausted from picking that stuff out. You want to come home and watch me eat them? I'm looking for a friend." I now realize that the only thing more uncomfortable than someone bagging my groceries has to be bagging my *own* groceries at a self-service checkout. As I ring up my purchases I always think, *When is this shift going to be over?* Sometimes I'll ask myself, *Hey, me, you want paper or plastic?* (sings) *El-vi-RA!*

HOT POCKETS:
A BLESSING AND A CURSE

Okay, let's talk about the eight-hundred-pound stuffed pastry in the room. If you don't know what a Hot Pocket is, all I can say is, congratulations or welcome to North America. If you are a resident of North America and don't know what a Hot Pocket is, I can only assume you are so rich you haven't gone grocery shopping for ten years or you have such a healthy and constructive lifestyle that you only shop at farmers' markets and don't watch television. Then again, you could also be another Unabomber.

There is nothing unique or innovative about the Hot Pocket concept. It is fundamentally just meat with a pastry-like cover. This is nothing new. I remember initially looking at the Hot Pocket product I saw in commercials and thinking, *Well, that's just a calzone.* I imagined all the South Americans exclaiming, "Hey! That's our empanada!" And the Jamaicans insisting, "No, that's our meat pie!" It seems like every culture has a version of the thing we Americans have come to call a Hot Pocket. While these other countries' dishes seem like real food with some special kind of history, the American version seems like a cheap imitation. The Hot Pocket is sort of a symbol of the way we eat in America. The early development of the Hot Pocket appears to have begun with the TV dinner, the hominid of the Hot Pocket evolutionary chain. In the middle of the last century, our lives got busier, and we got lazier in our food-preparation habits. In the 1950s, the TV dinner made it possible for us to conveniently eat in front of our television. The microwave made it possible for us to make the TV dinner faster so we could watch more television. The Hot Pocket made it possible for us to eat something from the microwave without a fork while we watch television. I imagine intravenous food streaming from the television is about a decade away.

It's almost embarrassing when I contemplate the impact Hot Pockets has had on my life. It truly has been a blessing and a curse. A blessing in that so many people relate so much to the series of jokes I wrote about this relatively simple micro-wavable food item that it changed my career, and a curse in that I certainly don't need more people yelling "Hot Pocket" at me in the airport. I'm never sure how I'm supposed to respond. "Uh, thanks?" Once I was on CNN speaking seriously about the good work that the Bob Woodruff Foundation does on behalf of veterans and, unbeknownst to me at the time, on the bottom of the screen I was identified as Jim "Hot Pocket" Gaffigan. I have no doubt that if an obituary were to be written about me at this point in my life, I would be remembered as the Hot Pocket comedian. Whether I like it or not, Hot Pockets changed my life. I might not be doing stand-up in theaters or writing this book if in the late '90s I didn't find the commercials for Hot Pockets so ridiculous.

No, I did not sanction this.

What seems like a hundred years ago, I was doing a spot at Caroline's Comedy Club in New York City. It was a showcase in which typically five or six comedians go up and do fifteen-minute sets of stand-up. It was a great opportunity to mix in new stuff with tried-and-true material while performing at a prestigious club. I had recently thought of a couple of jokes about a new product I had been seeing advertised a lot on television. The product was Hot Pockets. I thought the name was hilarious. Hot Pocket sounded like a euphemism for a sexual disorder.

GRANDPA TO TEENAGER: Look, Bobby, sometimes when fellas don't go on dates, they develop what's called a Hot Pocket. It doesn't mean you're bad. It just means you need a girlfriend. I used to have Hot Pockets all the time, and then I met your grandmother.

I thought the commercial was even more preposterous. It showed an overly happy mother pulling something out of a microwave that looked like a McDonald's apple pie and handing it to her overly happy son. Then there was this equally absurd, enthusiastic, two-word jingle: "Hot Pockets!" The commercial felt more like a *Saturday Night Live* parody than an actual commercial. I was simultaneously annoyed, amused, and intrigued. Who in their right mind would buy this product? I cobbled together a couple of jokes and did them that night on the stage at Caroline's. They got a couple of laughs in front of the late-night audience of local New Yorkers. Nothing remarkable. Nothing memorable. When I got offstage I approached my friend and host for the evening, Vic Henley. "That Hot Pocket stuff is funny," Vic exclaimed. I said, "Thanks," thinking he was just being nice, but then Vic repeated, "No, it's funny." Encouragement from another comedian you respect is really all most comedians are looking for when they are starting out. Rather than tossing aside the few observations, I began to gather more jokes on this odd product, Hot Pockets.

I think I got lucky with the timing of my Hot Pockets jokes. I got to them before other comedians realized the absurdity of the product. I certainly didn't expect Hot Pockets to gain the popularity it did. In hindsight, the success of Hot Pockets is perfectly logical. When I was a teenager, everyone ate frozen burritos that were heated up in a microwave. Usually the tortilla of the burrito tasted like cardboard, but it was easy to make. Hot Pockets were the next logical step. Something anyone could easily cook in the microwave that was edible. Well, kind of.

I actually buy Hot Pockets. I go into grocery stores, head to the freezer section, and think, *Yeah, I'll get these.* I've never eaten a Hot Pocket and then afterward thought, *I'm glad I ate that.* I always think, *I'm gonna die! I paid for that? Did I eat it or rub it on my face? My back hurts. Owwww! Wait, my watch stopped!* Hot Pockets should have a warning on the package.

> **⚠ WARNING!**
>
> **YOU JUST BOUGHT HOT POCKETS.**
>
> I hope you're drunk or heading home
> to a trailer, you hillbilly.
>
> Enjoy the next NASCAR event.

People sometimes ask if the Hot Pockets people have sued me or contacted me. The answer is no. I think the good people at Nestlé know Hot Pockets are not being paired with champagne. You rarely see Hot Pockets on a menu when you go out to dinner. "Let's see . . . I will have the Caesar salad and the Hot Pocket." You will never overhear the following conversation in a fine-dining establishment.

WAITER: Today's specials. We have Chilean sea bass, which is sautéed in a lemon beurre blanc, and we have a Hot Pocket that is cooked in a dirty microwave. And that comes with a side of Pepto.
PATRON: Is your Hot Pocket cold in the middle?
WAITER: It's frozen. But it can be served boiling-lava hot.
PATRON: Will it burn my mouth?
WAITER: It will destroy your mouth. Everything will taste like rubber for a month.
PATRON: Oh, I'll get the Hot Pocket.

Hot Pockets have not been in the public consciousness for that long. I saw a winner on *The Price Is Right* win a lifetime supply of Hot Pockets, which I'm pretty sure is technically a death sentence. Now Hot Pockets are part of our culture.

When they came out, I never imagined there would be over forty different flavors of Hot Pockets with new products being introduced on what seems to be a daily basis. Given the innumerable varieties of Hot Pockets available, people could play a game of Hot Pocket roulette in which a variety of Hot Pocket flavors are taken out of the packaging and placed in a freezer. Then the roulette participant can randomly choose a frozen Hot Pocket from the freezer. They have no idea what flavor or variety they will get until that first scorching bite. Actually, that wouldn't really be a fun game because no one would ever be sure which flavor of Hot Pocket they had chosen, given that they all pretty much taste the same.

A question linking me and Hot Pockets on
Who Wants to Be a Millionaire?

At times it feels like Hot Pockets are in the news more often than the latest tabloid starlet. Recently a large recall of Hot

Pockets was instituted because they were found to contain "unsound meat." To many of us who eat Hot Pockets, this was neither shocking nor newsworthy. I remember thinking, *I guess next they are going to tell us smoking is bad for us.* Mostly Hot Pockets are in the news for what humans do to a Hot Pocket or for a Hot Pocket. There was an almost biblical story of a teen who stabbed his older brother over a Hot Pocket in South Bend. There was another one about a college student at the University of Notre Dame who broke into a health spa and ate Hot Pockets. I'm less shocked that this behavior took place in my home state of Indiana and more surprised that a health spa was selling Hot Pockets. "After your therapeutic massage, may I interest you in our Hot Pocket cleanse?"

It wasn't that long ago Hot Pockets were probably just a twinkle in some drunk guy's eye. Or maybe some guy in a marketing meeting asked, "How about a Pop-Tart filled with nasty meat? No, really. This is different from my fish-stick-in-a-Twinkie idea. This would come in a sleeve." Hot Pockets come with a crisping-sleeve thingy. I don't recommend microwaving your Hot Pocket without the sleeve. I did that once and blew up my house. It takes three minutes to cook a Hot Pocket in a microwave. Coincidentally, that is how long it stays in your system. I believe if it took any longer to cook, people would have time to change their minds and eat something else. "Well, it's done; might as well eat it." It actually takes five minutes, because you're supposed to let the Hot Pocket cool for two minutes before eating it, which can be hard, because if you're like me, you want to feel sick right away.

Even if you haven't eaten a Hot Pocket, you are probably familiar with that jingle: "Hot Pocket!" It's not a very complicated jingle. It's as if someone had just been asked to sing the words "Hot Pocket." I'm not a music expert, but it seems like it's just three consecutive descending notes. Like something a four-year-old would play on a recorder. I can't imagine the "songwriter" worked very hard on that jingle.

> HOT POCKETS EXECUTIVE: Bill, what do you have so far on the Hot Pocket jingle?
>
> BILL: Was that due today?
>
> HOT POCKETS EXECUTIVE: Yes. Do you have something?
>
> BILL: (*beat*) Uh, yes.
>
> HOT POCKETS EXECUTIVE: Well?
>
> BILL: (*beat*) Uh, uh, (*sings*) Hot Pocket!?
>
> HOT POCKETS EXECUTIVE: That's good. Not as good as your "By Mennen!" jingle, but it's good. Now, what are we going to run in Mexico?"
>
> BILL: Uh, (*sings*) Caliente Pockets?
>
> HOT POCKETS EXECUTIVE: You've got a gift, my friend. Don't hide that under a bushel.

There really is a Hot Pocket for everyone.

Vegetarian Hot Pocket: There are vegetarian Hot Pockets for those who don't want to eat meat but would still like uncontrollable, explosive diarrhea. I always wondered if Hot Pockets were not just some elaborate scheme by the toilet paper manufacturers.

Lean Pocket: A Lean Pocket is the healthy version of the flagship Hot Pocket. I don't even want to know what's in the Lean Pocket. I imagine the directions: "Take out of box, place directly in toilet. Flush pocket." Possible slogan: "Half the calories, all the diarrhea."

Breakfast Pocket: My favorite is the breakfast Hot Pocket because I can't think of a better way to start the day. "Good morning, you are about to call in sick." The creative team at Hot Pockets has made it possible for you to have a Hot Pocket for breakfast, a Hot Pocket for lunch, and be dead by dinner.

Whole Wheat Hot Pocket: Now there are whole wheat Hot Pockets. As if that is what was holding some of us back: "I'm waiting for the healthy diarrhea."

Deli-Style Hot Pocket: There is a deli-style Hot Pocket that is made with real deli meat. This version only made me question what type of meat they were using before the deli-style Hot Pocket. Isn't regular meat the same as deli meat? "No, before it was iguana meat."

Hot Pocket Sliders: There are Hot Pocket sliders. This seems a little redundant. I expected White Castle to issue a press release that simply read, "Really?"

Hot Pocket Sub: I have no idea what this is, but I assume the Hot Pocket sub combines the disgusting meat of regular Hot Pockets with stale bread.

Croissant Hot Pocket: As if the French need another reason to hate us.

Chicken Pot Pie Hot Pocket: A couple of years ago when I saw a commercial for the Chicken Pot Pie Hot Pocket, I just assumed they were messing with us. I naively believed that they had run out of new product ideas. A Chicken Pot Pie Hot Pocket? I figured it was just a matter of time before I'd hear someone ask, "Have you tried the Hot Pocket Hot Pocket? It's a Hot Pocket filled with a Hot Pocket. It tastes just like a Hot Pocket. I'm going to go stick my head in a microwave."

Hot Stuffs

I perform regularly in Canada. A couple of years ago someone showed me the Canadian version of a Hot Pocket. It was called Hot Stuffs. It still confuses me how the Canadians somehow came up with a worse name than we did. Hot Stuffs? Aren't the Americans supposed to be the dumb ones in North America?

In the average box of Hot Pockets there are usually two Hot Pockets. One for you to eat and regret, and one to have in the freezer until you move. Or you can use the Hot Pocket as a measuring stick on how drunk you've gotten that night. (*Man opens freezer, looks at a Hot Pocket.*) "Yeah, I'm not eating that. I'm all right to drive. Let's head to Waffle House."

HE'S HERE!

Getting food delivered to my home combines two of my favorite activities, eating and not moving. There is something pretty pathetic about my ordering delivery. I usually have food in the next room that I could put in a microwave, but the task seems too daunting. I'm also normally ordering from places that are only a short walk away from my New York City apartment. "Yeah, I like your food. Just not enough to go down there and get it." The worst part of delivery for me is getting up and answering the door. "Well, this is a pain in the ass. Who am I, the butler? Well, at least I don't have to put on pants." Apparently I am not the only one being lazy about how I obtain my food. It used to be that pizza and Chinese restaurants were the only places that offered delivery. Now you can get just about anything delivered to your home. This is a pretty clear indication that as a society we are getting lazier. It's only a matter of time before we are on the phone: "Yeah, I'd like to get a delivery, and I'm going to need someone to feed me. No, no, I'll be in the tub. Yeah, the key is under the mat. Chip chop chip."

Given the amount of delivery I get, you'd think I'd be better at ordering. I've spent embarrassing amounts of time strategizing about what I want to eat, only to call up and find out they've stopped delivering at that hour. Generally I'm bad at ordering food over the phone. I think I'm ready, but I never am. It doesn't help that the guy on the other end of the phone is always impatient.

RESTAURANT: Delivery, what do you want?
ME: Uh, uh, uh, you got food there?
RESTAURANT: Yes, what would you like?
ME: Um, uh, let me call you back. I have to write it
     down. I wasn't ready for these trick questions.

I understand that many people order food online with their computer, which I think is unnatural and un-American. Do you think George Washington ordered his Thai food on a laptop? Of course not. He called on the phone and dealt with the person who didn't speak English because he was a patriot.

The most exciting part of the ordering process is when the delivery guy rings your buzzer or knocks on your door. It's like Santa has arrived at your house. "He's here! He's here! The delivery guy is here." Yet when I open the door, I don't treat the delivery guy like he's Santa. I behave like I'm in the middle of a hostage exchange. "Whoa, whoa. You wait there at the door. Here's the deal. I'll give you the money. You hand over the food. Then I want you to back away slowly. I don't need you casing the joint."

Then there's the awkward decision about how much you should tip the delivery guy. Everyone knows that at a restaurant a 20 percent tip is appropriate. Who's supposed to give us the guidelines for the delivery guy's tip? I always feel like saying, "Look, I'll give you twenty percent if you stay here and wait on me while I eat. Could you do something about the music in here? And bring me a glass of ice water right away." In reality, the delivery guys should probably get more of a tip, since they are going outside and getting in a car or on a bike and in my case carrying my food up five flights of stairs, which is actually way more than a waiter does. But still you just give him a couple of bucks and loudly lock the door behind him so you can open the paper bag and start eating your delivery before it gets cold.

I don't know why they include all that extra crap in the delivery bag. Even if I've only ordered food for one person, they still always stuff in twenty-five of the flimsiest paper plates imaginable and a bunch of tiny plastic utensils that look like they would break while cutting butter and that I imagine are from the stockroom of a prison. Why are they bringing disposable utensils to a home that presumably has a fully functioning kitchen? It's not like I'm ordering from a campsite. Judging from the poor quality of these "free" items, I am guessing that they are just trying to get rid of them. "What should we do with these five thousand worthless plates?" "Uh, just stuff them in the fat guy's bag. Let him throw them away. He's lazy enough to be ordering food from a block away, so he probably doesn't care about the environment."

Also in the bag of the delivered food is usually a menu for the restaurant. What is the purpose of that? Didn't I just order from the menu? I didn't just guess what they had at the restaurant. Did they get too many menus printed and they are hiding the mistake from their boss? I also have about five thousand pairs of chopsticks that came with random deliveries cluttering up my drawers. Who the hell is using chopsticks when they eat by themselves? Everyone knows you only eat with chopsticks to show off when you are actually *in* a restaurant. Also, in the delivery/garbage bag are enough condiment packets to get you through a zombie apocalypse. I never know what to do with all the packets. I feel bad throwing them out, but it's not like I can give them to a homeless guy. "In case you ever get that food you're begging for, here's some ketchup." Aside from these minor inconveniences, getting delivery remains my favorite nonsleeping activity. I mean, besides eating cheese.

SAY CHEESE

Drinking milk is a rather disgusting thing when you think about it. We are, in simple terms, drinking the breast milk of a cow. Growing up, we all heard, "Drink your milk." I wonder how we would have responded if our mothers had said, "Don't forget to drink that liquid that comes from one of the cow's six nipples." By that last statement I may have just killed any opportunity for me to do one of those creepy "Got Milk?" campaigns. I still don't understand why that advertising campaign worked. "Oh, this actor or athlete has a disgusting milk mustache. I guess I'll buy some milk."

Some people can't drink milk or ingest any dairy because they are lactose intolerant. For a short period I thought I was lactose intolerant because one night I drank four milkshakes and my stomach hurt pretty bad. Eventually I remembered I had also eaten four green-chile hamburgers that probably had bad meat in them. If you are lactose intolerant, you shouldn't be ashamed. It just means your sensitive tummy can't handle that spicy milk. "Do you have anything milder than milk? But not water. That gives me the runs."

While I find milk generally unappealing, what we make from the cow's breast milk is truly amazing: cheese, ice cream, whipped cream, butter. Cow's breast milk is really rather resourceful. Cheese is probably the most all-purpose dairy product. Everyone loves cheese. Supposedly the average American eats twenty-three pounds of cheese a year. That seems kind of low to me. I guess I'm making up for the non-cheese eaters. I'm not just referring to the rugged, lactose-intolerant folks. I'm including the people who don't like cheese. I don't mean little kids or people who don't like a really stinky blue cheese; I'm talking about people who don't like ANY cheese. I know. I can't believe those people exist either. These are usually the same people who don't like foods of certain colors or shapes. "I don't like eating food that is yellow, or square hamburgers." These food-complaining people are the first people I would eat if I were in the Donner Party, even though they probably wouldn't taste as delicious as the people who ate everything.

To me cheese is fantastic, and I've always loved it. I remember when I was a little kid I was kind of surprised when I realized the word *cheesy* was a negative. My older sister Cathy was complaining to a friend over the phone, "Yeah, that movie was kind of cheesy." This didn't make sense to the young me. I wanted to ask, "What kind of cheese?" Cheese and a movie sounded ideal to me. I wondered, *Did they have crackers too?* Part of me is relieved that eating tons of cheese makes you feel sick, so you stop. Otherwise I might be dead right now. Below is a letter I recently wrote to a block of Cheddar I met the night before.

Dear Cheddar,
    Last night was a mistake. Maybe it was the wine, but I acted impulsively and now I'm feeling a lot of shame and guilt, and, frankly, my stomach hurts. I know I said

I wanted to see you again tonight, but I can't. It's not going to happen. I just can't! Look, it was fun. I might even describe it as delicious, but it's over. Just because something is delicious and makes me feel whole for a moment does NOT mean it's good for me. Fine. I'll see you in the kitchen at 2:00 a.m. Jeez!

Yours truly,
Jim

Types of Cheese

Generally I like all types of cheese. Even the really stinky cheese that makes you almost gag before every delicious bite. On more than one occasion I've thought to myself, *This smell makes me want to hurl, but I can't stop eating it.* Below I give a quick overview that you didn't ask for on my feelings on the more popular cheeses.

Cheddar

When I'm lying in bed thinking about cheese, which is usually every night, I'm typically thinking about Cheddar cheese. It is the utility cheese. It works great everywhere. Great on a hamburger, great on a sandwich, even great with a piece of apple pie! Wow. You go, Cheddar! When I say *Cheddar*, I'm talking about sharp Cheddar. I usually look for "extra sharp" Cheddar, whatever that means. I just know, the sharper the Cheddar, the better. I don't understand why "mild" Cheddar even exists. It's like the nonalcoholic beer of Cheddar. What's the point?

Blue Cheese

I feel I became an adult when I started enjoying blue cheese. My siblings and I would cringe and snicker when my dad would order a salad with blue cheese as a dressing. "Is he crazy?" Blue cheese is an acquired taste. And I acquired it. It's not my daily cheese, but it is one of my favorites. It's hard to describe how I feel about blue cheese. Blue cheese is like the ice cream sundae of cheese. On a first-class flight they should fill the parfait cup with only blue cheese. No nuts on mine, please. My favorite blue cheese is Saint Agur's buttercream blue. I'm pretty sure Saint Agur was the Catholic saint of blue cheese.

Swiss

I've always viewed Swiss cheese as the grapefruit juice of cheese. Nobody really wants Swiss cheese, but it's nice to provide a choice for the occasional weirdo who wants something gross-tasting. I keep waiting for people to realize that Swiss cheese tastes like a pencil eraser. Swiss cheese is like an old dirty sock. It smells, it has holes in it, and if it's hanging on a doorknob, it means "Do not enter."

Brie

I was slow to get on the Brie bandwagon. I was never sure if I was supposed to eat the skin or shell or rind thing. Now I can eat three or four wheels of Brie during one episode of *The Biggest Loser*. I like the fact that cheese is one of the only food items that comes in a wheel. The cheese wheel is one of the greatest inventions since the actual wheel.

Goat Cheese

I'm a reluctant goat cheese consumer. I understand it's the healthy cheese (a description that always makes me distrustful), but I can't get beyond the fact that it comes from a goat. A goat? Goats always seem like characters from one of those *Lord of the Rings* movies. "Hey, you know that disgusting animal you'd never eat? Check out what we did with some of its breast milk!"

American Cheese

I don't want to create a Dixie Chicks–style cheese controversy here, but I hate American cheese. Hate it. I love my country and not just because it's God's favorite, but I don't understand American cheese. Maybe the idea was "Let's make a cheese that resembles real cheese but has no taste. You know, for people who like to melt things and hate themselves." Like a responsible citizen, I confronted this issue head-on by writing a letter to Kraft.

Dear Kraft,

I hope you are well. I wanted to write you regarding American cheese. I'd like you to stop making it, please. It's disgusting and completely unsatisfying.

Let me be clear up front. I am a huge fan of cheese. I love cheese. I realize an out-of-shape midwestern guy like myself enjoying cheese this much might be rare, but I don't care. I love cheese. Whenever I'm getting my picture taken and someone tells me to "say cheese," I smile because the word *cheese* actually makes me happy. I've gone to wine-and-cheese events *just* for the cheese. I bet if cows could talk and were asked what dairy product they are most proud of, they would say cheese. (Let's admit, ice cream is too reliant on sugar.) Cows even look like they eat a lot of cheese.

I love all kinds of cheese too, except for American cheese. American cheese is the worst of all cheeses. Well, to be honest, I've never tried headcheese. That sounds like it would be pretty bad. I guess I'm not interested in eating any cheese that has a body part in the name. Frankly, I was shocked when I recently learned that headcheese was not an actual cheese. Kraft, didn't you think headcheese was a cheese and some lame, casual, slang description for the president of an organization? Surprised me too. Can you believe they named a terrine of flesh from the head of an animal "cheese"? Isn't that like taking the name of cheese in vain? If I were you, Kraft, I would sue the headcheese people for copyright infringement. Wouldn't it be awkward if the person who came up with headcheese was reading this? "Hey, my last name is Head. I wanted to name it after myself. Jeez, this Jim Gaffigan is really mean. But he sure is good-looking."

Anyway, back to American cheese, which, while slightly better than headcheese, is disgusting. It doesn't even taste like cheese. I think the plastic that you individually wrap the slices in is tastier. You say in your commercials there is some part of a glass of milk in every slice. Is it the glass? I think that blocks of American cheese should be banned from the deli, where it sits like an imposter hiding among all the real cheeses.

Your cheese product kind of resembles cheese, but let's be honest, it's not even cheese. Why are you lying to our children? American cheese is like one of those fake presents that is just an empty box in wrapping paper I opened at the mall entrance last December.

Okay, here is the real reason you have to stop. Your so-called cheese is unpatriotic. Really? This is the cheese America gets? This great country that gave birth to the telephone, the car, and Jesus gets your so-called *American* cheese? It seems like every country contributed some important cheese. Even England, which almost prides itself on their nasty, bland food, has Stilton blue cheese *and* Cheddar. Yet all America comes up with is the shiny, gelled orange grease squares?

In summation, your American cheese is tasteless,

fake, and anti-American. If you can't stop making it, is it too much to ask you to change the name to "al-Qaeda" cheese or "I *can* believe it's not cheese" cheese? Kraft, I hope this letter will not stop you from coming to one or all of my theater shows.

Your friend,
Jim

By the way, those jerks at Kraft never got back to me. I think I can sue for that, right?

Other versions of cheese:

Vegan Cheese

You'd think with all of our technological advances, we'd be able to figure out a way to make edible nondairy cheese. We can pretend to put a man on the moon, but we can't create a nondairy cheese that doesn't taste like rubber? Jeannie has purchased every type of healthy cheese created, and they always make me prefer no cheese.

Cheese Curds

I don't really understand what cheese curds are. I guess they are like the cookie dough of cheese. Either way, cheese curds sound pretty unhealthy and are a key element of the Canadian national treasure, poutine. In Wisconsin they have deep-fried cheese curds, which taste like French fries and heaven had a baby.

Spray Cheese

We want our food easy. I've always found pre-sliced cheese rather pathetic. Nobody likes the double meaning of the term "cut the cheese," but even I've never been too lazy to take a knife to cheese. But we are a lazy bunch. How else would you explain spray cheese? I suppose there are some people who are, like, "You know I like cheese, but it is just too much work. You have to open it up, take the cheese out, slice the cheese. I don't have time for that. I have a job! I'd be willing to eat cheese if I could press something and have it just spray out. Maybe if I could write with it. Occasionally, I have to sign some checks to Mayor McCheese, and, as you know, he only takes cheese checks."

Cheez Whiz

Cheez Whiz is a cheese that comes in a jar that you can keep on a shelf. Apparently jar cheese is for people who are tired of throwing out cheese that has gone bad. This makes me wonder how long it takes some people to eat cheese. "Do you want this year's cheese or the cheese from ten years ago?" I'm less taken aback that there is a cheese that comes in a jar and more astounded that there is a product actually named Cheez Whiz. The people at Kraft must have been a little surprised the product worked. "Wow, people are actually buying that Cheez Whiz stuff. It was meant to be an April Fool's prank." When they came up with the name Cheez Whiz, don't you think there would have been one person at that meeting who would have said, "This cheese in a jar is an interesting idea, but *obviously* we're not going to call it Cheese Whiz, right?" It makes you wonder how bad the names were that they turned down before deciding on Cheez Whiz.

BOSS: Okay, let me hear your pitches for the jar cheese name.

EMPLOYEE: How about Cheez Squirt? Or maybe how about Cheez Runs?

BOSS: We need something gross that also communicates easy-to-use.

EMPLOYEE: Cheez Whiz?

BOSS: Brilliant. Cheez Whiz it is. Now get back to
    working on names for that jar of fluffy marshmal-
    low insides.

There are innumerable varieties of cheese. Most of them
are too fancy for me to understand, so instead of discussing
the rest of them here, I will just continue my research by eating them. There is cheese from just about every country in the
world except China. No cheese from China? Maybe tofu is
Chinese cheese. No wonder there was a cultural revolution.

CRACKERS: THE ADULT JUNK FOOD

Crackers are the junk food of adults. There are so many different types of crackers for adults to eat while they congratulate themselves for not eating potato chips. Of course, kids like crackers too. My children seem to enjoy Goldfish crackers and those Annie's Bunnies crackers, because apparently food shaped like animals tastes better to kids. Whenever I eat my children's Goldfish crackers (to make sure they are not poisonous), I'm always a little relieved they don't taste like fish. The bunnies don't taste as good as real bunnies either. Growing up, my family couldn't afford Goldfish crackers, or, in the less romantic version, my mom didn't buy them. I remember eating Saltine crackers as a kid. I'd grab a sleeve of Saltines, eat them one by one, and pretend I was in jail. Even as a child I had an active imagination and a strange appetite. People don't really eat Saltine crackers these days. They are mostly known for being the free stuff you get with soup or what to eat when you are sick. I imagine Saltines will have a comeback. If there are gourmet doughnuts, there might as well be gourmet Saltines. "These are Himalayan Salt Artisanal Saltines and cost ten dollars a cracker."

When I was a teenager, my mom upgraded the family to Ritz Crackers, which I guess she felt were classier than Saltines, even though I'm pretty sure Ritz Crackers have nothing to do with the Ritz-Carlton hotel chain. I wanted her to buy Doritos, Cheetos, and Fritos, but when I recommended that we get those, my mother looked at me like I suggested we move to a trailer park. My mom was a classy lady, and Ritz Crackers were more her style. Ritz Crackers do seem less pathetic than a bag of chips or Saltines, but of course they're not. They are still crackers. Occasionally, when I was out with my teenage friends, I'd buy Cheez-Its, which still remains the worst name ever for crackers. The appeal of Cheez-Its was that they were covered with a greasy cheese powder that was so toxic it would stain your fingers. They were a lot like that other junky stuff I was not allowed to eat at home, but they were disguised as crackers, which had a much better perception than chips and puffs. I think probably it was Cheez-Its that first taught me why crackers actually existed. They are the perfect platform for cheese.

Triscuits

Now that I am an adult, one of my favorite snacks is cheese and crackers. At a certain point Jeannie, in an attempt to curb my cheese-and-cracker-eating behavior, started buying Triscuits because they are a "healthier cracker" and hummus, a dip made out of chickpeas. While not a perfect substitute for cheese, hummus is pretty good. It comes in a variety of flavors, and you feel less guilty about eating a seventeen-ounce tub of hummus than you do eating a seventeen-ounce tub of Merkts cheese spread. I should clarify that I don't eat Triscuits because they taste good. I eat them because Jeannie makes me. Triscuits are just shredded wheat in cracker form. I always tell myself,

These are mostly air. No calories in air. Hearing something is better for me always gives me license to eat five times as much.

Being a late-night eater, I can hardly fathom how many Triscuits I've consumed. I'm sure the number is in the hundreds of thousands at this point. I wish I were exaggerating. I eat them like I'm training for some impending Triscuit-eating contest. If there were a frequent-eating program for Triscuits, I'd earn so many miles that I'd spend every other weekend in Hawaii. I typically eat Triscuits only at night. On an average night I'll do a stand-up show, go home, help Jeannie get our five children to sleep, and then sit down and eat five boxes of Triscuits. If I were murdered at my computer, there would most likely be a box of Triscuits in the crime scene photos. Lately Jeannie has only been buying Reduced Fat Triscuits, which are just like regular Triscuits but even less satisfying.

Wheat Thins

There are Triscuit people, and then there are Wheat Thins people. Everyone has his or her own brand of soda (Coke/Pepsi), ketchup (Heinz/Hunt's), and toothpaste (Crest/Colgate). We are a Triscuit family. Wheat Thins also have a healthy perception, mostly because they are smaller, thinner, and, I guess, wheatier than most crackers. "Well, there's even *thin* in the name!" I'm sure there is some delineating attribute that separates the Triscuit folk from the Wheat Thins folk. All I know is, Triscuit eaters are better-looking.

THE ROYAL TREATMENT

Eating in a fine-dining establishment is the closest many of us will come to being a king. We pick food from a list, someone makes it for us, and then someone else brings it to us. We don't cook. We don't clean up. We just sit there and people serve us like we are characters on *Downton Abbey.* When we order wine, the bottle is even opened and poured into a glass in front of us so that none of the peasants can poison us. I rarely get to go to fancy restaurants, but when I do I fully embrace it. Everything seems better in a fancy restaurant. Maybe it's the five sticks of butter they use in every dish, but everything is simply more enjoyable. Even a glass of tap water is more pleasing. "Oooh, this is good water." Being waited on makes us so self-important, we feel like we can critique the food. "How's your appetizer? Mine is a little rich." You can't do this when you have a dinner at a friend's house. "I didn't care for the chicken. I don't think we're coming back here unless your wife takes some cooking classes."

The royal treatment in a fine-dining establishment begins instantaneously when you are ushered to your table by the hostess or a maître d'. The maître d' becomes the king's guard, and the hostess is a lady-in-waiting who leads the way to your table with beauty and innocence. Upon arriving at your table you are greeted by your waiter, your personal servant for the night. Usually the waiter will tell you his name. Now that you are a person of royalty, you never give yours.

WAITER: (*warm*) Hello. My name is Phil. I'll be your waiter.

YOU: (*snotty*) I'll have the chicken.

I always feel uncomfortable when the waiter gives his name. I never use it. "I'm out of water, Phil. Yoo-hoo! PHIL?" Maybe they tell you their name to avoid your addressing them in other ways. "Waiter? Slave boy? Food bitch?—Oh, your name is Phil?"

Next you must determine what exquisite dish is worthy to enter your royal mouth. You are handed a menu, and the waiter begins to recite the chef's specials like he's announcing the lineup of your personal entertainment for the evening: "First the jester will perform a lovely . . ." "No! I don't want that. Off with his head!"

The specials are presented in a semi-conversational manner. "Tonight we have a coq au vin that is flambéed." Then there's a pause. I usually nod, but I always wonder if I'm supposed to say something. "Um, pass. Next." In an effort to be polite, I exert so much energy acting like I'm interested in the specials when I really don't care. "That's the soup of the day? Wow! I'm not getting any of these specials." The term *specials* seems a little confusing. Is the chef trying harder on the specials? "He'll cook the stuff that's written down, but he's not going to put any effort into it." I often think if the dish is that special, why don't they put it on the menu? By this time you've been handed your menu, which can come in varying sizes and shapes. Often the menus are unnecessarily oversize, so you feel like you are about to read a bedtime story to a young child. "Once there was a prime rib . . . for sixty-five dollars? That's a little scary." In general I don't know what I'm looking at when I read a menu in fancy restaurants. I usually recognize every other word. "All right, that means beef and I think that is a green leafy vegetable I wouldn't like."

When it finally comes time to order, a wave of panic usually crashes over me. It's a similar feeling to the one I have when ordering over the phone, but it's much more intense because I'm face-to-face. *What if I order the wrong thing? How adventurous should I be? How can I get Jeannie to order something I would like and then distract her so I can eat it?* In an effort to avoid mispronouncing things, I'll just point at items on the menu. "I'll start with the (*point*) and then I'll get (*pointing*) THIS." If someone orders something I was going to order, I suddenly feel like I have to change my order. I know it's irrational, but I don't want that person to think I'm copying, or I don't want the chef to get bored. The waiter is always there to provide advice and counsel. "Hey, waiter, you don't know me, but what do you think I should eat? Is it time for me to get a haircut? It's up to you, because you're a stranger and I'm an idiot." Occasionally a waiter will strongly recommend something from the menu. I always feel guilty not getting the waiter's recommendation. "I know you want me to get that, but I'm going to get what I want because I'm paying, right? Why don't you back off, Phil?"

Sometimes when out with a group of friends you are the last one to decide what you want on the menu. Throughout the ordering process you keep telling the waiter to skip to the next person. Now he's back to you for the final order, and you still don't know what you want and everyone is staring at you like you are holding all of them up and ruining the whole night. For me, this is when the *real* "order panic" sets in. I feel like I have to make this vital decision in less than a second, so I blurt out the first thing I remember, "Uhhh . . . burrito *puerte vejerta*!" Then it comes and it's like a snail and an egg. I just stare at it in utter disappointment. "Hey! Anyone wanna trade?"

When you go out to dinner, it is customary to order an appetizer in addition to the entrée. The appetizer is just an excuse for an extra meal. "Let's see, I will start with the eighty buffalo wings, and do you have a low-cal blue cheese? Because I don't want to fill up too much." It would be embarrassing trying to explain what an appetizer is to someone from a starving country. "Yeah, the appetizer—that's the food we eat before we have our food. No, no, you're thinking of dessert—that's food we have after we have our food. We eat tons of food. Sometimes there's so much we just stick it in a bag and bring it home. Then we throw it out the next day. Maybe give it to the dog."

In most fine-dining establishments a basket of bread is placed on the table. I enjoy bread in everyday life, but for some reason when I go out to dinner I suddenly crave bread. "Bread! They have bread here!" Bread suddenly becomes an unusual and fascinating delicacy. "Oh, we should have bread at home. We've gotta get the recipe for bread!" I'm not sure whose brilliant idea it was to give customers, often before they order, the most filling food for free.

MAN 1: You want a successful restaurant? Give everyone a basket of bread.

MAN 2: At the end of the meal, right? That way they leave full.

MAN 1: No, right when they sit down at the table.

MAN 2: Wouldn't they just fill up on the bread?

MAN 1: Exactly.

MAN 2: But then they would order less food.

MAN 1: Exactly.

MAN 2: And I'd make less money.

MAN 1: Trust me.

MAN 2: Okay, I'll do it.

Sometimes the bread in the bread basket is so amazing I can't stop eating it. This is usually when the basket of bread is an assortment of different types of fresh, warm bread. "Well, I should try the pretzel bread. Well, I should try that pumpernickel thing. Well, I can't skip the roll!" Also there is always that skinny breadstick in there that you have to eat because how often do you get to eat a skinny breadstick? I've eaten entire baskets of bread in restaurants. It can be kind of awkward asking the waiter for seconds on bread. "Yeah, can we have some more of that free bread, and can you cancel my entrée? I'm just going to load up on the bread and ice water. Are there other free things here? I prefer the free stuff more."

Most of the time I really should cancel my entrée. I'm rarely hungry when it arrives. It's often a little bit of a surprise when the entrée is presented. "Oh, I forgot about that. That's the thing that costs forty bucks, right? Is it too late to un-order it? I guess I'll just stuff it in while I think about what I'm going to eat for dessert." Other times the wait for the entrée feels like an eternity, and when it arrives you are given a stern warning about the temperature of the hot plate. I sometimes wonder if we are waiting for them to make the plates. "The steak is ready, but the plate is still in the kiln." On special occasions, while you're eating your entrée the chef will approach the table to see how you are enjoying your meal. You can tell it's the chef because they are usually dressed in some type of white karate outfit. A visit from the chef is a great honor and very generous because, after all, they are in the middle of their workday. It's the equivalent of me stopping during my stand-up show and approaching a couple in the fourth row. "How do you like the jokes so far? Well, enjoy." I usually awkwardly tell the chef everything is great, praying that he or she will go away. What else could you say? "I thought it would be better, but, hey, I'm here. Don't worry. I'll still pay."

It's usually after the second bite of your entrée that your waiter approaches and asks, "Can I interest any of you in dessert?" My first thought is *He's trying to kill us. I haven't been hungry in an hour.*

For some reason when you go out to dinner no one wants to be the one to order dessert. After eating a basket of bread and two courses of food, suddenly you decide that you don't want to overdo it. There is usually someone who wants to share dessert. "Hey, you want to share a dessert? Let's share a dessert." Why don't you get your own damn dessert? "Oh I just want a bite, just a bite." Then the dessert arrives and they turn into a vacuum. Apparently it was a bite from a shovel. "Yeah, I have a bit of a sweet tooth." No, you are a pathetic sugar fiend. I love the phrase "I have a sweet tooth." I always want to say, "You're ordering it for your tooth? That's interesting, because it's going straight to your butt. I think your butt owes your tooth an explanation." I guess we all have our own way of rationalizing. In defense of the friend with the sweet tooth, no one has ever really needed dessert. Who was the first guy to ask for dessert? "That was a good meal. I'm full. You full? Good. Let's eat a cake."

Following dessert and that necessary after-dinner coffee needed to provide you with the energy to move so you can eventually leave the restaurant, the check arrives. Your waiter always seems to delicately place the check on the table like he had nothing to do with it. "Some guy over there gave me this to give to you." The check is often in some type of leather folder like some kind of award. "What did I win?" "Bankruptcy." When you see the bill, you are reminded why the check comes at the end of the meal when you are too full to run away.

It can be startling how large a check can be when you go out to dinner. "How can it be that much? Did someone order furniture?" I remember the first time I paid when I went out to dinner. I was in my twenties. I thought to myself, *I have a job. I'm going to go out for a fancy dinner.* Then the check came and all I could think was *I'm moving home. I need my mommy and daddy to pay for everything.* The whole experience of going out to dinner is amazing until that moment the bill arrives. Your relationship with your waiter has gone from "Who is this stranger talking to me?" to "He's not our waiter, he's our friend" to "This guy is the reason we won't be able to send our children to college." When the check comes, the illusion shatters. You were never the king. You were just another john in a fancy food whorehouse.

NON-ROYAL TREATMENT

Of course, most of my eating-outside-the-home experiences are not at fancy restaurants. I'm normally in a hurry to eat or else on the road somewhere, so usually I end up in a place where it's less of an elegant adventure and more of a transaction. I'm just buying my food and sitting down and eating it. Sometimes I'm even standing up and eating it.

Homestyle

Sometimes after a show there's nothing open except the place across from my hotel that offers homestyle cooking. I never really understood the appeal. When I go out to dinner, I want restaurant-style cooking. When I hear *homestyle*, I always think of some guy in his underwear standing next to a micro-wave. "You want me to nuke a hot dog for ya? I got some old Chinese in the fridge, but I think it's my roommate's."

Dining Al Fresco

When people find out I live near Little Italy in New York City, they will often say, "Little Italy? You must eat well." I never understood that logic. It's not like they are giving the food away. Sadly, most of the food in Little Italy is not even the best Italian food, and most of the restaurants are tourist traps not even run by Italians. To maintain the illusion of authenticity, many of these not-really-Italian restaurants have quaint little outdoor seating sections on the sidewalk in front of the restaurant's entrance. When the Italian-looking Albanian waiter asks you if you would rather be seated indoors or dine "al fresco"—literally, "in the fresh" (air)—like it's some alluring vacation destination, you gladly choose the latter. After all, when pretending to be in Rome, do as the pretending-to-be-Romans do. Once you are seated, you quickly realize that "al fresco" in New York actually means, "Eating outside while you watch two drunk guys from Long Island yell at each other as a homeless man rummages through a garbage can."

Diners

There are different types of diners, but generally they all embrace the simple approach to mediocre food. There seems to be an almost deliberate lack of creativity. Don't get me wrong. I love diners. I love the booths, the subpar coffee, and the laminated menus that feel more like a catalog of every dish ever conceived of by humans. I usually want to ask, "To save time, can you just tell me the food you *don't* serve here?" The diner menu's description of food items is so hyperbolic that it borders on sarcasm: "World's 'Greatest' Tuna Melt." I especially love the diners that decorate their walls with actor headshots.

"Wow, look at all these people I've never heard of who have eaten this mediocre food."

Truck Stops

(See "Diners," but add in mud flaps and showers.)

Food Trucks

The chuck wagon of today, the food truck always looks to me as if it wandered away and got lost from the rest of the caravan. "I've been separated from my group. I'm selling coffee to raise money to help me find them." I don't really understand the appeal of a food truck. It is a truck, right? Are we supposed to be eating stuff served out of trucks? If they give you food poisoning, they have the ability to flee the scene quickly. I call them poison-and-run trucks.

On Portlandia, *my character worked in a food truck.*

Street Fairs

In order to increase traffic and block the entrance to perfectly good restaurants during the summer, most large American cities have street fairs. Suddenly food that is normally eaten only by drunk people is being sold in broad daylight, and sober folk are lining up to pay too much for it. I like to think of street fairs as stationary parades that are pretty insensitive to the homeless. "Sorry you have to live on the street, but we're having a PARTY!!! Can you move your box/house/bed thing? Thanks."

The Barbecue

There are other times when you leave your home to eat and you are not actually paying for your food. I'm not talking about a fancy dinner party or a casual meal at a friend's house. I'm talking about being invited to a barbecue. This gathering is a popular tradition in the summer months. You do not even have to know the host that well to be invited. As soon as it gets warm out, everyone suddenly has an uncontrollable desire to break out the grill and invite all their friends and friend's friends over for an obnoxious amount of food in their backyard. People are usually expected to bring something to the barbecue. As a result of this disorganized assignment, there are never enough buns, and an inordinate amount of disgusting, mayonnaise-based salads complete with their own clouds of flies. I know people love an outdoor barbecue, but to me it just means "Let's make the food more accessible to insects." I mean, I enjoy the wind blowing a plate of potato salad onto my shirt as much as the next guy, but whenever I am at an outdoor barbecue, I always think, *This would be so much better if it were indoors.* I realize I'm a man and I should love outdoor grilling, but eating, cooking, or even being outdoors just feels counterintuitive to me. There's just too much standing.

INTERNATIONAL RELATIONS

The term "ethnic food" is relative, of course. Germans don't think of German food as ethnic. I guess *ethnic* is code for exotic or unfamiliar food. I grew up in a small town in Indiana where my father's favorite ethnic restaurant was a place called Giovanni's that sold exotic dishes like spaghetti and chicken parmesan. I was raised on Wonder Bread, which is probably the whitest of the white breads. Frankly, I'm not even sure if Wonder Bread is bread. I don't think bread is supposed to catch on fire or be used to remove makeup. Anyway, my point is, I grew up thinking most food was ethnic food.

Asian Food

Asian food, or as 60 percent of the Earth's population refers to it, "homestyle cooking," is exotic, diverse, and amazing to me. Understandably, there are innumerable varieties and styles covering the enormous and culturally varied continent that is Asia. Having only a couple of paragraphs dedicated to Asian food is a little obnoxious, but then again, this book is titled *Food: A Love Story*. Not *Food: An Anthology*. Here's what I love about Asian food.

Thai

The best Asian food is undeniably Thai food. Congratulations, Thailand. I'm sure as a country you were waiting to learn what an out-of-shape pale guy from the other side of the planet thought of your food. I think Buddha was so peaceful and fat because of the Thai food. There are almost too many good dishes coming from Thailand. Pad Thai, Massaman Curry, and tons of other stuff I only know as numbers on a menu all come from Thailand. The Thai even figured out a way to make string beans delicious. The Thai combination of sweet, sour, hot, and spicy is incredible, really. I would be so fat if I lived in Thailand or near a Thai restaurant. Oh wait, I do. Well, at least now I know why I'm so fat.

Indian

I entirely agree with the Hindus in their belief that cows are sacred, yet for some reason beef is rarely an ingredient in Indian food. Thank God I'm not Hindu. Beyond a doubt, Indian food is the best non-beef food on the planet, which I feel is almost an impossible task. Indian food is either on the edge of too spicy or lethally hot. It's no wonder that Indian food also boasts the most delicious variety of breads offered at a single meal. We all know eating tons of different types of bread is the best way to effectively eat super-hot food. I'm a fan of any culture that is brilliant enough to justify this kind of bread eating.

Korean

I'm normally not a fan of restaurants where they ask me to do the cooking. I view fajitas as the IKEA of Mexican food. "Oh you want me to put my taco together myself? Um, okay." That being said, I'm a huge fan of Korean barbecue. It's like a self-serve Benihana where for some reason they don't allow me to toss knives.

Chinese

Given that the Chinese restaurant near my hometown growing up had a Chicago Bears poster hanging in it and no employees of Chinese descent, I like to think of myself as a Chinese food expert. Supposedly, eating Chinese food means you'll be hungry in an hour. This is a ridiculous statement, because after eating any food I'm hungry in an hour.

My family and I live near Chinatown in New York City. Like most Chinatowns throughout North America, there are live seafood tanks in the windows of many of the restaurants. Often I look at the windows filled with crabs and lobsters swimming in murky water and think, *Do you want us to come in there, or are these sea monsters protecting your establishment? Cause I ascared.* I eat a lot of Chinese food. One of the many things I admire about the Chinese is that not only will they eat anything, but they have an uncanny ability to make seemingly disgusting things taste good. The best example of this would have to be oxtail soup. This doesn't sound that appetizing. "Hey, you know how you'd never eat an ox? Well, how about the tail? Yeah, the thing it swats flies away from its butt with. Well, what if we put that in a murky soup, where you wouldn't be able to tell what was in it but you'd know there was a tail in there? Sounds good, huh?"

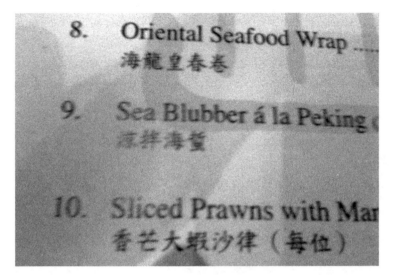

I know what I'm getting.

Chinese food is the most deliverable of all ethnic foods. Sometimes when I order Chinese delivery, it comes *too* quickly. I've been on the phone ordering from our local Chinese restaurant and the food has arrived while I was ordering, "Yeah, I'd like to order the General T . . . *DING-DONG* . . . oh, it's here already. How'd you know I even wanted . . . ?" Chinese food seems to be the fastest to prepare but the slowest to eat. I prefer the Chinese restaurants that have the silverware on the table when you arrive, because there's nothing more humiliating than starting with chopsticks and having to turn to the waiter and being like, "Uh, yeah, hi, uh, I'm too white. Do you have a shovel back there?" Chopsticks are fun, but I'd rather eat than play Operation. I always found it interesting that in China they use chopsticks, but in Russia they use forks. Does it change at the border? Or are there some border towns where it's mixed? I imagine the different groups don't get along. "I won't eat with those fork users!" I could see a real

Romeo and Juliet story coming out of one of those fork-chopstick border towns.

I have a lot of respect for the Chinese, and I'm not just saying this because in six months we will all be working for them. The Chinese have a truly amazing culture. Supposedly, three thousand years ago they were performing brain surgery in China. Yet they still haven't figured out dessert. There are endless food choices on the menu in a Chinese restaurant, but no real dessert. I'm not counting those fancy Chinese restaurants that have sticky buns or that tea ice cream that tastes like a pack of menthol cigarettes. I'm talking about a regular, generic Chinese restaurant where there are typically two dessert options. The first is sliced oranges. "Wow. I don't want to overwork the kitchen. Oranges? Where'd you get those? Did a schooner just arrive from the Caribbean? Looks like our scurvy is cured, fellas." The other choice is the fortune cookie, which is not even a Chinese thing, really. Fortune cookies are an American invention, and we gave it to them. The Chinese were probably like, "Uh, we don't want it." And we were like, "It's now part of your ethnic identity." Part of me feels like the fortune in every fortune cookie should just read, "You are about to eat a stale cookie." "Hey, my fortune came true!" It's almost like they wait for the cookies to get stale. "When were these made? 1984? Let's wait a little longer." Everyone seems to have the same reaction to fortune cookies. We all think, *These things are so silly. What a ridiculous concept . . . wait, what's mine say?* Like there's some ancient wisdom in that cookie that will provide guidance for our lives. As if Confucius himself were putting a tiny piece of paper into a tiny typewriter: "Happiness is . . . (*thinks*) a long journey. Um, I'll put some numbers here. Let's see . . . 17, 38 (*looks at watch*), 12. (*handing off*) Put this in a stale cookie." I do feel sorry for the baker who created the cookie that ended up being the fortune cookie. He was probably initially pretty proud.

BAKER: Oh, you have to try the new cookie I created. Tell me what you think.

SAMPLER: Okay. (*chewing*) Interesting. You know what this could use? Paper. This would be good for holding a note. Like maybe for a fortune or a recipe for a good cookie.

BAKER: Oh. How much could I charge for them?

SAMPLER: I'd give 'em away with the check. You got a spit bucket around here?

MY LONGTIME COMPANION

It's amazing how our attitude toward fast-food places changes over our lifetime. When you're a kid, a fast-food restaurant is one of your favorite places ever. A stop at a McDonald's or a Burger King is like a visit to a toy store or Disney World. What's for a kid not to like? Bright colors, French fries, an indoor playground. You even get a free toy with your meal. No wonder I begged to have my ninth birthday party at McDonald's. But as an adult, a practical wisdom sets in, and we see fast-food places for what they really are: a place for convenient, mediocre, super-unhealthy food. We view fast-food places like they are someone we used to date. You drive by and look at them like, "I can't believe I went there." Then a couple of nights later you find yourself at their doorstep: "It's late. I'm drunk. How about one for old times' sake?"

As sober adults we are embarrassed to eat in a fast-food restaurant. We sit by ourselves hunched over our food in a manner that communicates hurried desperation. "Don't tell my wife I'm here!" I'm convinced that if ski masks were sold in fast-food places, they would be a bigger seller than French fries.

Most regular restaurants try to set a mood or an atmosphere. French restaurants may have a quaint garden. Some Italian restaurants make you feel like you've been transported to a Tuscan villa. The atmosphere in a fast-food establishment looks like they are trying to re-create the environment of a mental institution. The bright lights, the smell of bleach, the employees with the smile and personality of kidnapping victims, and for some reason the furniturè is bolted down. "Oh, good, I'm eating in a place that also appeals to a segment of the population that is likely to steal furniture from restaurants." It almost seems like fast-food places are attempting to stage a scene from *One Flew Over the Cuckoo's Nest*, but with milkshakes. They should just make everyone dress in robes. The food is even served in paper wrappers so we don't try to hurt ourselves.

The fast-food industry knows that many of us don't want to be seen in their establishments or eating their food, which is why the drive-thru was created. The drive-thru is the fast-food industry's way of saying, "Look, no one has to see you. Just drive around back, and we will hand you the food out the window. You can eat it in your car." The drive-thru is a pretty convenient idea except for that final arm stretch you have to do to get your food. I always ask, "Um, can you bring your building closer to my car?"

Of course, every aspect of the fast-food experience is constructed around convenience. In a way they've ruined how I view dining in a normal restaurant.

ME: Let's see, I will order the cheeseburger. (*beat*) Where is it?

WAITER: Sir, how would you like your burger done?

ME: Uh, right now. Where is it?

WAITER: I'll place your request with the chef.

ME: Can you have the chef wrap the burger in paper so I feel like I'm opening a present? Or maybe put it in a Styrofoam clamshell and present it like an engagement ring? Then we can do that scene from *Pretty Woman*. How about it?

The Food

After a lifetime of going to fast-food places I've come to the conclusion that the only food that can be prepared quickly is food that is bad for you. Anyone over the age of eight knows eating fast food is a form of killing yourself. I'm still waiting for a burger named "The Euthanasia." If you are going to a fast-food place, you're probably not that concerned about your health. The latest trend (or court order) of posting nutritional charts provides us with no new information. "Wait, since when are French fries unhealthy?" The food at fast-food places is so unhealthy, it's not even considered odd that milkshakes are offered as a beverage with your meal. "Well, I shouldn't, but I'll have the cheeseburger and fries. And to drink, I'll have the ice cream you can drink through a straw. Do you have an EKG machine back there?"

LOOKING FOR MR. GOODBURGER

You can't talk about fast food without crediting the hamburger and French fries. It's what fast-food empires like McDonald's, Burger King, and Wendy's were built on. Even fast-food places that don't serve burgers and fries know they are the odd ones. Taco Bell had an ad slogan begging us to "think outside the bun." The baffling success of Subway was basically constructed on *not* selling burgers and fries. "Eat Fresh" was a creative apology for not having French fries.

McDonald's

I like to tell people I go to McDonald's. As a matter of fact, I like to tell people I go to McDonald's more than I actually like going to McDonald's. I just love how people respond. There's sometimes a shocked silence, like I just admitted I support dog fighting. "How could you?" Occasionally, people give a smirk that says, "Oh, I didn't know I was better than you." These pompous responses are because no one admits they go to McDonald's. McDonald's sells roughly six billion burgers a day, and there are only three hundred million people in this country. I'm not a calculus teacher, but I figure some of these people are lying.

I have to admit that many times a cloud of depression appears over me when I enter a McDonald's. In my head I hear the sound of a buzzer, like I got something wrong on a game show. "*BZZZT!* Not equipped to be an adult." The worst is when I'm in McDonald's and I see a friend. I always think, *Oh crap*, and then, like the brave man that I am, I try to hide behind a garbage can. I'm always seen. My friends never seem to be in there for the food. "Oh, I'm just in here to use the ATM. What are you doing here, Jim?" Not wanting to embarrass and humiliate myself by admitting I'm there for the food, I say, "Oh, I'm just meeting a hooker. He should be here by now."

We all know how bad McDonald's is for us. We've all read the articles and seen the documentaries. It's the same message: "Look, McDonald's is really bad for you. It's very high in fat and calories, and we don't even know where the meat comes from." We all respond with the same shock and disgust right before we bite into our juicy Big Mac. There is a McDonald's denial, and we embrace it. We all know McDonald's is like a casino for heart disease. Yet we gamble we can beat the house odds. "I'm feeling lucky. I'm going to double down on the Quarter Pounder. And I'll raise my digestive system a shake." No one goes into McDonald's innocent. We're walking into a red-and-yellow building with a giant *M* over it.

DUMB GUY: What's this, a library? Oh, what a surprise! It's actually a McDonald's. Well, I guess I might as well get some fries while I'm here.

It's hard to be in a McDonald's and not order the fries. They are that good. I try to rationalize eating them. "Well, these fries are too thin to have calories." Has your mom ever made anything as good as a McDonald's fry? Not even close. No sane adult has ever had too many McDonald's fries. There never seem to be enough of them. You can see confused people in McDonald's after they've finished their fries. They always look around their tabletop like their fries disappeared into thin air. "What happened?" Then they'll scrounge in the bag for the fry crumbs or that loose fry at the bottom of the bag, or, as I call it, the bonus fry. Sometimes there is even a bonus fry in the bag when you order the apple pie. The bonus fry is the dividend for all the good deeds you've ever done. It's like Jesus is up in heaven and decides, "You know what? Give him an extra fry. He'll pay it forward." The bonus fry is never a regular-size fry. It's always extra long. "Bonus fry, how did I not see you? You deserve your own ketchup packet." You savor that last fry. turning it into multiple bites. "I'll catch up with you guys later. I got a bonus fry." McDonald's fries are truly that amazing . . . for roughly about eight minutes. Then the fries turn into something that's likely not biodegradable. They become edible cold shoelaces. We've all made the mistake of reheating McDonald's fries in the microwave, transforming them into packing peanuts. This of course doesn't stop me from eating them.

McDonald's fries can't get cold, and McDonald's milkshakes can't get warm. Once I left a chocolate shake outside for an hour and reality set in. It was definitely not a milk product. The contents turned into some kind of disgusting chocolate mucus. However, by the time I finished the shake I got used to it.

McDonald's has many strange McProducts with broad appeal, but the oddest has to be the McRib. I'm not sure why a McRib is even called a McRib. There's no rib in there. The overly processed pork is shaped to look like ribs and then covered in barbecue sauce and two pickles. If the McRib patty's resemblance to a bloated futon with ripples was meant to be visually disturbing, it worked. I guess they decided against naming it the McPork or the McGlob. If the name or shape weren't odd enough, the McRib has a strange "here today, gone tomorrow" existence. Like a serial deadbeat dad, the McRib arrives with great fanfare only to skip town without warning.

Children have a strange obsession with McDonald's. Even kids who have never been to McDonald's or seen a McDonald's commercial want to go there. No one knows how they found out about McDonald's. Most children's first complete sentence is "Can we go to McDonald's?" It's almost as if children are born with an innate love of McDonald's. "She has her mother's eyes and her father's love of McDonald's."

Growing up, I was so used to McDonald's soft-serve I was disappointed when I first tried a scoop of real ice cream: "Well, this is okay, but it's too hard. How do they even get it through that pump? Wouldn't these scooped balls clog it?" The things that appeal to children about McDonald's are innumerable: the clown, the playground, the colors of a nursery school, and, of course, the Happy Meal. I'm not sure why they call it a "Happy Meal" when it seems to turn children into monsters. "Can we go to McDonald's? Can we? Well, after that, can we?" Children get a free toy with their Happy Meal. I didn't even get a napkin at home when I was growing up. We are setting our children up with false expectations. In San Francisco they made the Happy Meal illegal, a decision that caused a backlash because it was a sad day for freedom when a parent no longer had the right to poison his or her own child. The strange obsession McDonald's has with children is kind of creepy. "Hey kids, come in here and Uncle McDonald's will give you a toy." My kids only want that damn toy. On road trips they beg for the Happy Meal, get the free toy, and don't eat the food. Some "free toy."

Given all children's obsession with McDonald's, we shouldn't be surprised that their spokesman is a clown. In a way it feels like they are mocking us, the consumer.

"Who should our spokesman be? Burger King has a king."

"It doesn't matter. These idiots are going to come here no matter what."

"How about a rat?"

"No, not a rat. Too cute. What really freaks out little children more than a rat?"

"Um, a witch, a clown, a weatherman . . ."

"Let's go with a clown with a creepy weatherman vibe."

McDonald's used to have a whole group of spokespeople. The Hamburglar, Grimace, Mayor McCheese, and others. I was never sure what Grimace was or why he was named after a pained facial expression. Maybe he represented the look on everyone's face after they ate McDonald's. Whatever the case may be, all the spokesmen disappeared except for Ronald McDonald. I think we have our suspect. Someone needs to call Detective Olivia Benson. Maybe they did a reality show elimination of spokespeople and Ronald won. More likely, it was a Destiny's Child situation. Ronald was the breakout. The entertainment manager for McDonald's characters was like, "Hey, you guys are all great. Grimace, Hamburglar, Mayor, we love what you guys do, but we're thinking of going with just Ronald for a while. Maybe we'll do a reunion tour at some point."

All clowning aside, somehow McDonald's gets us in there. We know those McDonald's commercials are not realistic. I'd just like to see one commercial that showed people five minutes after they'd actually eaten McDonald's. "Ugh, now I need a cigarette. I deserve a cigarette break today." Yet we keep going back because the one thing McDonald's does well besides fries is consistency. You know how much it's going to cost. You know how long it's going to take. You even know how sick you are going to feel after you eat it. We are also lured in by the McDonald's deals that are so good they seem cruel. "Two Big Macs for Two Bucks." I drive by and think, *Well I don't want to lose money on this. I'll get eighty of them.* We are further lured by the promotional games like Monopoly, even though we have no possibility of winning. "I got Boardwalk. All I need is sixty-three more pieces. You know, I could probably make some money here." During the Olympics, commercials tell us that eating at McDonald's is a way of winning free food and supporting Team USA. It's like our own private decathlon of unhealthy eating.

There also used to be McDonald's gift certificates. There was even a commercial where people were hanging McDonald's gift certificates on their Christmas trees, just as Jesus would've wanted. When I was ten years old I was actually given McDonald's gift certificates for Christmas by my mom. Yes, my own mother. I guess she couldn't find gift certificates for a vending machine. I like to think it was her way of saying, "Merry Christmas. Here are some coupons for poison." McDonald's introduced the gift certificate prior to the obesity epidemic. I'm not saying that McDonald's gift certificates caused the obesity epidemic, but in retrospect, the timing is kind of suspicious. It was a more innocent time back then. I remember there was another commercial where a kid gave Santa Claus a gift certificate. These days there would probably be public outrage and a demand that Santa be given a gym membership instead. "It's abusive and enabling to give that to an obvious food addict."

I'm sure some of you are reading this and thinking, *Sorry, white-trashy guy. I don't eat at McDonald's.* I have friends who brag to me about *not* going to McDonald's. "I would *never* go to McDonald's." I always think, *Well, McDonald's wouldn't want you because you're a jerk.* I'm tired of people acting like they are better than McDonald's. You may've never set foot in a McDonald's, but you have your own McDonald's.

Maybe instead of buying a Big Mac, you read *US Weekly*. That's just a different type of McDonald's. It's just served up a little differently. Maybe your McDonald's is telling yourself your Starbucks Frappuccino is *not* a milkshake, or maybe you watch those *Real-Housewives*-of-some-large-city shows. It's all McDonald's. It's McDonald's of the soul: momentary pleasure followed by incredible guilt, eventually leading to cancer. We all have our own McDonald's. It may take me a decade to digest my Quarter Pounder with Cheese, but that tramp stamp is forever. In a way, it's all McDonald's out there in our society. Why can everyone name three people who have dated Jennifer Aniston? It's McDonald's! And we gobble it up just like those McDonald's fries. "Who's she dating now? Yum, yum, yum. I know I shouldn't, but it's so salty! Yum, yum, yum. Is she pregnant yet? That's not even my business! Yum, yum, yum. Scarlett Johansson got a haircut! Why do I even a care?" Because it's McDonald's! *McDonald's of the soul.* By the way, if you actually care about the British royal family, that's Burger King. That's not even *our* gossip.

I truly enjoy the societal outrage directed at McDonald's: "McDonald's food has no nutritional value! There are no vitamins!" I always imagine McDonald's' confused reaction to be "Um, excuse me? We sell burgers and fries. We never said we were a farmers' market. Heck, our spokesman is a pedophile clown from the '70s. What do you want from us, America?"

We treat McDonald's horribly. We behave like hormonal teenagers dealing with their parents. "I hate you! You're gross! When's dinner? I have some friends coming over." Really, going to McDonald's is similar to attending a family reunion. You're initially always excited to go. "This is going to be great." Then, after you're there for a while you think, *I don't know if I should be here.* Then, when you're driving back from the family reunion you're thinking, *I'm going to kill myself. I can't believe I had to eat with that clown in the room.*

We shouldn't be so ungrateful. McDonald's has given us so much. We wouldn't know when breakfast ends without McDonald's. I'd be eating eggs at 5:00 p.m. like a moron. Thank you, McDonald's. How would we know Saint Patrick's Day is coming up without the Shamrock Shake? Thank you, McDonald's. Who's going to keep all the cardiac surgeons employed? Thank you, McDonald's.

Burger King

The thin, healthy, smart people are really missing out on some horrible food at Burger King. It's so ironic that Burger King is called Burger King when McDonald's is the true king of the burgers. Burger King is the imposter king. I realize there are likely Burger King fans reading this right now who will vehemently disagree, but my whole view toward Burger King seems to be an ongoing "What are they thinking?" It's not as if I have that high of a standard for fast-food places, but it seems like Burger King purposely does it worse. Like when they are planning the recipe for their burgers and fries, the taste testers are saying: "No, no, no. This tastes too good. It has to be way more flavorless. Remember our motto, 'Not as good as McDonald's'? Let's stick with that, people!"

Recently Burger King, a place that sells mostly burgers and fries, introduced the French Fry Burger, a burger with fries tucked under the top bun. Now, I know this concept has been done very well in some of my favorite regional sandwich shops, but on a burger at a fast-food burger place? It seems staggeringly uncreative. How lazy do they think we are? I'm pretty sure every single fast-food consumer at one time in their life put some French fries on a burger, usually when they were eight. Not a proud moment in anyone's life, but at least we didn't dedicate millions of advertising dollars toward telling people that it was an innovative new product called the French Fry Burger. I think you can order extra shame with the French Fry Burger. I guess "Have it your way" means "Have it the way you thought of doing it when you were eight."

Wendy's

If McDonald's is the one true king of burgers, then Wendy's is the king slayer. Wendy's is just my all-time favorite of the big fast-food chains. It's the high-end McDonald's. In my heart I know it's fast food, but I always think of Wendy's as a real restaurant. They have a salad bar, chili, and free crackers. Maybe it's the fresh, never-frozen ground beef. Maybe I'm drawn in by the "old-fashioned" slogan. Maybe it's that smiling face of the sweet, red-haired girl looking at me like, "Hi, I'm pale too. I'm your people. Now come on in and make yourself at home." Wendy's is the other woman in my life, playing hard to get with her delicious Frosty. Wendy's Frosties, like the White Witch in *Narnia*, are dangerous. They are too thick to be a shake and served in a cup so that we can deny we are eating six scoops of melted ice cream. The Wendy's Frosty goes down way too fast and easy. I have yet to eat a Frosty without getting a crippling brain freeze, or, as I call it, "the Frosty Headache." Wendy's is the best. I sometimes walk by Wendy's and think, *Shoot, I wish I didn't just eat.* But then I just get a Double anyway.

White Castle

Some people make fun of White Castle, and these people are called everyone. White Castle is just too easy of a target for comedy. They are famous for their sliders, and their initials are

W.C., as in "water closet." Insert punch line. *Sack* is an actual unit of measure in the kingdom of White Castle, as well as the way you will measure yourself after eating at White Castle. You can get a "sack" of Sliders, a "sack" of Chicken Rings, a "sack" of Clam Dippers, and, of course, a "sack" of Fish Nibblers. Are they serious? I'm not describing the products sold at the Krusty Krab in a *SpongeBob* episode. These products are really on the menu at White Castle, along with, for some reason, applesauce. I assume the applesauce is made fresh in individual restaurants with the same utensils they use to make the Clam Dippers. If any place is up to code on cleanliness, it's White Castle. Good ol' White Castle applesauce. I'm sure I'm not the only person who's thought to himself, *I could go for some applesauce. Well, off to White Castle.*

I recently walked into the White Castle near beautiful Penn Station in New York City for lunch because I care that little about being alive. It had been a couple of decades since my last visit to the kingdom, so I was surprised to see that White Castle was still in business and even open during the day. I just assumed White Castles were legally allowed to be open only during those early-morning hours after all the bars in the city have closed, since there is a direct correlation between binge drinking and eating at White Castle. I was even more shocked to discover that the Penn Station White Castle offered seating for people to eat the White Castle food in the restaurant. I had never seen this before. I always assumed White Castle intentionally didn't provide seating because they didn't want you in the room when the Sliders kicked in.

There are many other fast-food burger chains. Here's a quick overview:

In-N-Out: The California Shake Shack. Amazing fast-food burger, which is actually embraced by celebrity chefs and the good-looking me. Anyplace where you can get a burger "animal style" (cooked in a thin layer of mustard) is a place of magic.

Steak 'n Shake: This is one of the better ones, but it could be that I am just imagining it because the name is so good.

Jack in the Box: You have to admire the audacity of a place that serves a burger with something called "Jack sauce."

Roy Rogers: Roy Rogers was one of America's favorite cowboy singers. I only view Roy Rogers as a place to go when I'm looking for a fast-food place more disappointing than Burger King.

Sonic/Rally's/Checkers: These places are great for people who really like to eat in their car.

Whataburger: The Texas Carl's Jr.

Carl's Jr.: The West Coast Whataburger

Hardee's: The southern Carl's Jr.

COMIDA RAPIDA

Given the power and beauty of Mexican food, it is surprising how few great Mexican fast-food chains exist. For every Chipotle there are a dozen Del Tacos. Of course, Mexican fast food would not exist without Taco Bell.

Taco Bell

I don't normally fall for expert testimonials in advertising, but Taco Bell's most well-known spokesperson was a dog. The Taco Bell dog would say, "*Yo quiero* Taco Bell," which means, "I want Taco Bell." Sure, it's cool they found and hired a talking dog that spoke Spanish, but it's not that impressive of an endorsement, considering it came from a dog and dogs will eat just about anything, including their own throw-up. I'll never forget when I found out about the death of the Taco Bell dog. It was announced on CNN, and I remember telling myself, *Wow, real journalism is dead.*

It seems Taco Bell will do just about anything to get people into their restaurant, or, more specifically, their room with a microwave in it. None of the food is cooked *at* Taco Bell. It's reheated and assembled on-site. Taco Bell is fundamentally one step up from an office break room. For a while there was a commercial actually promoting the "Taco Bell Diet," which I'm pretty sure was constructed on the belief that once you eat Taco Bell, you won't want to eat again. If you are going to Taco Bell for your diet, you have a bigger problem than your weight.

I NEED A HERO

Sandwich and sub shops have emerged as strong fast-food players. They can range in quality from Panera to Blimpies, but I still prefer a burger and fries. Here are two notable sandwich chains.

Subway

Subway is just the McDonald's of delis. It is a fast-food sandwich shop that has positioned itself as the healthy alternative to the burger-and-fries places, which is already a turnoff for me. Previously, I brought up the Subway slogan, "Eat Fresh," but if you've bitten into a Subway sandwich, you mostly think, *not so fresh.* Subway shops seem to be everywhere. It's hard to walk a block in most major cities without passing a Subway restaurant. You've probably walked by and breathed in the bread exhaust that is pumped into the street. I always think, *Ah, the smell of bread that was just baked in a dirty dishwasher.* I never know if it's making me hungry or concerned about the ozone.

All this being said, I still go to Subway, and not just because it's fun watching a clinically depressed person throw together my sandwich. They are assembling my sandwich right in front of me. You'd think they'd do it with a little bit of flair. I'm not expecting the enthusiasm of a Benihana chef, but it's always a little awkward while they sloppily slap the ingredients onto the bun. I usually stand there wishing the sneeze guard were facing the other way as I watch them do everything in those plastic *CSI* gloves. Those plastic gloves are always a little suspicious because they're wearing them before they even start on my sandwich. "Let me just ring up this other guy's order, tie up this garbage bag, scoop up these heroin needles . . . Now, what type of triangle of cheese would you like on your sub?" There are mice that would turn down that triangle slice of cheese at Subway. If you prefer your cheese melted, you can get your sandwich heated up in the crumb-filled toaster oven it appears someone stole from a dorm room. The Subway toaster oven always makes me wonder, *Wait, is this even a restaurant?*

Subway is another place that shows you how lazy we've gotten in our society. I can understand the appeal of fast-food burgers and fries. Who has the time to make a burger? Who owns a deep fryer? But we are too lazy to make a sandwich? "I could make a sandwich at home for like twenty cents, or I could watch this sociopath make it." To be fair, the Subway employees are not sociopaths, but they do have that kind of faraway look in their eyes as they hold the squirt bottle of goo. "In my country I was attorney general. Would you like Santa Fe sauce?" (*SOUND EFFECT: farting squeeze bottle*)

You have to go through a bunch of steps before your sandwich is ultimately slid into that plastic Subway airsickness bag. The first step is, you have to pick out your bread. And by that I mean, pick out the color of your bread, because all Subway bread seems to taste the same. "Do I want the whole-wheat-colored bread? Or the Italian-colored bread?" After you select your bread you must identify the toppings you would like on your sandwich. Subway makes a big deal about how all the toppings are free at Subway. "Free lettuce? No way! How do you guys pay the rent? What's next, free napkins?" I think the toppings are free at Subway to distract us from the fact that we should not be paying for the meat. Once I asked a Subway guy, "Is that chicken or a really old piece of ham?" Subway is also very stingy with their undesirable meat. It's preportioned and peeled off like a Mafia kingpin wannabe handing out dollars. "Here's three slices of ham. Get yourself something nice, all right? Don't say I never did nothing for youse."

Subway, like other fast-food restaurants, always has deals that they advertise as an incentive for eating at Subway. I had to hire a witch doctor to get the "Five-Dollar Footlong" jingle out of my head. I like cheap deals as much as anyone else, but I wish they would keep the word *foot* out of my food.

Someone told me they saw a Subway with a drive-thru. I'm not sure how that would even work.

SUBWAY EMPLOYEE: All right. Pick out your bread.
Now drive up six inches. What kind of meat? Drive up six inches. Lettuce, onions? Oh, you want it toasted? You gotta circle back around.

Have you tried the soup at Subway? I'm not talking about the tuna salad. I always get the tuna sub at Subway, where they ladle the tuna onto the bread. The tuna is in that giant metal tub with the white puddle of tuna water, like a tuna gazpacho. Very appetizing. I'd love to ask them for a glass of that tuna water. Or maybe bring in a really long straw and just start drinking it. Too much? Did I cross the line? "I was reading this guy's book until he brought up drinking tuna water. I found it offensive. My fiancé is allergic to tuna water. It's nothing to joke about."

Subway built its reputation as the healthy alternative, mostly through the successful weight loss of spokesman Jared Fogle. We all know the story. Jared lost all that weight eating only Subway sandwiches. This makes me kind of wonder what Jared was eating before he started going to Subway. Cases of doughnuts, maybe. We all like Jared. He seems like a decent guy, but deep down we all secretly want to see the fat Jared again. "Come on, Jared! We all struggle! Eat a burger!" I can't imagine how desperate Subway must be to keep Jared thin. "Merry Christmas, Jared. Here's another treadmill and bag of laxatives. Dig in, buddy. Do you mind if I leave this case of my diet pills here for a couple of years? Feel free to help yourself." But Jared's hung in there. He's been a Subway spokesman for so long that there is a generation of kids who don't even know about the fat Jared. I have a ten-year-old nephew who thought Jared was the *owner* of Subway. I explained that Jared "was a big fat guy who ate all these Subway hoagies and now he's thin." Even my nephew was like, "Well, that's bullcrap." I'm not saying Jared didn't lose the weight, but I'm just suspicious that Jared hasn't aged in fifteen years. I don't feel sorry for Jared. I feel sorry for every other guy in the United States who happens to be named Jared. I'm sure some of them have started to tell people, "Actually, my name is pronounced 'JeROD.' "

Of course, Jared didn't lose the weight just eating Subway sandwiches. He switched from eating burgers and fries every day to eating Subway sandwiches every day. So as a result we think of going to Subway as a healthy activity. "Well, I could go jogging or I could go to Subway and have a meatball sub." What level of denial are we in when we view eating a meatball sub as a healthy alternative to a hamburger? Isn't a meatball sub just five hamburgers rolled into balls, covered in cheese, and put on a bun that can hold five hamburgers?

There's always an open door behind the counter at Subway revealing a back room. What's going on back there? I know it's not the kitchen, because the kitchen is the toaster oven. Do you think maybe Jared is back there? Is he secretly running all the Subway shops like the Wizard of Oz? "I am the great and powerful Jared!" More likely it's probably a safe room for all the employees to hide in when the Health Department shows up. Eat Fresh!

Arby's

Arby's is famous for its roast beef. You've probably driven by the Arby's hat sign, which I always found confusing. "The food tastes like eating a hat?" I always thought someone had to eat their hat when they lost a bet. Maybe the bet was that Arby's used real roast beef in their sandwiches.

I'm not sure, but I think it's supposed to be a cowboy hat, since Arby's signature dish is the roast beef sandwich and cowboys are associated with cattle and Arby's wants to give the impression that their meat comes from cows. Keeping with the cowboy theme, Arby's offers a sauce called "horsey" sauce. It may be a reference to a horseradish sauce, but I'd think a fast-food place would make a stronger effort to not associate itself with horse meat.

Arby's is like the cousin of the other fast-food places, but it's that weird cousin you never see, and when you do, you always think, *Oh, yeah, you exist.* I love a Beef 'n Cheddar, but there's nothing really impressive about Arby's. You'll never hear, "Well, I met him at Arby's, so you know he has good taste."

About ten years ago Arby's tried to replace the cowboy hat with a talking oven mitt. I guess the idea was to emphasize the "oven roasting" that they do to their bologna-like roast beef loaves. Unfortunately, the oven mitt just made people buy more Hamburger Helper, so Arby's went back to the hat. Maybe they'll try the saddle next. Giddyup, horsey!

CHICKEN DANCE

KFC

Fried chicken is not good for you. Anyone who has left a piece of fried chicken on a paper napkin and returned to discover that the napkin has turned into liquid knows this. No one ordering a bucket of fried chicken at KFC believes they are making a healthy decision. Anything that comes in the serving size of "bucket" can't be that good for you. A bucket, after all, is how we feed farm animals. "Yeah, I'll have a bucket of fried chicken, a silo of Pepsi, and a trough of pig slop. Make it the *diet* pig slop." The company was aware of the health perception when it changed its name from Kentucky Fried Chicken to KFC. They didn't stop selling fried chicken, but they supposedly added non–fried chicken "healthy items" to their menu, like the DoubleDown, which is the strange, two fried chicken patties without a bun, and Popcorn Chicken, or Original Recipe Bites, which I'm pretty sure is just leftover crumbs from making their fried chicken. I guess selling these crumbs as a dinner menu item is less disturbing than selling them as a breakfast cereal.

The most successful new KFC product would have to be the

KFC Famous Bowl. I'm not sure what makes these bowls famous, but it's certainly not their health benefits. It almost seems like someone at KFC decided, "You know how all our side dishes are unhealthy, disappointing, and taste the same? Why don't we just throw them all together in a Styrofoam bowl?" The Famous Bowls are like a shepherd's pie of unhealthiness. They have a layer of mashed potatoes, a layer of corn, a layer of cigarette ashes, and a couple of apple cores. The bowls are like paying homage to the character of Templeton, the barnyard rat in *Charlotte's Web.*

I was lucky enough to meet the actual Colonel Sanders statue in the Louisville airport.

Popeyes

KFC, Brown's, and Church's all have fine fried chicken, but my favorite is Popeyes. That's right, "Popeyes." I didn't forget the apostrophe. That is how the name of the restaurant is spelled. It's not possessive, it's . . . plural, I guess. I don't know. Since I'm generally horrible at grammar, the absence of the apostrophe in the name Popeyes almost makes me feel smarter. How many thousands of people did that slip by before I, Jim "bad at grammar" Gaffigan, caught it? Anyway, I'm still waiting for someone to explain to me what Popeye the sailor man even has to do with fried chicken.

> OWNER: I'm going to name my fried chicken restaurant Popeyes.
> FRIEND: Didn't Popeye eat spinach?
> OWNER: Spinach, fried chicken . . . what's the difference?
> FRIEND: Oh, I get it. Popeye was a sailor, and your food goes through me like a torpedo.

Supposedly the name Popeyes has nothing to with the cartoon character. Maybe the name is a reference to what happens to your eyes after you eat the spicy Cajun recipe.

PIZZA: THAT'S AMORE

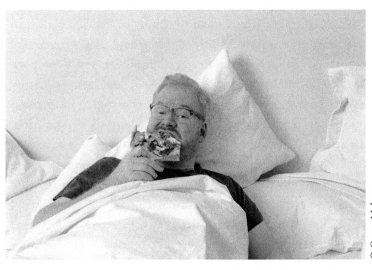

© Corey Melton

The standards are set pretty low for pizza. There is even a brand of frozen pizza called Tombstone. Yes, *Tombstone*. I guess someone figured, "This pizza tastes worse than death. It actually tastes like the cement slab placed on top of a grave."

When you're a kid, you don't know the difference between good pizza and bad pizza. You just love pizza. I grew up eating and loving Tombstone pizza and fondly recall bragging to friends, "I just ate an entire Tombstone." I guess I've always considered all pizzas to be personal pizzas. Now I'm too lazy and impatient to cook a frozen pizza or to go out for pizza. I get delivery.

The most amazing thing about delivery pizza is how critical we are of it. Pizza from Domino's, Little Caesars, and Papa John's is considered automatically bad. "Oh, that place sucks!" Oh really? It's pizza. That you ordered by phone most likely after midnight. That some underpaid college student or overqualified immigrant personally brought to your home. I'm sorry if it doesn't meet your high-end culinary standards. I live in New York City, one of the many places that claims to have the best pizza on the planet. My friends will often make comments: "How is Domino's even in business in New York City?" You know the biggest difference between some guy making your pizza at a local pizzeria and some guy making your pizza at a Domino's? Nothing. Well, mostly nothing. The two guys making the pizzas are probably paid the same and even emigrated to America from the same country. I'm not saying I don't care about good-tasting pizza, but often the largest discernible difference between a Domino's and the local pizzeria is that the latter one offers pizza sold by the slice. I never understood the big appeal of buying pizza by the slice. "Can you reheat a slice from that pizza that has been sitting out for a couple of hours?" It feels like you are eating someone else's pizza. My major issue with the pizza delivery chains is their interpretation of sizes. Based on Domino's "large" pizza, a small pizza would be roughly the size of a dog bowl. Because you are not actually in the restaurant, you can't complain about the size. You're not going to have the delivery guy send it back to the kitchen. Of course, I prefer pizza from Lombardi's to Domino's, but in the end all pizza is great. Everyone loves pizza. When the moon hits your eye like a big pizza pie, *that's* an indication you have an unhealthy obsession with pizza. I know I do. The following are pizza places I've probably called late at night when I should've just gone to bed.

Domino's

Domino's became famous for their now-defunct promise of delivering your pizza in thirty minutes or less. They stopped it when a couple of delivery cars ran over some people while trying to deliver a pizza before the deadline. Now I think Domino's may be trying to kill us with their food. I can never figure out those Domino's deals. It always seems like you can get one large pizza for $15.99 or you can get two large pizzas for $15.99. If not trying to slowly kill us, I think Domino's is definitely trying to get us fat. "If we get them superfat, so fat they can't leave the house, then they *have* to call us again." I call it the "Domino's effect." A ridiculous idea? Consider this. All the dishes Domino's sells are carbohydrates: pizza, breadsticks, pasta, and the poorly named Cinna Stix. Is there anyone who desires that many carbs in one meal? (*excited*) "Why don't we get a pizza, and as an appetizer let's have bread! And for dessert, how about this . . . bread? Maybe I'll open a nice bottle of bread. Then we can rub bread on each other."

A nice bottle of bread.

Every Friday night in my house is family pizza night, which involves me calling Domino's and attempting to order four large pizzas from some guy who is making them faster than I can order them. During these phone calls fraught with miscommunication, I'm usually pitched Domino's latest new product. "You wanna try our new sandwiches?" Whenever Domino's introduces a new product, there's always a part of me that thinks, *I don't know if you guys have mastered the pizza yet. I think you still got some work to do. I don't think the pizza crust and the box are supposed to taste the same.* A couple of years ago, Domino's introduced the Bread Bowl Pasta, which is a bread bowl filled with pasta covered in cheese. I guess the only thing missing was a suicide note. I don't know what it says about our culture when there is a market for a bread bowl filled with pasta. I'm pretty sure eating the Bread Bowl Pasta is a sign you have a serious eating disorder, right? It sounds like something someone would confess at an Overeaters Anonymous meeting. "I knew my eating was out of control when I started eating pasta out of a bread bowl. It was just a matter of time before I'd cover it with cheese."

I don't know how you would even come up with the idea for the Domino's Bread Bowl Pasta.

NEW PRODUCT HEAD: We need a healthy alternative to the pizza, something like a salad.

JOHNSON: Do you mean like a bread bowl filled with pasta covered in cheese?

NEW PRODUCT HEAD: Uh, not really. No, I was thinking more like a salad with lettuce in it.

JOHNSON: We could do that, *or* we could fill a potato with a sweet roll and inject it into people's butts!

NEW PRODUCT HEAD: Do you even work here?

JOHNSON: No.

In full disclosure I have tried the Domino's Bread Bowl Pasta. When I was eating the cheese-covered pasta out of the bread bowl, all I could think was, *This could use a side of mashed potatoes.* It was carb-a-licious. I like to imagine the folks back at the Domino's headquarters are fighting over credit for creating the Bread Bowl Pasta.

DOMINO'S CEO: Johnson, you came up with the Bread Bowl Pasta, right?

NEW PRODUCT HEAD: Well, actually it was me, sir.

JOHNSON: It was me!

DOMINO'S CEO: Well, either way, we've been contacted by The Hague. We are being prosecuted for crimes against humanity.

JOHNSON AND NEW PRODUCT HEAD: (*pointing*) It was him!

I love how Domino's presents the Bread Bowl Pasta as some traditional entrée from the old country. (*Italian accent*) "Ah, da pasta bread bowl! Justa like a Mama Domino used to make. Every Sunday she saya, 'You gettoutta my kitchen when I maka da pasta bread bowl. What's a matta for you? I breaka ur face!" (*and other stereotypical Italian phrases*) Good old Mama Domino!

Pizza Hut

I guess at some point somebody thought it would be a good idea to name a pizza restaurant Pizza Hut. "We want a name that communicates quality food *and* third-world housing!"

"Is the pizza good?"

"It comes from a place called Pizza Hut. Need I say more?"

Papa John's

There are few things I'm certain of in this world, but I'm confident I'll never hear someone say, "I order pizza from Papa John's because I like their commercials." It's just the owner of Papa John's pitching his restaurant in a monotone voice. I sometimes wonder if the Papa John's commercials are trying to get us to order from Domino's. The owner of Papa John's may not be the best pitchman, but he's the worst at acting. Papa John's commercials actually make me yearn for a Men's Wearhouse commercial.

Little Caesars

On the low end of delivery pizza is Little Caesars. Little Caesars doesn't even bother to tell you how their pizza tastes. It's about price. Their deals are always like "Five dollars for five pizzas!" In a way, their prices are almost too low. I always think, *Maybe charge a little more and use better ingredients.* Little Caesars is the ninety-nine-cent store of pizzas. I seem to see a lot of Little Caesars shops in Kmarts, which is not really helping the Little Caesars' perception, or Kmart's perception, for that matter. I'm not sure who thought this was a good idea. Maybe someone who'd never been to a Kmart or a Little Caesars.

Sbarro

When Sbarro recently announced that it was filing for sbankruptcy, I was sbad. I wasn't sburprised, given that Sbarro is a pizza chain that doesn't deliver pizza. That doesn't seem sbmart. "I can get that mediocre fast-food pizza impersonal touch without the convenience of delivery?" I'm not looking to be sbanned from Sbarro or sbound sbtupid here. If you enjoy mediocre Italian food or dry pizza with ziti on it, Sbarro is . . . well, still disappointing.

The Johns

"The Johns" is how I refer to a group of fast-food chains that all have *John* in their name, so I assume they are all related under the John family corporate umbrella. There is Papa John, his son, Jimmy John, and his first-generation immigrant grandfather, Taco John. Tim McGraw and Norah Jones somehow fit into this family tree, but they have not yet agreed to take one of those genealogy DNA tests. I did figure out that Long John Silver was a distant cousin or maybe just named after Papa John's favorite underwear. Maybe I think this way because I've eaten so much fast food my doctor told me I might need the Jimmy John surgery.

Whether good or bad, I will always love pizza. The Italians really knew what they were doing, combining all the major food groups into something we can eat without a fork. Even less work for me in that I can have it delivered. It's great hot and even great cold for breakfast after I wake up with my face in it after I passed out eating it the night before. Pizza is pretty much an ideal food.

THE PEOPLE'S COURT

If eating fast food were a sport, the food court would be the gymnasium, where there is a whole different type of body-building going on.

There are many varieties of fast-food places in food courts. You can have pizza, Chinese, and a burrito within a few feet of each other. The food court is like the United Nations of crappy food. You and your friends or family can order from different restaurants and still sit at the same table as you compare everyone's version of fake ethnic fast food.

Sometimes the food court is totally deserted, and all the employees are standing behind their counters staring at one another like jungle animals in competition over their prey. When you pick the place you want to go, you feel like you have to ignore the others' guilt-tripping stare-down: "What's wrong with *my* food?" The only thing worse than an empty food court is probably a really crowded food court, which always has the energy of a refugee camp. Masses of families, coworkers, and teenage girls are milling around with trays looking for an open table, trying to steal chairs. There's always that group hovering over you with their trays, waiting for your table. "I think you have stayed past the fifteen-minute limit, buddy." The worst is if you are by yourself at a table. If you are over the age of eighteen, it is impossible to eat alone in a food court and not look like a serial killer. "I'm here to eat and find my next victim." Everyone at the food court has been found guilty, and there appears to be no parole.

KETCHUP: KING OF THE CONDIMENTS

Jeannie really appreciates condiments. No, really. She puts mayo on both sides of a sandwich. She puts mustard on her burger and then dunks her burger in mustard! The more condiments, the better in Jeannieland. I affectionately refer to her as Condi because she loves condiments that much. She has hot sauce sitting on her desk right now. Yeah, she's one of those people. Condiment-prepared. Jeannie loves hot sauce, but she's not obnoxious about it. It seems that most people who are really into hot sauce feel the need to challenge other people. "You have to try this super-hot fire engine sauce." I always explain, "That's okay. I don't want the super-hot fire engine diarrhea. I'm not a fan of wearing a diaper." All I need to be condiment-prepared and satisfied is ketchup.

Ketchup is the undisputed king of all condiments. When you enter a diner, ketchup is already on the table. It's the diner's way of saying, "Look, you are going to need this." Ketchup is that important. There really isn't any condiment competition for ketchup. Mustard, the closest competition, is the Mets to ketchup's Yankees. Mustard has its fans, but there really is no comparison. My children love ketchup but would rather go to bed early than taste mustard. Ketchup simply consists of tomato paste, vinegar, and sugar. There are two major brands: Heinz and Hunt's (I'm a Heinz), and they have had the same recipe forever. There is no improving ketchup. You never see ketchup sold as "Now even more ketchupier!" It's just ketchup. The only variety in ketchup is in the way to spell it: *ketchup* or *catsup*. Mustard, on the other hand, seems to be constantly reinventing itself in a desperate attempt to compete with ketchup. It's pretty sad, really.

KETCHUP: Hey, Spicy Brown Mustard.

MUSTARD: Uh, actually now I'm Honey Dijon Mustard.

KETCHUP: Weren't you also just Chipotle Mustard?

MUSTARD: That was last week. Now I'm Honey Dijon Mustard.

KETCHUP: Right. Oh, how's that going? Are you on the table in diners yet?

MUSTARD: Well, in some high-end delis and a few hot dog carts. (*beat*) Do you think I should go back to being Spicy Brown Mustard? I guess I have to face the fact that I'll never ketchup.

KETCHUP: Was that a pun?

MUSTARD: Yes. Was it funny?

KETCHUP: (*beat*) I should go. People want to see how I taste on tamales.

I am an avid ketchup user. Jeannie thinks I use too much ketchup, especially on my sushi, but I find it drowns out the fish flavor. It seems you can put ketchup on anything. When you are using ketchup you are really saying, "This food is so good. I want it to taste like ketchup." If you are using ketchup, you are probably eating something unhealthy. We never put ketchup on anything healthy like broccoli or asparagus. Ketchup is only there to assist unhealthy food. Ketchup is like that friend who's always encouraging you to do the wrong thing. "Why don't you get fries? If you get fries, I'll help you out. Or you could get a burger. Get a burger. I'll be there. Oh, you're ordering a salad. I gotta go. I don't get along with lettuce." Ketchup is important. You only realize how important ketchup is when you don't have it. Ever eat fries without ketchup? It just feels wrong.

Yes, this is a photo of my son Patrick drinking ketchup.

There are some people who don't like ketchup. I think they are called losers. Almost universally everyone loves and uses ketchup, which always makes me surprised when I see a television commercial for ketchup. What a waste of money. Who are those commercials for? "You know, honey, we should try that new product called 'ketchup.'" We are all going to buy the ketchup anyway. Once I saw a ketchup commercial that touted lycopene, an antioxidant found in ketchup, as a reason to buy ketchup. If ketchup is the healthy part of your diet, you probably need to be on the Taco Bell Diet.

The only ketchup news in the past fifty years has been the advancement of the bottle. We've now had the upside-down plastic squeeze bottle for about ten years, but don't you think it's a little embarrassing how long it took us to come up with that? It wasn't that long ago someone had the realization.

DESIGNER 1: You know how we have to hold ketchup bottles upside down and it takes a ridiculously long time for the ketchup to come out of the glass bottle? Why don't we put the cap on the bottom and make the bottle plastic and squeezable?

DESIGNER 2: Wait, have people been complaining that ketchup is hard to get out of the glass bottle?

DESIGNER 1: For like a hundred years!

DESIGNER 2: I guess we could try it. I don't know why someone would want easy access to ketchup.

The most inefficient form of ketchup delivery is those tiny glass bottles they give you when you order hotel room service. The bottle is too small to pour and often a knife won't even fit in the top. "This is adorable, but I asked for ketchup, not a Christmas ornament."

Ketchup goes well with everything.

Every culture has its own ketchup. Salsa is the Mexican ketchup, marinara sauce is the Italian ketchup, and I guess vinegar is the British ketchup. How bad is your food when adding vinegar is an improvement? What can I say? The British just have a different attitude toward food. In London, you have to pay for ketchup packets in fast-food places. It's that type of behavior that started the Boston Tea Party.

Packets

Thankfully, in American fast-food places you don't have to pay for ketchup packets, but what is with the single-serve size of those ketchup packets? I'm not saying I need a gallon of ketchup, but maybe enough for more than one fry. Tearing open twenty packets with my teeth, I end up looking like a heroin addict. "I'm gonna party once I get set up here!" Has anyone ever used just one of those ketchup packets? "Do you have a half of a quarter of an ounce of ketchup? It's just so darn rich. Maybe a resealable ketchup packet? One I could store in my purse." Most often fast-food places give you two or three packets, and if you go back up to ask for more, they make you feel like you are trying to score drugs. "You think you could hook me up with some more of the good stuff?" Sometimes fast-food employees act like you are taking from their personal stash. "Looks like my kids won't be getting ketchup tonight because you are a ketchup glutton!" There's no good place to put the empty ketchup packets; they are always such a mess. "Should I put it on the napkin, the table, or stick it to my sleeve?"

Sometimes the packets will have printed on them "Not for resale." I didn't even know that was an issue. I've been to a lot of flea markets and have never seen anyone reselling ketchup packets. I didn't even know there were people looking at ketchup packets and thinking, *eBay here I come. Ca-ching!* If you are in a position where you have to sell ketchup packets, I don't know if anything written on the packet is going to hold you back. "We need money. Maybe we should sell these ketchup packets. Shoot, it says here on the packet 'Not for resale.' Dang it!" I doubt there are people even interested in a resold ketchup packet. Personally, I only want ketchup packets that are fresh from that box behind the counter.

If you're lucky, you'll occasionally come across a packet labeled as Fancy Ketchup. I usually think, *Fancy? Ketchup, you are being modest.* I'm not sure what would make ketchup fancy. Who's using ketchup at a black-tie event with the elites of our society? "Is this the ketchup that I sent my butler to get?" I guess it's all relative, but what kind of life would you be leading if you considered ketchup packets fancy? "Well, we're not rich folk, but on special occasions we will break out the ketchup packets. Like on Grandma's birthday. Let her know it's a celebration. Why not let her feel like a celebrity with a ketchup packet? Then we put her back in her cage."

Some fast-food places like Wendy's offer an in-store ketchup pump instead of packets. It's like a keg of ketchup that you pump into tiny paper shot glasses. I like to hang around the ketchup keg and try to meet ladies. Whenever a woman approaches, I'll just starting pumping ketchup for her in a masculine manner. "Here, I'll pump for you. You come to this Wendy's often? My roommate and I got a ketchup pony keg back at our dorm. You like that song "Elvira"? Here's an extra shot of ketchup for your cute friend." I'm never sure how many shots of ketchup I'm supposed to get when I'm eating in a Wendy's. I usually get three shots of ketchup, but if I'm having a bad day I'll get five.

JUST DESSERTS

Dessert is special, and as a result it is treated differently. In some restaurants, desserts get their own menu. In diners and truck stops, desserts are sometimes put in a rotating glass case like they are an artifact or some of Queen Elizabeth's jewelry. I'm not sure what the intended response is supposed to be. "I didn't want dessert before, but now that I see pudding at that angle, I gotta get me some!"

When I was growing up, my family had dessert only on special occasions like birthdays or holidays. My children live in a different world. Dessert is not a luxury. It's a right. If my four-year-old, Katie, doesn't ask about dessert four times in an evening, I assume she is sick or there is going to be a tornado. Dessert is special for everyone. That's why it's saved until last. If that exclusive spot after the meal were not reserved for dessert, what would stop anyone from just ordering dessert instead of the meal?

It is my belief that all desserts are just a form of either ice cream or cake.

ICE CREAM: FOREVER YOUNG

Just about everyone has a fond memory of eating ice cream as a child. It is rare to find a child looking disappointed while eating ice cream. As much as eating ice cream can make a child look happy, indulging in the exact same ice-cream-eating behavior makes an adult look pathetic. This is because ice cream is for children. Everyone *likes* ice cream, but it's really for kids. Ice cream trucks, ice cream cones, and the sprinkles that go on the ice cream are for children. Kids get ice cream. Adults get alcohol. It's only fair. Unfortunately, just like kickball, silly birthday parties, Disney, and diapers, ice cream has been co-opted by adults. Admittedly, I am an adult and I eat ice cream, but I'm not proud of it. I'm not going to walk around in broad daylight eating ice cream like some kind of fat, good-looking loser. Some things are better kept behind closed doors in the privacy of your own home. Every adult should know that the appropriate place to eat ice cream is on the couch in front of the TV, watching TLC. "*(mouthful of ice cream)* See, those *Hoarders*, they're the ones with the problem!"

The way we adults rationalize eating ice cream is rather pitiful. "It's hot outside. Let's get some ice cream." "My boyfriend broke up with me. I'm going to have some ice cream." "My name is Jim Gaffigan. I'm going to eat some ice cream." It's always bitter-sweet when there is no ice cream in our home. Mostly because this means I just ate a pint of ice cream. I'll try to blame it on one of the babies, but I find it hard to explain the ice cream stains on my shirt. I mostly eat ice cream at night in sweatpants, the uniform of ice cream eating. I'll toss the lid even before I start eating the pint, because I'm not a quitter. Occasionally Jeannie will inquire, "Are you going to eat the entire pint of ice cream by yourself?" I answer, "Hopefully. Unless you selfishly want a bite."

There was a time back in the '80s when adults remembered that ice cream was for children. Frozen yogurt was presented as a healthier, adult version of ice cream. There was even nonfat frozen yogurt that meant you could eat delicious frozen yogurt without the fat. I don't know why I find fro-yo so annoying. Some friends in college would replace lunch with nonfat frozen yogurt. "We are going out for fro-yo." They would announce it like they were about to eat a salad or go jogging. I couldn't express my joy enough when it was revealed that nonfat fro-yo, while it had no fat, had all the calories of regular ice cream because it was loaded with sugar. People again had to face the fact that eating ice cream really was for children. So the grown-up ice cream eater went back into hiding.

Suddenly in the '90s an ice cream company from Vermont named Ben & Jerry's burst onto the national scene and made it not only possible but also cool for adults to come out of the closet as ice cream eaters. The Ben & Jerry's feel-good social agenda helped soften the reality of eating ice cream for adults. "I can eat ice cream with candy in it *and* help the environment? I'm eating this pint for the Earth." My dream job would be to be the guy who comes up with those Ben & Jerry's recipes. Now, *that's* a great job. How could anyone complain about that job? I imagine that guy or gal just comes into work early in the afternoon. "What do I feel like binging on today? Let's see . . . Reese's, Snickers, vanilla ice cream, and a caramel swirl. Let's call it, um, 'Fat Daddy.' Well, see you guys tomorrow. I'm going to go take a nap."

Two hands!

LET THEM EAT CAKE

People tend to behave differently around different food. For example, being around vegetables can make people lose their appetites and the close proximity of cake turns people into neurotic messes. Cake has such a magnetic effect. It is difficult to pretend you are not mesmerized by its captivating presence. Everyone wants to devour the cake as soon as they see it, or at least dip a finger in the frosting, but you have to exercise restraint around your peers lest they discover that you truly have no impulse control. To cover up your greediness, you have to act bashfully ignorant of the existence of cake. "What is this called, *cake*? Well, I guess I'll try it. I've never tried cake before." We can't simply enjoy cake. People eat cake like they are committing adultery: "Don't tell my husband I'm doing this." This strange behavior is driven by the fact that cake is a true symbol of gluttony. If you eat a whole pizza, your friends might respond, "Wow, you were hungry." But if you eat a whole cake, friends will say, "You have a problem." Eating cake is not like drinking alcohol.

You never hear someone brag, "Yeah, last night I had four pieces of cake."

"Why are you telling us?"

"I just wanted you to know I partied."

Mikey takes after his father.

Cake is a social food. It must be eaten with someone else or in a group. There is something profoundly sad about eating cake while you are alone. Believe me, I do it all the time. The bonus of cake is that it's not just cake. It's usually cake with frosting on top. *Frosting* is a fancy name for sugar mixed with grease. I'll never forget the time I found a tub of frosting in a cabinet when I was ten. I remember thinking, *Wow, it would be really pathetic to eat this, but here goes.*

Given that we all know cake is bad for us, we often try to hide the fact that we are eating it. We have masterfully created socially acceptable ways to disguise cake so we can eat it whenever we want. "It's breakfast and I obviously can't eat cake. I'll have a muffin." You know the difference between a muffin and a cupcake? Nuffin. A muffin is just a bald cupcake, and we all know it. If the muffins weren't absurd enough on their own, there are also mini-muffins. How much denial are we in when we are eating mini-muffins? "Oh, I'm just going to have one or twelve. They are so small they don't really count. They are like muffin vitamins, really. When I eat them, I feel like an astronaut." We all know we are not supposed to have cake for breakfast, unless it's a *pan*cake. I'm not sure how that one slid through. "Young man, you're not having cake for breakfast! You're having fried cake with syrup for breakfast. Now, load up on that and try not to nap." Pancakes definitely make you lower your expectations for the day. "Well, looks like I'm not showering today. I'll be digesting those carb-cakes for the next eight hours."

The Power

Cake's power over us is undeniable. How else would you explain anyone's participation in a cakewalk, which is just musical chairs with the possibility of winning an entire cake? It should be noted that it is a cakewalk, not a cakesit. Maybe the chance of winning a cake is used as a way to motivate people to move. Cake is so powerful, it can actually bring people together.

OFFICE WORKER 1: It's Bill's birthday.
OFFICE WORKER 2: I hate that guy.
OFFICE WORKER 1: There's cake in the conference room.
OFFICE WORKER 2: Well, I should say hello. See how he's doing.

Take the picture so we can eat the cake.

If there was any doubt about the importance of cake, we need look no further than the milestones of our life. Cake is how life is celebrated. Birthdays, weddings, and retirements are honored with cake. Cake is a symbol for celebration. There is no replacement for cake at these events. Especially not pie. Pie, while delightful in its own way, can't compete with cake. If you see candles in a cake, it's someone's birthday. If you see candles in a pie, someone is drunk in the kitchen. You never hear of a showgirl jumping out of a pie announcing, "Happy Birthday!" Jumping out of a pie would only make the showgirl look like she's re-created the prom scene from the movie *Carrie*. "Take a shower, showgirl." If someone is getting married, there is a wedding cake. If someone dies, you bring over a pie, because bringing a cake would be inappropriate. Cake is too celebratory. Cake is way more important than pie. There is a popular band named after cake. *Cake* is a term used for wealth. A sad song was even written about a cake that was left out in the rain. Pies, on the other hand, just seem disposable. Pies are thrown in clowns' faces.

There are innumerable types of cake. Here I analyze some of the more important ones.

Birthday Cake: Cake's strongest association is with birthdays. Whether you are celebrating someone's first or hundredth year alive, a birthday cake is usually presented to the honoree. Yet whenever you hear the "Happy Birthday" song, all you are really thinking is *Hey, I'm about to get some free cake!* While you sing the song you are mostly wondering what kind of cake it is. "Happy birthday to you. *Hope it's chocolate for me!*" Birthday cakes typically have candles and writing on them, which is strange, because cake is the one food that needs no decoration or fanfare. A loaf of sugar bread smothered with a quart of icing has an appeal all on its own. How spoiled was the recipient of the first birthday cake?

MOM: Happy birthday, son! Mommy made you a cake.
SON: NOT GOOD ENOUGH! I WANT FIRE!
I WANT MY NAME WRITTEN ON THERE!
AND I WANT EVERYONE SINGING!

If I hold the kid, I get the first piece, right?

Rum Cake: I guess rum cake makes sense. Who hasn't been eating cake and thought, *You know what this needs? Booze. A shot of liquor. I don't have time to eat cake and drink alcohol at the same time. I only have two hands and one of them is holding a cigarette.*

Funnel Cake: Just a giant French fry covered in powdered sugar.

Cupcakes: It's always been a mystery to me how I could simultaneously love cupcakes and hate cupcake shops. The prices are too high in cupcake shops. A cupcake at a cupcake shop is roughly the same price as an entire sheet cake in a grocery store. I guess I just hate what the cupcake shop represents. Cupcakes are designed for people who love cake but are not fans of sharing. "I want my *own* cake!" Cupcake shops are just clubhouses for selfish people. Okay, I guess I kind of like cupcake shops.

Cake Pops: I understand there are plenty of fans of these stale-cake-balls-on-a-stick, but I'm convinced cake pops are an indication that the wheels have come off the bus of our culture. I'll never forget the moment I first became aware of cake pops. I was standing in line at Starbucks and saw them. My first thought wasn't *Oh cool,*

Would you like a delicious reindeer?

cake pops. All I could think was *Wait, now we're eating cake on a stick? Maybe we* are *the infidels!*

Ice Cream Cakes: I never really understood the appeal of an ice cream cake. They are so temporary. They just end up stressing me out. "Hurry up, we have to eat this thing before it melts."

Cheesecake: Did you ever encounter a day with perfect weather? You know, it's not too hot, not too cold, but it has that perfect feeling? I feel that way about cheesecake. Cheese plus cake? Perfect. Cheesecake is a double positive. Cheesecake is like a food all-star. With cheesecake, you *can* have your cake and eat cheese too. There's never a strike at the Cheesecake Factory.

Pound Cake: It's pretty impressive that a baker was confident enough to name a cake after one of the side effects of eating cake. "Should I have the pound cake or the seat belt extender cake?"

Flower Cake: At some point those weirdos over at 1-800-Flowers created the "flower cake," which is made completely of flowers. No, not frosting flowers. Real, live, inedible flowers. I've never received a flower cake, but I can only imagine the awkwardness that the flower cake has created for some relationships. How is receiving a flower cake supposed to be interpreted? "I got you a flower cake. You know, you could stand to lose some weight."

Carrot Cake: Cake is so powerful it can even make carrots appealing. This is accomplished in the form of carrot cake covered with cream cheese frosting. The best part of all? It doesn't taste like carrots. That's why instead of a salad, I normally just order a carrot cake.

Fruitcake: The most disappointing "real" cake has to be fruitcake, which is rated one step above a urinal cake.

You'd think fruitcake would be better. It doesn't add up. Fruit, good. Cake, great. Fruitcake, nasty crap. I don't even think fruitcake is made with fruit. Whenever I've made the mistake of tasting fruitcake I always think, *Did I just bite into a Skittle? Or was it a thimble?* It seems the recipe for fruitcake is "anything but fruit." It's like the baker was cleaning off his counter: "Put all this crap in there." I'm convinced nobody eats fruitcake. They just mail it to their relatives around Christmas. Rumor has it that there are only ten fruitcakes that keep getting regifted every December.

AIRPORTS: MY HOME
AWAY FROM HOME

Being a stand-up comedian, I travel a lot. As a result I spend an enormous amount of time in airports. I could provide some details and specifics, but I don't like to think about it too much. It's depressing. Let's just say I'm on a first-name basis with some TSA screeners at LaGuardia. If your job involves traveling, you understand. It's too exhausting. If you are a businessperson who travels out of town even once a month, it's too much. If you don't travel for a living, you probably think I'm being a baby. "Oh, poor Jim! He has to take a two-hour flight from New York to Chicago. Let's build him a statue where he's holding a rattle." The mistake in this logic is that the length of a flight is usually how we measure the time of air travel. "It's only a two-hour flight! That's not bad." This doesn't factor in the time it takes to get to and from the airport. For example, the Denver Airport, for some reason, is in Missouri. Additionally, the airlines want you at the airport hours before your flight. "Your flight is in two days? You should go to the airport now." Add in packing, going through security, flight delays, and picking up checked luggage—a flight from New York to Chicago takes a week. I'm not exaggerating. Okay, maybe a little. It's actually more efficient to take a six-hour flight. You're killing the whole day anyway, might as well get across the country.

Initially when you start to do extensive amounts of air travel, you look for a silver lining. "Well, at least I'm getting all those frequent-flyer miles." Then you quickly realize that what you earn for doing all this air travel is *more* air travel. "So if I travel by plane on your airline for a hundred thousand miles, I can earn an opportunity to travel some more on your airline?" This is equivalent to eating a hundred cans of beans so you can earn a free can of beans. At that point you don't want beans. "I don't want beans. Can I get a hot dog instead of beans?" "No, but if you buy a hot dog on this beans credit card, you can get some beans." "I can't stress to you enough how much I don't want beans!"

Air travel is amazing, but no one enjoys it. You are being transported thousands of miles in a couple of hours. It's really an unbelievable feat, yet on the plane everyone is grumpy and complaining. Even when the trip is over, a deep-seated paranoia sets in around baggage claim, like someone is really going to steal your ugly luggage filled with clothes that only fit you. I think I've figured out why we find air travel so annoying. Air travel is a direct simulation of spending time with your parents. Think about it. The pilot is your dad, and the flight attendant is your mom. You get on the plane and the flight-attendant-slash-mom instantly starts in with the nagging. "You need to fasten your seat belt." "Okay, Mom." "You need to turn off your phone." "Okay, Mom!" "Would you like some juice?" "Okay, Mom." When the plane takes off, the pilot-slash-dad bores you with one of his stories. "I just want to let you know how we are going to get there blah blah blah . . . you know, if you look out to the left, you'll see the blah blah blah . . . ." "We don't care, Dad! Just fly!"

Because I'm getting to the airport early and enjoying all those flight delays, I spend a lot of time in airports. I spend lots and lots of time in airports. To me airports are like museums of boredom. The Austin airport sometimes has musicians, but generally you are just left sitting in a seat at a gate, hating humanity. Sometimes I'll play mental games to entertain myself. One is to try to find the person at the airport who doesn't look suicidal. Unfortunately, this game takes longer than Risk, and nobody is a winner, because you are at the airport. Everyone is stumbling around miserable. We should rename airports "*Walking Dead* Reenactment Centers." Another game I play is Imagine Excuses to Wake Up People Who Are Sleeping at the Airport. "Are you sleeping?" "Are you tired?" or "Why aren't there more movies with strong female leads?" are some of my favorites.

Often I'm at airports early in the morning, when humanity is at its worst. I'm usually less surprised that I'm at the airport at five in the morning and more mystified by other people's behavior at that ungodly hour. I'm not a morning person (is anyone?), so when people are outgoing and happy before noon, I'm stunned. Once I had a sweet woman at Boston's Logan Airport ask me, "Do you have an early flight?" I responded as anyone would, "No, I just like hanging out at the airport at six in the morning."

My answer to this horrible airport predicament (and virtually every other problem in my life) is to eat. For no particular reason other than I always eat when I'm in airports. It drives Jeannie crazy. I could have eaten at home right before I left for the airport. But I still have to buy food at the airport. It is an involuntary behavior at this point. I'm not even aware of it. Like a superstitious Catholic doing the sign of the cross as they pass a church or a graveyard. It just happens. I get to an airport, check in, go through security, and immediately have to find food. I justify this behavior by telling myself that

I don't want to be hungry on the plane, but it's pretty shoddy reasoning. "Well, what if the plane goes down? I don't want to have to start eating people." I also tell myself I don't want to eat the food on the plane. Airplane food used to be the only exception to my all-free-food-is-delicious rule, but now you have to pay for it. I realize I'm going out on a limb being a comedian who criticizes food served on airplanes, but everyone knows that airplane food is an oxymoron. Of course I still eat it, but I don't *enjoy* it. Airplane food is unique in that it actually tastes like someone tried to make it taste bad. I mean, how can you screw up chicken and pasta? Somehow all the food on airplanes tastes like an airplane seat. Did they cook it in a seat?

Sometimes I tell myself I'm having a Quarter Pounder at the airport as a reward for dealing with the unnecessarily difficult task of getting to the airport, checking in, and going through the security line. I'm like a mouse getting the piece of cheese at the end of the maze, but *my* piece of cheese has a patty of ground beef and a bun with it. It's a good thing I'm not a healthy eater, because it's virtually impossible to eat healthy in airports. Healthy items are not even sold in some airports. Once I tried to buy a piece of fruit in the South Bend Airport and was informed it was only for display. Usually room-temperature prepackaged salads are the only option. "Well, I could either eat a salad that was prepared eighteen years ago, or I could eat something that won't make me cry."

Not all airports have the same food options. Some cities make a real effort to offer local specialties like Shake Shack at JFK and Rick Bayless's Tortas Frontera at O'Hare, and the San Francisco International Airport is filled with some of the city's great restaurants, bars, and cafés, but these are the exceptions. Most airports have a fast-food chain or two and then the standard airport places that you would never see or eat at unless you were trapped in the airport.

Auntie Anne's Pretzels

If you like your pretzels doused in that fake butter they put on popcorn in movie theaters, then you would love Auntie Anne's pretzels. Of all airport food options, I consider Auntie Anne's a last resort. I have some dignity. I'd rather eat a bag of nuts from a Hudson airport bookstore than an Auntie Anne's pretzel. Don't misunderstand me. I love pretzels and have contemplated a world with only pretzel bread on many occasions, but Auntie Anne's is not for me because I don't find a grease-soaked pretzel appealing. One would think a shop that sells greasy pretzels couldn't stay in business, but the airport is a captive audience, and pretzels have a great reputation. To be fair, Auntie Anne's is not just pretzels. They also have . . . pretzel dogs and . . . pretzels with pepperoni on them and, um . . . pretzels rolled in cinnamon sugar and . . . um, that's it. There are dipping sauces at Auntie Anne's that are distinguished by the different ailments they cause. "This sauce causes heart disease. This sauce causes liver failure." I'm not sure if the origi-

nal Auntie Anne is still alive, but it would've been interesting to be a nephew or niece of hers. "We're going over to your Auntie Anne's. Bring your Lipitor and diabetes medication."

Would you like a greasy pretzel or a greasy pretzel?

Chili's Too

It seems you can find a Chili's Too restaurant in most airports. If airports were a country, Chili's Too would be the ethnic food. I appreciate that they add the hilarious "Too" to the name so we don't confuse Chili's Too with the regular Chili's. I guess they didn't want the mediocre food at Chili's Too to be confused with mediocre food served at a regular Chili's. After eating at Chili's Too, you wonder if the misuse of "Too" was not a cute idea but an actual spelling error by the people who started Chili's Too. I love going to Chili's Too when I'm in an airport. Where else could I sit and watch a middle-aged guy with a mullet chew dry eggs with his mouth open while I listen to Wham! at six in the morning? Bucket list complete. "Wake me up before you go, go!"

My old stomping grounds.

Cinnabon

I do try to rationalize what I eat when I'm at the airport, but some things just can't be justified, like a Cinnabon. It seems every airport has a Cinnabon kiosk that sells the oversize frosted cinnamon buns. I'm pretty sure Satan himself is the largest shareholder in Cinnabon. Cinnabon only sells buns with that sugary paste. There is no reason to ever eat a Cinnabon, especially not at the airport. "Well, I'm about to get on a plane. Maybe I should eat eight pounds of cake." You usually have to take a nap halfway through eating one, which is why you see so many people sleeping in airports. The first time I ate a Cinnabon, I thought I was going to need some insulin and a wheelbarrow for the other half of my bun. It's kind of generous referring to a Cinnabon as a *bun*, or a *bon,* for that matter. It is the size of a beanbag chair. "Should I sit in it or eat it? I guess I could sit in it *and* eat it." There's always a strange Cinnabon odor emanating from the Cinnabon store. It always smells like someone poured cinnamon-flavored tequila into a humidifier. On more than one occasion I've walked by a kiosk and gotten a cavity. Everyone knows Cinnabons are horrible for you. You can see it in the shame on the faces of patrons in line to get a Cinnabon. I've done some humiliating things in my life, but standing in that Cinnabon line is up there. There's such a sense of defeat. "Hi. Yeah, can I get a Cinnabon? You can just staple it to my behind. It's going to end up there anyway. Why am I doing this to myself?"

If it isn't hard enough to deal with the indignity of my airport food problem, there is the added guilt I feel facing Jeannie when I get home from the trip. "Did you eat airport food again?" "Not really. I mean, I wouldn't call it *food . . .*" Before I get home, I always try to rid myself of all the incriminating evidence of my shameful addiction, such as napkins or empty containers with the names of these objectionable establishments boldly printed on them in primary colors, but something always gives me away. Jeannie has been known to be holding my credit card bill as I return. "Auntie Anne's, Jim? Really? And who is this *Wendy* you've been spending so much money on?"

BREAKFAST:
A REASON TO GET OUT OF BED

I love breakfast. I just wish it weren't served in the morning. I am a night person, so I don't really understand why people would want to wake up early and immediately eat something. I'm not even hungry in the morning anyway, mostly because I usually ate a couple of hours earlier. The perfect situation for me would be to sleep until I'm hungry again. Unfortunately, given the

fact that most businesses are open during daylight hours and young children are too dumb to sleep in, I have to get up. The only consolation prize for getting out of bed in the morning is that the meal of breakfast includes some very tasty items.

Too dumb to sleep in.

You would feel guilty about eating most traditional breakfast items at any other meal during the day, but since it's the morning, somehow these foods are considered okay. There is an unspoken agreement: "Because you dragged yourself out of that warm, comfortable bed, you can have this stack of cakes covered in syrup glue and a half package of sausages." What is socially acceptable to eat for breakfast seems to have neither rhyme nor reason. Sausage patties or links are fine, but having a hamburger or a corn dog from 7-Eleven is somehow just not appropriate at 8:00 a.m. Similarly, what we drink at breakfast makes no sense either. The idea of someone waking up and drinking alcohol seems rather pathetic, unless of course it's a Bloody Mary or a mimosa. Then it's somehow chic. We also understand that drinking fruit juice of any form is akin to drinking a sugar-and-carb shooter, and ordering a glass of orange juice with dinner would evoke a perplexed look from your waiter. Somehow at breakfast, again it is okay. When I was a kid, grapefruit juice was the Pepsi to orange juice's Coke in the morning. "Would you like orange or grapefruit juice?" This is no longer the norm because I guess at some point everyone eventually realized people would rather be constipated than drink grapefruit juice. My dad used to eat half a grapefruit for breakfast. There was a special grapefruit spoon with a ridged tip to dig out the grapefruit sections. Now you'll only see that spoon in museums or on *Boardwalk Empire*.

There are other healthy options at breakfast, like oatmeal. Everyone knows eating oatmeal in the morning is good for you, and we know this because oatmeal has no taste. Sometimes my kids will eat oatmeal for breakfast, but they only like the flavored kind in those pouches that include a cup of sugar. I've discovered I'm not good at making them oatmeal, but I'm really good at making them oatmeal soup. Whenever I eat oatmeal I always feel like a prisoner or an orphan. "Please, sir, may I have some more?" Nothing like starting off the day eating the same thing Oliver ate before he started singing the song where he and the other orphans were fantasizing about real food.

Keeping it healthy!

If I'm waking up and I'm going to be eating, I want eggs. Eggs are like the flagship item of breakfast. There are things that taste better than eggs (pancakes and waffles) for breakfast, and there are things that taste worse than eggs (oatmeal, fruit) for breakfast, but eggs are the breakfast standard. Eggs are what separate a continental breakfast from an enjoyable breakfast. There are so many ways to prepare eggs. Here are some of my favorites:

> **Breakfast Burrito:** If you like eggs, cheese, potatoes, and sausage in each bite and also napping after a meal, then the breakfast burrito is for you.
>
> **Quiche:** The egg and cheese pie. If you can't decide between breakfast and dessert, then quiche is for you. WARNING: Supposedly, eating quiche isn't manly, and

occasionally when I eat quiche, my gynecologist will make fun of me.

Best quiche ever: Tartine in San Francisco.

Eggs Benedict: For a traitor, Benedict sure knew how to eat breakfast. In all fairness, poached eggs over ham on a buttery, toasted English muffin covered in Hollandaise sauce would make anyone betray their country.

Other Countries

As a touring comedian I have the privilege of visiting other countries. Now, I enjoy other cultures as much as anyone, but what they are serving for breakfast I find baffling.

Europeans are all proud of their muesli, which I'm pretty sure is what we here in the USA feed our cattle. In some European countries a tray of deli meat is sitting on the table at a breakfast buffet. Initially I thought the deli meat was there because a refrigerator broke or someone accidentally left it out from yesterday's lunch. There's no bread or condiments. Just a big tray of different varieties of sliced ham and salami. Eating slices of cured meat for breakfast sounds to me like something that would occur in a frat house while standing in front of an open refrigerator. Not an appealing image first thing in the morning.

English Breakfast

I was equally shocked and relieved when I discovered that Americans don't have the unhealthiest breakfast. The English win the "Oddest and Unhealthiest Breakfast" award for the traditional English breakfast, which, for some reason, includes baked beans. That's right, baked beans, with all their undesirable side effects, are consumed first thing in the morning in England. The other items in a traditional English breakfast include a fried egg, a fried piece of toast, a stewed tomato, a sausage link, *and* a strip of bacon, *and* a piece of fatty ham. Yes, the "traditional" English breakfast, for some reason, includes

all the breakfast meats. This makes the Denny's Grand Slam breakfast look like a bowl of cut fruit in comparison. I've heard that waking up and smoking a pack of cigarettes is better for you than a traditional English breakfast.

Traditional English breakfast.

Irish Breakfast

The traditional Irish breakfast includes many of the traditional English breakfast items plus something called "black pudding," which is most definitely not pudding. It never even was pudding or anything close to pudding, and that is extremely obvious upon first sight. Black pudding appears to be a sliced, oversize, sausage-shaped thing with something that looks like seeds in it. Apparently the "black" in black pudding is a reference to blood, which I always understood should be colored red, not black, unless it is the blood from a zombie or an otherwise undead creature. There is also a "white pudding," which is also not a pudding or white or made from blood. Scientists worldwide are still trying to decipher the molecular composition of white pudding. Personally, I think it's made from ghosts. The Irish might be unfairly associated with drinking too much, but whoever decided to call black pudding "black pudding" or white pudding "white pudding" was definitely drunk. "Let's call that stuff pudding! Ha, ha. No, I'm not drunk. Okay, I had one drink . . . every two minutes for an hour. Ha, ha. Oh, it's black. Call it 'black pudding'! Ha, ha. The other one? Call it 'white pudding.' Can I pass out now?"

Traditional Irish breakfast.

Breakfast in Bed

Breakfast in bed is a glorious fantasy for me, and not just because I'm a fan of lying down and eating bacon (which I believe is how people kill time in heaven). Breakfast in bed is such an amazing concept because it gives you the option of going right back to sleep when you are finished eating. "Well, it would be rude to eat and run, right? Wake me up when lunch is ready." I'm always amazed there aren't restaurants with beds instead of tables. "We'd like a bed for two . . . with a view of the TV if you have it." I think the ultimate experience is lying in bed and watching TV while people bring me food on a tray. It's too bad hospitals have that whole sickness-requirement thing. If it weren't for that minor detail, I would check into the hospital mañana!

"What are your symptoms?"

"I'm hungry AND I could go for a nap, STAT!"

You can't turn down breakfast in bed. If you see someone walking into your bedroom with a tray of food in the morning, it is impossible to say, "Sorry, I just ate." Although that is usually true for me.

THE BAGEL: MY EVERYTHING

I have loved living in New York City for the past twenty years. Everything happened here. I started stand-up comedy, met my wife, Jeannie, and became a father of a basketball team in New York City. The energy, the people, Broadway, Central Park, and even the subway still captivate me, but probably my favorite part of New York City is the bagel. I realize saying New York City has the best bagels is a bit of a cliché, but there is just something truly special about a New York City bagel. Maybe it's the water, maybe it's purely a psychological phenomenon, but bagels taste different in New York City.

I wasn't always a bagel snob. Back in Indiana I could go through a sleeve of frozen Lender's Bagels before they were thawed. As a college student in Washington, DC, I worked in a café and discovered the masterpiece that is a cinnamon raisin bagel with cream cheese and bacon. But it was in New York City that I received my bagel education. I gained a respect for the power and art of a New York City bagel. Bagels in New York City are more dense, more flavorful, and, when toasted, develop this crunchy outer crust that becomes its own entity.

When you bite through that crunchy outer layer and experience the warm, chewy insides of a New York City bagel, you will become a believer too, and you will forsake all other bagels. Bagels outside of New York now just taste like stale round rolls with holes in them. They feel like the bootleg DVD of bagels.

As a struggling new comedian in New York City, late at night I would often shuffle, defeated, into H&H Bagels on Second Avenue after a less than stellar show a block away at the Comic Strip comedy club. The scent of bagel perfection was like a comforting welcome from an old friend. I'd meekly ask, "What's hot?" and then I would be handed happiness in the form of the freshest, hottest bagel in New York City. Eating the delicious bagel was like a reassuring hug telling me that even if the audience didn't get me, the bagel did. The bagel knew how to make me happy. Bombing so often at the Comic Strip allowed me to drown my frustrations in freshly baked versions of every traditional variety of bagel. Sometimes I'd get butter or cream cheese on the almost-too-hot-to-hold bagel, but often I would just consume it au naturel. During those early years, H&H Bagels was a shield from the awkwardness of figuring out stand-up comedy. A safe haven where I could escape from the harsh rejection I felt at the club. A bagel even sort of looks like a shield. A delicious shield you can hold up in front of you with your finger in the hole, and nothing bad can happen. Holding my bagel shield, I was like the little Dutch boy saving the village of my ego from the flood of audience disinterest.

I've never been the same. Now my daughters go to school on the Upper East Side, and going to Tal Bagels has become my reward for getting up early and transporting them to the other side of Manhattan while barely conscious. Now whenever I make it to the Upper East Side, which at that hour feels like I've traveled to another planet, I feel like I've earned a bagel. I heard someone talking on the phone describing a "delicious gluten-free New York City bagel," and it made me angry. How dare you call *that* a New York City bagel? I know New York City bagels. Well, I've eaten a whole bunch of them, and there is no such thing as a delicious gluten-free bagel. I just shook my head, sneered at my wife, and walked away to get something to eat.

Bagels are pretty much universally loved. Everyone has *their* bagel. Their bagel of choice. Mine is the "everything" bagel. The everything bagel is a toasted mixture of poppy seeds, sesame seeds, onion, garlic, and salt. I like all bagels, but an everything bagel is something more than special to me. I love my children, but I can't articulate the depth of feelings I have for a toasted everything bagel with cream cheese. They say you can't be everything to someone, but I think the everything bagel is my everything. If reincarnation is real, I'd like to come back as an everything bagel. Then I could guarantee that I'd be loved. I've recently decided that the next time I have to cry in an acting scene, I'm just going to imagine a world without New York City everything bagels. What a horrible world that would be.

DOUGHNUTS: THE CIRCLE OF LIFE

Cops love doughnuts. Ha, ha, ha. Cops and doughnuts. They go together like, well, doughnuts and cops. I find this an interesting stereotype, because you know who else loves doughnuts?

Absolutely everyone. "Yeah, we'll get those cops back for having power by saying they love that thing everyone else loves." Of course cops love doughnuts, because they know the difference between right and wrong. And not liking doughnuts is wrong. Have you ever met someone who doesn't like doughnuts? Of course not, because those people are in jail. The cops probably caught them murdering puppies because they never knew the love of the doughnut. As ridiculous as the cop-doughnut cliché is, I will admit that I'm always excited when I see a police officer in a doughnut shop. I feel as though an angel has just gotten its wings. Maybe I'm just high from the smell of the doughnuts.

Many mysteries surround doughnuts. I think it was Plato who struggled over the question "What is the difference between seeing a doughnut and wanting to eat a doughnut?" The answer is, of course, "One second." We all know seeing a doughnut happens occasionally. Wanting a doughnut is a continuous desire. See, now even you want a doughnut. I had a doughnut recently. I was with my friend Tom and we were walking by a doughnut shop, and I asked him if he wanted to get a doughnut. He responded that he wasn't hungry. Understandably I replied, "What does that have to do with it?" As if there has ever been a good reason to eat a doughnut. "My doctor says I need more powdered sugar in my diet. Well, another day on the doughnut cleanse." Everyone knows doughnuts are bad for you. Whenever I eat a doughnut I always think to myself, *Looks like I'll never know what it's like to be a grandpa.* Of course I am aware that doughnuts are bad, horrible things to eat, and according to my health-nut wife, they are not appropriate for a trail mix. I've repeatedly tried to explain to Jeannie that I'm on a different trail. Mine leads to the emergency room. Trail mixes have nuts, and my favorite nut is most definitely a doughnut.

There is no nutritional value in a doughnut. There may be

the odd study that found somehow that chocolate and wine can help you live longer, but no one even contemplates doing a study about the doughnut. The doughnut is all about taste. In Los Angeles there is a doughnut shop chain named Yum-Yum Donuts. The name cuts right to the chase. I suppose you need an IQ of maybe two to understand the concept. "Yum, yum? Me like yum, yum!" I imagine their target audience is cavemen. "Me know yellow fireball rise in sky, and Yum-Yum Donut."

Dunkin' Donuts

You can't really discuss doughnuts in the United States without bringing up the omnipresent Dunkin' Donuts. Many cities have their own local doughnut shop or chain, but they usually always also have a Dunkin' Donuts. In New England, Dunkin' Donuts is not just a local favorite. It is engrained in the New England provincial identity. "Dunkie's" is a favorite son. It seems like New Englanders view that doughnut shop like a relative or a childhood friend. "Dunkie's is awesome. It's wicked awesome!" They are so passionate and vocal at times, it makes me question whether Dunkin' Donuts is making doughnuts or playing for the Red Sox.

I like Dunkin' Donuts, and judging from the fact that there is a Dunkin' Donuts on every city block in most major cities of the United States, I am not alone. This is not to say that Dunkin' Donuts shops are the most appealing destinations. I don't think I've been to a Dunkin' Donuts that didn't have a homeless guy standing in front of it. It's possibly part of the design plans. I picture the architect showing his model to a prospective franchisee. "There will be an entrance here with a deranged lunatic standing outside." Maybe they find the lunatic first. "Hey, there's a guy living in a cardboard box who is yelling about the end of the world. Why don't we put a Dunkin' Donuts there?" Either way, there's always some character standing at the entrance of Dunkin' Donuts serving as a freelance Ronald McDonald. "Welcome to Dunkin' Donuts. Can you spare some change?"

Dunkin' Donuts may be the most successful doughnut chain, but all doughnut shops are generally an interesting concept. It's almost as if Alcoholics Anonymous opened their own restaurant. "What should we have at our place? Coffee . . . doughnuts . . . maybe a little honesty! And definitely a place to smoke outside." I've never really understood how Dunkin' Donuts stays in business. Of course, they sell coffee, but even if they sell three thousand doughnuts in one day, what would they make, thirty bucks? Additionally, whenever I go into a Dunkin' Donuts, it seems like they're always trying to get rid of the doughnuts. Allow me to recount my recent visit to Dunkin' Donuts:

ME: I'll have six doughnuts.
DOUGHNUT LADY: That'll be three dollars. But if you get a dozen, it's a nickel.
ME: A nickel more?
DOUGHNUT LADY: No, just a nickel.

I heard a rumor that if you get two dozen doughnuts, Dunkin' Donuts gives you five bucks. Okay, fine. Maybe they aren't paying us to eat them, but it does seem like Dunkin' Donuts is trying to get us addicted to doughnuts.

Whenever I buy a couple of doughnuts for the family—well, for me, really—the Dunkin' Donuts lady always throws in some Munchkins for free. Munchkins are like the gateway doughnut. Like a classic drug dealer, Dunkin' Donuts follows "the first time is always free" rule. At some point during my adult life, Dunkin' Donuts absorbed the ice cream parlor Baskin-Robbins. Dunkin' Donuts and Baskin-Robbins are a marriage made in obesity. I guess the marketing idea was that Dunkin' Donuts could finally offer dessert.

Krispy Kreme

Over the past decade or two, doughnuts have witnessed a rebirth in popularity. When I was a kid, a doughnut seemed like this unattainable item that grown-ups would eat in offices and occasionally at gatherings after church. While that hasn't changed at all, doughnuts do seem more popular. We all witnessed the Krispy Kreme wave as it overtook the nation and then suddenly disappeared. At first, Krispy Kremes were so popular that several years ago some friends of ours, Chris and Emily, gave out entire boxes of Krispy Kremes as the parting gift at their wedding. I ate the whole box on the way home. Biting into a Krispy Kreme is a unique experience. The doughnuts melt in your mouth so easily that for a short time I tried to convince Jeannie they were a liquid. "I'm thirsty. I think I'll have a doughnut." Then out of nowhere Krispy Kreme doughnut shops disappeared. Of course they didn't completely disappear, but their presence diminished significantly. It is possible that a group of district attorneys threatened a class-action lawsuit.

Portland

Many American cities have great doughnut shops, but Portland, Oregon, seems to have a vibrant doughnut obsession. I don't know if this has to do with its geographic proximity to coffee-obsessed Seattle or its—well, let's just say—"late-night eating" culture. Whenever I announce that I'll be performing in Portland, my Twitter feed is peppered with advice to go to

Voodoo Doughnut. Often the comments are not suggestions but demands. "You have to go!" "If you don't go, I'll kill you." The actual word *voodoo* means something like "mysterious forces or powers that govern the world and the lives of those who reside within it," which is pretty much the same way I feel about the power of an actual doughnut. Voodoo Doughnut has a doughnut called "Captain My Captain" that has Cap'n Crunch cereal on top of a doughnut. I call it the "Mutiny of My Diet Doughnut." At Voodoo, I always get the maple-bacon doughnut and then nap in the cab back to my hotel. Well, it's more of a "passing out in a sugar coma" than a nap, but you get the idea. Not to play favorites in destroying my health, I must also add that Voodoo Doughnut is not the only doughnut shop that Portland is known for. There is also Coco Donuts. At Coco's I always get a lavender doughnut so I can feel fat AND fresh.

Tim Hortons

I love Canada, and Canada loves Tim Hortons. I'm no Canada expert, but I know they like their hockey, poutine, and Tim Hortons. Tim Hortons is the Canadian version of Dunkin' Donuts, or maybe Dunkin' Donuts is the American version of Tim Hortons. Either way, I'm applying for dual citizenship.

Gourmet Doughnut Shops

Gourmet doughnuts. Yes, gourmet doughnuts. I believe they are deep fried in gold. We can't stop dressing up junk food. It started with the boutique cupcake shops. Now we have gourmet doughnuts. It's an evolution. I can't wait for the Sloppy Joseph. What will bored, rich people eat next?

Specialty, or gourmet, doughnut shops now can be found in

most major cities. I'm not sure how anything deep fried can be that "gourmet." Gourmet doughnut shops are a perfect destination for those of us who want to waste money *while* we gain weight. I recently purchased a gourmet doughnut. At the time I didn't realize I was buying a gourmet doughnut. I was in a doughnut shop. I suppose being in a doughnut shop never really leads to a healthy or smart purchase. You never hear, "I was in a doughnut shop and I found these great probiotics." Anyway, there I was in a doughnut shop. I pointed at a square doughnut and told the doughnut guy, "I'll have the square one." As he started to ring it up on the cash register, he said, "That will be $3.99." I politely said, "Oh, no, I only want one." He then in a matter-of-fact manner informed me, "That *is* the price of one." At that moment there was this long, awkward pause where the doughnut guy stared blankly at me and I waited for him to lean forward and say, "Just kidding." But he didn't. He just looked at me with a smug smile that said, "Got ya, tubby!" He knew I would pay for the doughnut because I was in a doughnut shop, and it's not like I was there to buy a yoga mat. Like the great philosopher Plato, he knew the difference between seeing a doughnut and eating a doughnut is but one second.

HOUSE OF CARBS

A very important subsegment of the restaurant industry is breakfast restaurants. Well, *I* call them breakfast restaurants. Many of my single friends enjoy going out to fancy places for breakfast or brunch on weekends. They meet up, gossip, and giggle about the adventures they had the night before. I'm not talking about those places. I'm talking about the breakfast restaurants where I can take my five screaming children and feed them for around twenty dollars while I witness them do about forty dollars' worth of damage to the establishment. These are usually chain restaurants that serve other meals besides breakfast, but breakfast made them famous because it's the only thing anyone wants to eat there. You are more likely to get the pancakes than the veggie burger at the IHOP. You'd rather go to Denny's for the Grand Slam breakfast than the avocado salad. You get the idea. I seem to be in chain breakfast restaurants either in the morning with my screaming children or late, late at night after shows with slurring adult-children. It's really not that different of an atmosphere.

IHOP

The most famous breakfast restaurant chain is probably IHOP, which seems like a strange name for a place. Whenever I've eaten at IHOP, I never really feel like hopping. ICanBarelyMove feels more appropriate. Maybe INeedA-Wheelchair. The IHOP is famous for its pancakes, yet the entire restaurant seems like a syrup exhibit. Every table in IHOP is equipped with its own caddy filled with an assortment of syrups (maple, strawberry, blueberry, butter pecan, and boysenberry). Each of the syrup containers is personally licked by a similar assortment of five-year-olds. As a result of the syrup being preplaced on the table, there is not an inch of an International House of Pancakes that has not been touched by syrup, even the bathrooms. To prepare for the next morning, at the end of the night an IHOP employee even mops the floor with syrup.

Waffle House

My favorite of the breakfast restaurant chains is Waffle House.

Waffle House is similar to the International House of Pancakes, but instead of pancakes they serve waffles. I'm not sure if it's intentional, but the Waffle House vibe feels more like that of a halfway house or a mobile home than an actual house. I'll never forget the first time I walked into a Waffle House. It was in Tampa, Florida, in 1989. All I could think was *Wow, I owe the IHOP an enormous apology.* The moment you enter most Waffle Houses, you get the sense the staff stopped caring a long time ago or never did. You'll never hear "Nice job cleaning up" in a Waffle House. If you've never had the chance to visit a Waffle House, simply imagine a gas station bathroom that serves waffles. That sums up the atmosphere pretty well.

I love everything about the Waffle House experience and not just because watching someone fry an egg while they smoke a cigarette reminds me of my dad. I love how the waitress approaches the table with an attitude that says, "Okay, I'll pretend to be your server before I go back to the kitchen area and pretend to be your chef." I mostly go to Waffle House after midnight with comedian friends following shows, when the clientele is at its ripest. Many of the patrons are drunk, which explains why there are pictures of the food on the menu. I'm not sure how drunk someone would have to be to not remember what a waffle looks like. "Oh, yeah, it's like a plaid pancake." The folks in a Waffle House after midnight are a motley bunch of twenty-year-olds, Vietnam vets, and elderly couples ignoring each other. It feels a little like a family reunion for me, or maybe a white-trash convention. Waffle House is so filled with white trash, it actually makes the International House of Pancakes appear international. Everyone seems to be dressed in camo, on the verge of passing out, or muttering into a coffee cup, regretting the past twenty years of their lives. It's like you walked into a scene out of *The Deer Hunter*. I've seen a gun up close five times in my life, and three of them have been in a Waffle House. There is always an air of danger after midnight in Waffle House. The Waffle House sign, with its individual block letters, is even reminiscent of a ransom note. Occasionally there will be a letter burnt out in the electric Waffle House sign, so the sign will read AFFLE HOUSE. You never hear of anything good happening at a Waffle House after midnight. "Another disease was cured at Waffle House last night." Even the hash brown section of the Waffle House menu reads like a serial killer to-do list: "Smothered, covered, diced, and scattered." Despite all these unbecoming attributes, Waffle House is where so many nocturnal folks, including myself, seem to go for a late-night meal. The Waffle House slogan should really be "It's 2:00 a.m. There's still time to make one more bad decision."

THE CELEBRATION OF FOOD

Everyone seems to gain weight during the holidays. Unfortunately, the way I eat, I often find myself gaining weight *for* the holidays. The positive spin on my approach is that it makes the holiday weight gain seem less dramatic. As we all know, holidays are special days to commemorate historical and cultural events or famous dead people. For some reason we typically celebrate these events or honor these dead famous people by overeating on holidays. To clarify, I am talking about holidays in the American sense of the word, because, for some reason, people in the British Commonwealth call any vacation a "holiday," which is weird and somewhat annoying, but it actually applies here too, because on a holiday (a day, not a vacation) we eat like we are on vacation (a holiday for you English-speaking foreigners). This is what you call a cross-cultural reference. I don't know why a holiday or a vacation naturally leads to overeating. Maybe we feel like we've earned it. Well, I feel like I have earned it. Don't judge me. You're the one reading a book about food.

In a way, holidays chronicle my unhealthy living throughout a given year.

First Quarter

I start off the year with the best intentions. It's a new year filled
with hope and possibility. I resolve to lose weight, live healthier,
and overall be more like Oprah. In almost reactionary behavior
to December, I stumble through January somberly observing
Martin Luther King Jr. Day and contemplating who is actually
attending those white sales on Presidents' Day. It seems to be
going along nicely until the first Sunday in February. The first
attack on my impressive few weeks of somewhat healthy living
is Super Bowl Sunday. While not an official holiday, the Super
Bowl provides the strongest competition to Thanksgiving on
the food-overconsumption front. Unlike Thanksgiving, there is
no facade of gratitude or family time . . . it's all about football
and food. Thanksgiving may go food, then football, but Super
Bowl Sunday is simply eat food, watch football while you eat
food, and then eat more food. The food served on Super Bowl
Sunday is all handheld and makes the Thanksgiving meal look
like a health shake. It's like a college fraternity catered a fu-
neral. Buffalo wings, pigs in a blanket, chips and guacamole
are usually the healthiest offerings, and this is right and good
because, after all, it is called the "super bowl," not the "diet
plate."

Barely guilt ridden after my Super Bowl binge, I slog through
early February with its horrible weather and no football and
brace for Valentine's Day. Around Valentine's Day is when I
really lose my way. The fatigue of winter has set in, and even
though by some miracle I am in a relationship, the awkward
romantic pressure of Valentine's Day seems to prompt unjus-
tifiable chocolate consumption. Valentine's Day seems to be a
day shaped to create failed expectations. The whole idea of a
day constructed around romance seems counterintuitive. It's
like a surprise birthday party that you know about and aren't

in the mood for. You can stop a surprise birthday party, but you can't stop Valentine's Day. Everything seems a little forced on Valentine's Day. This is even evident in the amount of candy consumed. One of the Valentine's Day traditions is giving each other those big red heart-shaped boxes filled with the gamble chocolates. I've never eaten any chocolate out of those big red hearts with any confidence. I always think, *This could either be really good or totally nasty, but I'm just pig enough to find out.* I usually get the piece filled with the pink toothpaste. Then naturally I have to eat another nine to get rid of that flavor. There seems to be no logic in why certain chocolates were included in the heart-shaped box. One time I'm pretty sure I bit into a chocolate-covered acorn. Valentine's Day also offers the tiny chalk heart-shaped antacids that are one of the few things that make unsweetened baking chocolate seem appealing. "I know I make you nauseous so here's a Tums with 'hug me' written on it."

March brings Saint Patrick's Day, which is also known as the "Overdrinking Academy Awards." Saint Patrick's Day is supposed to be an ethnic celebration based on an English saint who converted Ireland to Christianity and drove the snakes out. It usually feels more like sanctioned binge drinking. They say, "Everyone is Irish on Saint Patrick's Day," and I'm starting to think that is most certainly not a compliment. I always imagine Saint Patrick looking down from heaven mumbling, "What are they doing? I hated beer." Some of the overconsumption of alcohol on Saint Patrick's Day is a function of the Irish stereotype of a love of drinking, but I think it has even more to do with how bad corned beef and cabbage tastes. I am an American of Irish heritage. You may recall earlier that I mentioned the Saint Patrick's Day traditions of my childhood—that we would eat corned beef and cabbage for dinner. After that my mom would encourage my siblings and me to go into the yard looking for a leprechaun. If we caught a leprechaun, we would supposedly get a pot of gold. I realize now she probably just wanted some time alone so she could eat something delicious that was not corned beef and cabbage. Even she knew she made it wrong.

It's strange being an Irish American. Alcohol is woven into the ethnic pride. As a teenager I felt pressure to like Guinness. It's an acquired taste, but Guinness is presented to the Irish American as being as familiar as mother's milk. This is probably because Guinness has the same chemical composition as your Irish American mother's milk. As a teenager I remember thinking, *I want to like this, but I don't see it happening.* Now I sometimes enjoy a Guinness, but I'm not crazy about the wait. You could write the entire *Guinness World Records* book while you wait for a Guinness to be poured in a bar. Often, instead of ordering a Guinness, I'll just tell the bartender, "I'd like to wait an hour for my beer." He knows what I mean.

Second Quarter

Spring is a period of renewal. To celebrate this period of joy and rebirth, I eat candy. Easter is one of the most sacred holidays for Christians, yet the rituals always felt very strange to me. I don't understand where most holiday traditions came from, but the egg seems to play a particularly confusing role at Easter. I always imagine how the conversation occurred.

GUY 1: Easter is the day Jesus rose from the dead. What should we do?
GUY 2: How about eggs?
GUY 1: Well, what does that have to do with Jesus?
GUY 2: All right, we'll hide them.

GUY 1: I don't follow your logic.
GUY 2: Don't worry. There's a bunny.

It's not just the involvement of eggs that makes Easter traditions so bizarre. It's also the absurdity of letting young children handle the fragile eggs. Thank God the colorful eggs are hard-boiled because, wait for it, LITTLE KIDS BREAK EGGS. Kids can't even dye the eggs without breaking them. Every year on the Thursday before Easter, Jeannie and I dye hard-boiled eggs with our young children. Let's just say there's usually a lot of egg salad eaten on Good Friday. To make matters more interesting, since we live in New York City, Jeannie and I hide the remaining unbroken eggs in our apartment and then ask our children to find them. That's right. We are voluntarily embracing the great likelihood of a rotten egg being hidden in our small, smell-friendly apartment.

Painting eggs and looking for them is amusing, but like most five-year-olds, I focus on the more unique Easter food. Chocolate bunnies, chocolate eggs, and, of course, Peeps, which are the candy corn of Easter. Nostalgia is the only thing keeping Peeps in circulation. Fact: Stale Peeps are far better than fresh Peeps, so take care to break the plastic wrapper the night before Easter to allow appropriate hardening. I'm talking the night before Easter a year before the Easter you plan to eat them.

Recently Americans started celebrating Cinco de Mayo, perhaps less out of respect for the large number of Mexican Americans here and more to provide an excuse to have a party in May. Cinco de Mayo serves as almost a sequel to Saint Patrick's Day, but instead of just binging on alcohol, we overconsume alcohol AND food. Excitement for spring and the fact that tacos, burritos, enchiladas, and pretty much all

Mexican foods are some of the greatest things on this planet made Cinco de Mayo an inevitable American holiday. In a lot of ways, the American celebration of Cinco de Mayo feels like a marketing stunt by the makers of Corona beer and Old El Paso products. For some reason I don't understand, Cinco de Mayo always seems to be on or around the fifth of May.

Third Quarter

During summer the weather is nice, which means people love to eat outside. To kick off these warmer months, Americans observe Memorial Day to honor the heroes who gave their lives for this country and, more important, to celebrate the first day they can break out the grill. This love of grilling and picnicking is most notable on Independence Day. The day we as a country became free to eat whatever we wanted. The Fourth of July is another fine example of how we use holidays as an excuse to overeat. "Normally I don't eat a burger, a brat, AND a steak, but it *is* the Fourth of July, and I'm gonna need the energy if I'm going to be blowing things up. Besides, that is what the Founding Fathers would want." August feels like a month-long rehearsal of how we will barbecue, eat, and celebrate Labor Day.

Fourth Quarter

My favorite holiday is Halloween, and not just because women use it as an excuse to dress like prostitutes. You ladies totally do.

"I'm a witch."

If she were a hooker.

"I'm Little Miss Muffet!"

I'm sure you are.

A cautionary note: Never shop with your children for their Halloween costumes online. You're sitting there with your four-year-old daughter and google "Little Red Riding Hood costume," and what comes up looks like it should be on the cover of an X-rated video. Not that I know what the cover of an X-rated video would look like.

No, Halloween is my favorite because it is the ultimate candy holiday. When you're a kid, Halloween is amazing. You dress like a superhero, you bang on your neighbor's door, and they give you candy. I do that today, and my neighbor wants me arrested. Probably because I make such a hot Cat Woman. "Purrr! Kitty wants some *candy*." Pumpkin—the only real food associated with Halloween—is purely decorative. People buy pumpkins around Halloween, but it is never to eat them. When someone wants pumpkin bread or muffins or a pumpkin pie, they go to a bakery. It is way too disgusting to try to obtain actual food out of a raw pumpkin. Who the heck gets hungry while scooping out that nasty, tangled mess? Hannibal Lecter? In our family, we always try to roast the slimy seeds, but they

just turn into burnt, overly salted choking hazards that scrape your intestines for the next two weeks after eating them. We only buy the pumpkins to make jack-o'-lanterns. "Let's carve this healthy food up into a scary face and let it rot while we eat some candy."

Thanksgiving is uniquely an American holiday. Sure, Canadians have a Thanksgiving, but I think they have theirs in October or something. Weirdos. I don't think they even have a Fourth of July. Thanksgiving is intended to be about gratitude. A day of gratitude. Thank God there is a day for us to focus on being grateful because I'd hate the idea of having to be grateful year-round. We express this gratitude by overconsuming turkey, an enormous assortment of side dishes, and, of course, pies. There is very little complexity in the concept of the Thanksgiving holiday. It seems as if very little effort went into the planning.

"How about at Thanksgiving we just eat a lot?"

"But in America we do that every day!"

"Well, what if we eat a lot with people who annoy the hell out of us?"

Thanksgiving is all about overeating. Even one of the main dishes is actually called "stuffing." Stuffing? What names did they turn down? "Cram It In"? "Eat Till You Can't Breathe"? In some parts of the country, people call stuffing "dressing." Actually, the term *stuffing* makes a lot more sense than "dressing," which normally refers to something done externally rather than internally. By calling it dressing instead of stuffing, it almost seems as if they are purposely hiding the location where this dish is actually cooked. It's borderline dishonest. "Here's your 'dressing' (*wink*)." Admittedly, I'm not completely comfortable with the fact that stuffing (or dressing) is, in reality, cooked inside a dead animal. I'm not sure how this is supposed to be appetizing. We are basically shoving a loaf of bread up the carcass of a turkey. This is a rather humiliating thing to do to anything after it dies. Talk about an outrage of personal dignity. I hope the turkeys never find out about this practice of "stuffing."

TURKEY: You guys are going to kill me?

HUMAN: Oh, it's going to get a lot worse.

The Thanksgiving meal represents the opening day of the holiday season, and it is a very unprofessional season at that. Santa may be watching, but nobody is being good in December. Christmas is the Las Vegas of holiday eating. From the moment December begins, you get a free pass to overindulge. There's even candy in Advent calendars. Regardless of your faith or belief system, all Americans find themselves invited to a never-ending buffet of holiday parties. All dietary rules are suspended. You navigate your way through each day facing an onslaught of hors d'oeuvres, the French phrase for "trays of fattening stuff no one can identify." Cookies, cakes, and candies are exchanged with friends for virtually no reason at all. During December we are all ingesting, imbibing, and spending with a reckless abandon like a bachelor party on a guilt-free boondoggle. Everyone has the unspoken agreement that what happens in December stays in December.

If Christmas consumption doesn't kill or bankrupt you, you get one more chance on New Year's Eve, the prom night of holidays. New Year's Eve is the pinnacle of the alcohol over-consumption category, but it also is the culmination of all the indulging of the entire year in a final fit of hedonistic madness. It's the overconsuming of overconsumption. The pressure is on. We get one last hurrah before we head back to the war of regular life and responsible living. Over the course of December's gluttonous rampage we've committed to turn over a new leaf come January. We can't go on like this. We *can* be healthy, but only if we first get one last night. One last drink. One last piece of cake. One last cigarette. Like the Frog Prince, a kiss at midnight from our sweetheart will turn us into a new person. And *poof.* It's a new year.

First Quarter

I start off the year with the best intentions. It's a new year filled with hope and possibility . . .

FAMILY DINNER

When I was growing up, every Sunday my family would have a family dinner. "Sunday dinner"—or as I called it, "torture"—was my parents' attempt at being civilized and having at least one meal a week with the entire family. Mom, Dad, and the six kids would gather around the dining room table. There was no getting out of it. My friend's mom could offer to take me to meet Jesus and I wouldn't be able to go. It was "family time," and I remember hating it. There was a formal-dress requirement. Well, not formal but more fancy, so wearing scratchy clothes was a necessity. The dinner had to take place in the dining room, and my mom had to use her wedding china that was so nice it could never go into a dishwasher. It had to be carefully washed by hand. And preferably dried with a kitten. And it had to be a white kitten.

Sunday dinner would start around 6:00 p.m. We would say grace to thank God for all His blessings. Then we would try to rip each other apart over the first serving as my mother yelled orders at us from the other room. She never had time to eat. She would be scooting back and forth combining elegance and warmth with absolute frustration. "Eat the coleslaw!" would be bellowed from the other room. My dad would hack a productive smoker's cough before he began every sentence. "(*cough*) This is great, Marcia," my dad would mumble as he slid a carving knife into a pork roast, a turkey, or a rack of lamb. He would use a low voice as if to indicate to the rest of us "Compliment your mother or you die." My siblings and I would quickly chime in with "It's great. Thanks, Mom." Then a silence would fall over the table as bowls and plates were passed and food was voraciously consumed. I remember being a kid and never being able to find a multicourse meal appealing. I couldn't understand why we couldn't just have McDonald's for Sunday dinner. My eight-year-old palette was already accustomed to fast food, and expanding it beyond that has been a lifelong struggle for me. My mom could make thick and juicy home-cooked hamburgers on some fancy roll, but I still preferred a thin, tasteless McDonald's hamburger on that wonderbun.

At the end of dinner, my dad would light a cigarette (yes, in the same room with all six of us kids) and begin a discussion that to me always seemed like awkward small talk: "Someone (one of the kids) broke the clicker (remote control)." Or: "(Someone we don't know) is dying, so we should all feel horrible." Or even worse: "What do you want to be when you grow up?" As a ten-year-old I remember announcing, "Mike says I'd be a great proctologist." No, I had no idea what it was, but I figured out I'd said something wrong when everyone laughed at me and my dad gave me the deadeye stare.

Occasionally my father would ask us about historical events. "Jimmy, what do you think of the Vietnam War?" It didn't matter that the Vietnam War was long over or that I was ten years old at the time and pretty much unaware of the existence of Vietnam. I'm sure my answer was nothing very insightful and probably pretty ignorant, much to the delighted mockery of my older siblings. "Um, it seems fun on *M*A*S*H*." (*gales of laughter*) "That was *Korea,* you idiot!"

Many of these Sunday night family "discussions" would inevitably lead to massive arguments, and normally someone would end up crying or getting punished. The punishment was pretty harsh and usually involved cleaning up after the Sunday dinner, which was the only thing worse than the actual Sunday dinner. Cleaning up after an eight-person Sunday dinner that you don't even want to be at should probably be added to Amnesty International's list of torture techniques. But we were dressed nicely, so it seemed like very civilized torture. It's no wonder I still love McDonald's. You can just eat it, then throw the bag away.

LAST SUPPER

Sitting and eating a meal with someone is intimate. I try to eat as many meals as I can with my kids. Sure, I try to eat as many meals as I can in general, but eating with my children is important. There we are together, eating and talking, spilling and throwing food. Sometimes my kids misbehave too. It's a great time to force myself away from all the other distractions in life and sit around a table sharing an experience with my family. Even baby Patrick in his high chair knows it's important. He laughs along and babbles in agreement. He is in the mix. The entire family is participating in something together. Jeannie and I try to teach manners and civilize these little monsters, but anyone with young children knows it's never a relaxing experience. It's just good to eat together. It's a unique time you can share with your family, and it's been going on for thousands of years.

My board of directors.

People of every culture have shared a family meal to commemorate their most important customs. On Passover, Jewish people eat lamb, bitter herbs, and unleavened bread in communion with their ancestors. It's pretty brilliant, really. Imagine if years from now people thought of you while they ate bratwurst. "Well, on this day we eat brats to honor Jim Gaffigan." Eating a meal with your family or friends to honor someone or something heightens the experience of eating, and eating heightens the experience of the tradition. It was on a Passover over two thousand years ago that Jesus hosted the Last Supper. It was the "Last Supper," not the "Last Seminar," for a reason. Jesus was getting at least twelve men together. There had to be food.

JESUS: Tomorrow I'd like to get everyone together.
APOSTLE: Is there going to be food there?
JESUS: (*annoyed*) Yes, there will be food.
APOSTLE: Are we talking appetizers or like a meal?
JESUS: (*frustrated*) It will be a supper.

APOSTLE: A supper? So it's casual? I can wear a robe? I mean, if you said dinner I would wear a tie.

I always found it odd that this momentous event was given such a seemingly casual name. The word *supper* sounds like a potluck with Jed Clampett as the party planner. I can just see Jed in his floppy hat: "Hey ya'll, Jesus is having a Last Supper. Let's rustle up some grub. Sissy, you bring your Jell-O salad. Jesus will fry up the fish. I'll be playing fiddle."

I'm sure the Last Supper was anything but casual. It was the last meal Jesus shared with the apostles before things got really messy. Anyone who has organized a gathering with a large group of friends knows this is never an easy task, even if you are not about to be crucified. No matter how intimate the event is, there is always someone who shows up at your dinner party with uninvited strangers. You know, one of the apostles arrived in this manner. "Hey, Jesus, Happy Last Supper! I hope it's okay, but I brought my friends Frank and Weezie. They're visiting from Cleveland, and they are HUGE fans of yours. Is it cool if they get a selfie with you?"

Of course, at the Last Supper there was no Jell-O salad or people from Cleveland. It took place in the Middle East, and, given Jewish dietary laws, the bread Jesus broke and shared with his apostles was probably not that tasty and had all the leaven taken out. Think how different things could have been if the Last Supper had occurred in Mexico. Jesus probably would have said, "Take this, all of you . . . but not the chips. I'm saving those for the guacamole." We all know the importance of guacamole. Now, I know the Last Supper did not occur at a Mexican restaurant, or in any type of restaurant in the modern sense of the word, although I love the idea of an interrupting waitress at this momentous event.

JESUS: Take this, all of you—
WAITRESS: Can I get anyone coffee?
JESUS: We are good, thank—
WAITRESS: Dessert? We have a key lime pie to die for!
JESUS: Just the check, ple—
WAITRESS: I'm going to bring you guys a slice of the
    pie with a bunch of forks. On the house. You only
    live once, right?
JESUS: Something like that.

I hope I haven't offended anyone with my lighthearted take on the Last Supper. I certainly don't mean to offend. I understand that religion jokes make some people uncomfortable. Especially the people who are going to hell. It is my belief that God has a great sense of humor. How else would you explain the appearance of the duck-billed platypus or the manatee? Doesn't it look like God didn't try very hard on the manatee? "Let's see, make him a gray blob of fat, flip-flops . . . what the heck, let's go with the goatee. Stick him around Florida; he'll fit right in."

THE FINAL MEAL

I have five young, energetic children whom I love with every ounce of my existence and who I always joke are going to be the death of me. Whoever said "Kids keep you young" was being sarcastic. The reality is that eventually we are all going to die, even though no one wants to think about it. Whenever the news tells us someone famous has passed away we always think to ourselves, *I'm glad that's never happening to me.* But when you have kids, you have to start talking about wills and life insurance and all other kinds of morbid stuff, so you are forced to acknowledge that death eventually will happen. Whenever I am confronted with the thought of death, I am faced with the same perplexing question that has puzzled both philosophers and religious leaders since the beginning of time: What do I eat for my last meal?

Supposedly, death row inmates get to request a last meal before we take their lives. Often these criminals have done horrible things, so it's kind of confusing to me that we are executing them but, just beforehand, offering them a little treat. As if it somehow makes taking their lives more civilized. Suddenly we as a society are like a James Bond villain: "Before I kill you with my evil contraption, would you like some caviar?"

Most of us don't know when or how we are going to go, so for us non-death-row inmates, the last-meal question presents an interesting conundrum. How do we plan? I don't like to have forgettable meals in normal circumstances. Even worse than that are the meals that are bad or unsatisfying. You wouldn't want to spend the afterlife regretting your last meal. "I can't believe I ordered the fish." "What was I doing eating applesauce from White Castle?" We want to leave the people here with the knowledge that we have loved them dearly but also that we have no regrets and lived our lives to their fullest. Therefore, I conclude that we should be full. Full of something delicious.

Jeannie told me the Bible says that the Kingdom of Heaven is like a wedding feast, but what if I'm not invited? I figure I'd better do some carb loading to increase my stamina for when I have to start the heavy negotiating with Saint Peter. I'm sure I will be standing outside the ropes. "I know my wife is in there, and I'm almost positive she got me on the list. No? Maybe you could just give her my mobile number? If I could just talk to her, I'm sure we could straighten this out. Her name is Jeannie. She may be going by Saint Jeannie up here?"

But how to plan the last meal? For the answer to this age-old question, I needed only to turn to my brilliant and funny peers. Most of the great advice I've received in my life I've gotten from fellow comedians. Sure, we are a ragtag bunch of self-destructive narcissists, but there is an inherent bravery and wisdom found in stand-up comedians. Comedians examine life from a unique point of view. There are so many influences I could mention, but, really, each of my stand-up comedian friends and predecessors has taught me so many things. Once, a friend told me he tried to treat every performance like it might be his last. Similar to the football coach instructing players to give 100 percent or leave "everything on the field," it is always possible any stand-up performance could be your last, so make sure it matters. No comedian would want his last performance to be uninspired or "phoned in." I think unconsciously I've also applied this advice to my eating. I'd never want my last real meal to be a kale salad or a PowerBar. Maybe this whole eat-every-meal-like-it's-your-last approach to life is what really inspired me to write this book.

My advice to you, dear reader, is to eat well and eat frequently. Our time here is pretty short. It's filled with disappointments and drama, and food can make it better. I'm not proposing that every meal be a Shake Shack burger or a falafel from Mamoun's on MacDougal Street, but it is important that you enjoy your life. That's why a decent cheeseburger is always a good decision. Yes, I am saying that a cheeseburger and fries would be a great last meal. Make it a double. Since we don't know how or when we will go, I make it a point to eat a few cheeseburgers throughout the day just in case.

I am a firm believer that the meal should always fit the occasion, so I also have suggestions for last meals depending on the way you go, just in case you are a planner and also a clairvoyant.

- If you are going to go down in a private jet, I would suggest a Kobe beef steak dinner.
- If you are murdered by a junkie, your last meal should be a doughnut.
- If you are fatally hit by a foul ball at a baseball game, you should be eating a hot dog.
- If you die from a gunshot wound, you should be digesting Waffle House.
- If you are stabbed to death in jail, it should be over a bologna sandwich.

- If you have a heart attack watching a football game, you should be reaching for a brat at the time.
- If you die from dysentery, it should be from a Hot Pocket.
- If you take your own life, it should be after you ate kale because you don't deserve a good last meal if you do that.
- If you die abroad, may it be in Mexico or Thailand after an amazing feast.
- And, of course, if you choke to death, it should be on bacon.

Thank you, my friends, for reading this book. I hope your worst eating experiences are behind you. May you enjoy only great meals, mostly with family and close friends. I hope your coffee is strong, your cheese is sharp, and your guacamole is chunky. This is my wish for all of you, but, most important, I hope you don't dance. People look really silly doing that. Am I right or what?

ADDITIONAL ACKNOWLEDGMENTS

Jeannie and I have written two books. The first book was *Dad Is Fat,* which was all about my conversion from happy loner to grateful, exhausted father of five. This second book compiles many of the observations I've made about food over a lifetime. I wasn't sure how to acknowledge everyone, so I'm going to thank some of the people who bought me free meals or exposed me to amazing food.

First and foremost I'd like to reiterate that Jeannie is the reason this book makes any sense and that I'm not a serial killer. Everything Jeannie touches is delicious. In an ideal world I would eat all meals with Jeannie. My favorite dish she makes is Königsberger Klopse. No, that is not a made-up name.

I must thank my beautiful children, Marre, Jack, Katie, Michael, and Patrick, who constantly provide a fresh perspective on food and how it can be consumed or rubbed on one's face for no reason. They remain the only people I don't mind sharing food with.

I thank my father for his love of steak and an appreciation for going out to dinner.

My mom was the bacon of all humans. No, really, she was. Her spaghetti with two pounds of ground beef remains one of my favorite dishes. She would have loved how much my son Jack adores her recipe.

Thanks to my amazing manager, Alex Murray, who has bought me tons of Chipotle, and his tireless associate, Jerilyn Novia, who brought me to an excellent Mexican bakery in Los Angeles.

I'd like to thank my editor, Suzanne O'Neill, and the whole gang at the Crown Publishing Group, who still owe me a dinner at Nobu: Maya Mavjee, Molly Stern, Tina Constable, Tammy Blake, Julie Cepler, Tommy Cabrera, and Jenni Zellner.

Thanks to Nick Nucifaro, Martin Lesak, Greg Cavic, Simon Green, John Sachs, and all the CAA folks, who I hope will continue to bring me to expensive steakhouses for years to come.

Thanks to all the New York City–based comedians who I've eaten tons of shawarma, pierogi, pizza, and bagels with over the years.

Thanks to Greg Giraldo, who introduced me to the power and majesty of rice and beans.

Thanks to Angela Muto and Ken Formen for exposing me to cold borscht.

Thanks to Tom Shillue, who never makes me feel guilty when we eat a steak after one of our theater shows.

Thanks to my sister Cathy, who brought me to my first dim sum and allowed me and my brother Joe to eat everything in her house that one spring break.

Thanks to my sister Pam, who not only gave me a packet of hot dogs, a six-pack of Dr Pepper, and a hot-air popcorn maker for my birthday but also brought me many times to

Godfather's Pizza while I was in high school. I still love those rabbit-turd sausages they put on their pizza.

Thanks to my brother Mike, who brought me to Taste of Chicago and began my love affair with all Chicago food.

Thanks to my brother Mitch, who always gets Schoop's to bring free burgers to my shows when I perform in Northwest Indiana. Mitch also makes a great blue cheese burger.

Thanks to my brother Joe, who bought me innumerable meals, including my first Portillo's hot dog. Thanks also for punching me repeatedly when I accidently bought Happy Jose tamales.

Thanks to my aunt Katie, who bought me pints of ice cream as a child and has tried to make me enjoy steamed crabs for decades.

Thanks to Rob Hubbs, who allowed me to eat all the good food in his house when I was a teenager. Say hi to your mom, Bev.

To Chris Carrera and Emily Chen, who have taken me out to dinner at many restaurants that I could never afford.

To Nancy Gagliano and Emily Chen, who ate really mediocre sushi with me in college.

To George Alexis, Dan Currie, Kevin O'Connell, and Jim Depersia, whom I scavenged for food with during college.

To Nora and Trey Fitzpatrick, who brought me to Andy Nelson's barbecue in Baltimore.

To the Noth family, who opened my eyes to the glory of Wisconsin food.

To Dom Noth in particular, who taught me to love and also to pronounce *aioli*.

To Gary and Tracy Thiel, whose Hotel Thiel remains one of my favorite places to stay. Thanks for those morning pastries.

To Justin Sundheimer, who told me about the great Mexican place in the Phoenix airport that I can't remember the name of.

To Ian Bagg, who brought me to my first In-N-Out Burger.

And to all my Internet friends on Twitter, Facebook, and Instagram for all the local food suggestions. I blame my impending diabetes mostly on you.

ABOUT THE AUTHOR

Jim Gaffigan is a *New York Times* bestselling author, comedian, and actor who only wishes he was as thin as the caketopper groom on the cover of this book. When he is not eating in airports before flying to some city to eat and do stand-up comedy, he overeats in New York City and also lives there with his five young children and much smarter and thinner wife, Jeannie.

© Corey Melton